CAN DREAMS CHANGE YOUR LIFE?

A bride at the altar suddenly realizes she's forgotten her lines. A man goes fishing—and catches a dog. No matter how common or uncommon, lucid or disjointed, many dreams offer helpful clues to your state of mind and your deepest feelings—if you know how to decode them. During difficult, stressful times, our dreams can help us confront and explore our situation—and lead us to a new enlightenment....

"ALAN SIEGEL PROVIDES AN INVALUABLE KEY TO UNDER-STANDING...This is a great gift for anyone interested in dreams."
— The Reverend Jeremy Taylor,
author of *Dream Work*

"A WEALTH OF COHERENT ADVICE...READ IT."
— *New Frontier*

"INNOVATIVE AND BEAUTIFULLY RESEARCHED."
— *San Francisco Chronicle*

"THIS BOOK *CAN* CHANGE YOUR LIFE if you focus on your dreams as turning points."
— Association for Humanistic
Psychology *Perspective*

"EXCELLENT...This is a book that can be confidently recommended to anyone wanting to draw on the wisdom of their dreams."
— *The California Psychology*

DREAMS
THAT CAN
CHANGE
YOUR
LIFE

NAVIGATING LIFE'S PASSAGES
THROUGH TURNING POINT DREAMS

ALAN B. SIEGEL, PH.D.

BERKLEY BOOKS, NEW YORK

For Tracy and Zoe

This Berkley book contains the complete
text of the original hardcover edition.

DREAMS THAT CAN CHANGE YOUR LIFE

A Berkley Book / published by arrangement with
St. Martin's Press, Inc.

PRINTING HISTORY
Jeremy P. Tarcher, Inc., edition published 1990
Berkley trade paperback edition / September 1992

ISBN: 0-425-13483-0

A BERKLEY BOOK ® TM 757,375
Berkley Books are published by The Berkley Publishing Group,
200 Madison Avenue, New York, New York 10016.
The name "BERKLEY" and the "B" logo
are trademarks belonging to Berkley Publishing Corporation.

PRINTED IN THE UNITED STATES OF AMERICA

10 9 8 7 6 5 4 3 2 1

Contents

Foreword

SINCE TIME IMMEMORIAL, the great cultural myths of native people have served several functions. They explained the world's creation and the workings of nature. They forged a connection between a community of human beings and the realm of spirits. They also provided a society's framework for work, play, and human relationships, establishing behavior patterns based on age, gender, and social class. Finally, cultural mythologies assisted community members during times of developmental passage—birth, coming of age, marriage, having children, coping with illness and death.

For example, there are three wedding ceremonies among the Filipino Bisayasi. In the first, the future groom announces his intentions; in the second, the extended family gives its blessings at a wedding feast; in the third, vows are exchanged. There are mythic antecedents for each of these events.

In West Africa, a newborn child is raised into the air by his father so that the universe can take note of its newest inhabitant. In many Native American tribal groups, adolescents embark on "vision quests" to discover their secret name, totem animal, or curing song. Among some mountain tribes of Southeast Asia, older community members are given the responsibility of initiating young people into the joys of sexuality.

Voodoo devotees in Haiti worship Baron Samedi, the lord of sex and death, portraying his skull-like countenance in paintings, dances, and carved masks. Elaborate funeral rituals characterize the Tanya Toraja tribe of Indonesia; they provide a special home for the corpse while the family raises the money for a proper funeral—a task that might take years. Until then, the deceased individual is not considered "dead," only "sleeping"; children take turns keeping the corpse company until the rituals can be observed.

The complex worlds of work, play, and art were also regulated by a culture's myths. Vocational activities were dictated by one's social caste in Hindu societies. Pre-Columbian athletic events in Central America often ended in death for the captain of the losing team. Balinese dance movements were carefully choreographed, leaving no room to improvise or innovate. On the other hand, shamanic practitioners were allowed considerable latitude to be creative, especially when treating illnesses, locating game, protecting the tribe from danger, or interpreting dreams.

Among hunting and gathering groups, shamans were the custodians of tribal myths. They took this role seriously, as they sang, danced, and acted out the tales and legends of gods and goddesses, heroes and villains, lovers and warriors. Later, priests and priestesses codified these teachings, making them the basis of organized religion and the institutionalized doctrines that accompanied permanent settlements and agriculture. Much later, the mythologies of dogmatic religion were bypassed altogether with the advent of technology and industrialized societies.

Today, in our technological age, various mythologies have competed for individual and group allegiances. Some individuals, bewildered by the plethora of beliefs, doctrines, and admonitions that exist in their societies, simply withdraw from the fray, allowing whim or habit to govern their moral choices or to settle internal conflicts when critical life decisions need to be made. Others fall back on the faith of their ancestors, or jump on the bandwagon of the most charismatic cult leader who passes their way.

Nevertheless, another option is available. Each of us has what my colleague David Feinstein and I refer to as an "inner shaman" who is able to create a personal mythology that represents the most profound wisdom we are capable of mustering for dealing with the turning points of our existence. Myths, both cultural and personal, are imaginal statements or stories that address the core issues of our lives, influencing our daily behavior and decision-making. Personal myths reflect what we have learned from our bodies, our cultures, or interpersonal encounters, and our spiritual experiences. Sometimes these myths are dysfunctional (as when we mutter, "I can never do anything right" or "Everyone is against me"); but they can also empower us (as when we tell ourselves, "I will put my best effort into this task" or "I cannot expect perfection from myself or from those I love"). Largely unconscious, these mythic statements and stories have filled the gap created by the disintegration of these monolithic cultural mythologies that gave direction to social groups for millennia—and that still affect the behavior of the few native societies that attempt to maintain their traditions in isolated areas throughout the globe.

Our dreams can give us the most direct access to our much-needed personal myths. Four, five, or six times each night, our lower brains initiate a random firing of nerve cells, probably in an attempt to provide some sort of neurological equilibrium during sleep. These nerve cells stimulate the higher brain, or cortex, evoking images and memories—most of them visual or kinesthetic. To make sense of these images, the brain weaves them together into a narrative, and in many cases, this narrative is one of the ready-made myths that have gradually coalesced in our unconscious over the years. When the randomly evoked images trigger a mythic framework that begins to integrate them into a meaningful narrative, that particular myth usually is reinforced and bolstered. And when we recall a dream of this nature, it can yield a valuable insight into the inner working of our minds. It can, for example, point out how a myth has outlived its usefulness. It can portray how current myths can help us solve problems. And it can assist our detection of emerging myths that might serve us in the future.

Alan Siegel has worked with these types of dreams for many years, finding them a critically important personal resource. He has been able to decode the metaphors and symbols in these dreams, discovering that they were not necessarily disguises but a remarkably cogent way to represent life's conflicts and possible solutions. By respecting the dream's narrative quality, Dr. Siegel was able to elucidate the dream's content and message. Dr. Siegel has also read widely about cultural myths and about Native American "vision quests," integrating this material into his dream workshops and classes.

Although Freudian and Jungian approaches to dreams differ, Dr. Siegel has been instructed as well by these great psychoanalytic pioneers, both of whom read widely on the topic of cultural myths, the results of which can be found in the essence of their work. However, Dr. Siegel departs from the psychoanalysts in a vital way: he endorses carefully focused do-it-yourself dreamwork as well as leaderless dream groups, which rely on mutual respect and common sense to illuminate dreams.

This book is unique in that it focuses on "turning point" dreams, those dreams with life-changing potential. Unlike native cultures, modern societies have few meaningful rites of passage. However, according to eminent mythologist Joseph Campbell, facilitating developmental transitions is a key function of cultural mythologies, as can be seen in the three-stage wedding ceremonies of the Bisayasi.

Like the instructions given in the "Books of the Dead" common in many cultures, this is a "Book for the Living," describing ways in which mythic dreams can identify turning points in one's life, such as mid-life "crises," menopause, and fears of death. He shows how these dreams can galvanize one's personal potentials in coping with misfortune and taking advantage of opportunity. And just as cultural myths once provided the template for courtship and marriage, personal myths—as revealed by Dr. Siegel's dreamers—show how our feelings regarding intimate relationships can emerge from dreams, guiding the interpersonal transition at hand.

Each cultural mythology had its unique interpretation of conception, pregnancy, and childbirth: personal myths about these events also differ dramatically, as illustrated by Dr. Siegel. Yet each set of dreams paints a vivid portrait of the dreamer, just as each set of myths bears the stamp of the tribe that lived out its dictates. To assign a dead body to its own room would be laughed at in a society where space is at a premium.

Cultural mythologies assist—and often mandate—vocational pathways; dysfunctional personal myths can be just as inflexible as the caste system which assigns "untouchables" and their descendents to menial work. These dictatorial myths can bind people to inappropriate careers or to unsatisfying jobs because "Your family has always put its life into this business" or "You have a family to support and cannot risk failure." But breakthrough dreams can reveal alternative myths and job choices that are more appropriate to the dreamer. Dr. Siegel's detailed suggestions on exploring and even "incubating" career dreams will be both revelatory and practical for many readers. Working with a series of dreams rather than only a solitary dream can be especially pertinent in exploring our relationships with employers, employees, or with the job itself.

Some neuroscientists and psychotherapists still take the position that dream content is without significant meaning or that dream material is better forgotten. These debunkers should read the stirring accounts of how nightmares often reflect post-traumatic stress, and how, if skillfully explored and worked through, they can help resolve trauma.

I suspect that dreams often help us rehearse future behavior, sort out our day-by-day memories, and make sense of our ongoing experiences, whether we recall them or not. I believe that dreams can be even more effective if we give them the attention that they deserve. In *Dreams That Can Change Your Life*, Dr. Siegel has provided an excellent guide for those who are able to accept this challenge.

I have a final, quite personal reaction to this brilliantly conceived book. Dr. Siegel gives credit to the late Gordon Tappan of Sonoma State University for stimulating and mentoring his original work with dream rituals. Professor Tappan was one of our first doctoral students at Saybrook Institute; his decision to complete his doctoral work with us helped give our neophyte graduate school valuable support and credibility during its early years. Professor Tappan touched the lives of many students, profoundly affecting the course of their development. In many ways, this book is a tribute to his sensitivity and his genius.

Stanley Krippner, Ph.D.
Professor of Psychology,
Saybrook Institute

Acknowledgments

IRST AND FOREMOST, my gratitude goes to the many men and women who contributed their time and their dreams. Their stories were a continuing source of inspiration.

The consummate editorial skills of Alan Rinzler were crucial to the completion of this book. His responsiveness helped me to find a creative rhythm, and his deft red pencil refined the words and ideas but respected my voice. Peter Beren helped me launch the book and develop my concepts. Connie Zweig and Hank Stine also provided incisive editorial and conceptual suggestions. Jeremy Tarcher provided inspiration and support throughout.

I want to offer a special note of thanks to my colleagues who generously shared their research and clinical expertise with me: Adrienne Aron on the dreams of Central American political refugees, Jane Hawes on earthquake victims, John Prendergast on the dreams of people with serious illness and those facing death, and Dale Westbrook on premarital dreams.

For their critical comments and consultation on the art of writing and publishing, I want to thank Saul Rosenberg and Patrick Gannon. My thanks also to my friends who read parts of the manuscript and offered support and constructive suggestions: David Donner, Mary Ford, Robert

Lewis, Josie Lismay, Teresa Pantaleo, Julie and Michael Searle, Daniel Sonkin, and Gary Stolzoff.

Finally I want to thank my family for their support and encouragement: my mother and father, Perle and Jerry Siegel; my grandmother, Sarabelle Siegel; my in-laws, Mae and Sam Green; my daughter, Zoe, for giving my life a wonderful new dimension; and most of all my wife, Tracy, for editorial and emotional support beyond the call of duty and for dreaming with me through all our important turning points.

Introduction

THIS BOOK WILL show you how to use dreams to resolve crucial turning points in your life. It's based on the ways I've used dreams in my life, in my work as a psychotherapist, and in dream workshops and courses I have taught.

Inspired by undergraduate courses on Freud and Jung at Johns Hopkins University, I began a daily dream journal in 1971. After some time I noticed remarkable patterns in the symbolism of my dreams. Without any conscious attempt to control or shape them, I experienced recurring images of certain people, places, and events.

During the first year of keeping my dream journal, I had repetitive vivid dreams about the two houses I lived in as a child. Almost every week I would make a dream pilgrimage back to my old neighborhood, to my family's home and the room I shared with my brother before I was ten years old. Sometimes the house would be remodeled. Other times I would see the old carpet and furniture and wait for the wind to cool me as it did on hot Florida nights in the mid-1950s.

Having these nostalgic dreams about my childhood home while I was in my sophomore year of college showed me that I was more connected to my parents than I had imagined in my nineteen-year-old fantasies of being an independent adult. The dreams made me more aware of the difficulty I was having in striking off on my own. Being able to acknowledge the strength of my lingering emotional ties helped me to be more realistic in my quest to develop my own adult identity.

During the early period of keeping my dream journal I also had a puzzling dream series involving plane crashes. In these dreams I would see an airplane and know it was about to crash. I would watch helplessly as the plane lost altitude and went down in flames. These dreams were so vivid and recurred so many times that I was tempted to take them literally. I wondered whether the dreams were an omen that I should give up flying. For a while, I even became convinced that I would witness a real plane crash.

I began to document many associations to these dreams in my journal. I had suffered from a mild fear of flying in the past. My father and uncle had both been fascinated by planes and were pilots when I was a child. I had read voraciously about the development of the space program. When I was seventeen, I'd been on a plane that was hijacked to Cuba and then quickly returned.

This dream series had more than one meaning for me. As I documented the life events surrounding the plane crash dreams, it became clear that they were not literally about planes. They were a metaphor for stressful events and periods in my life. They occurred when I was becoming too frantic, working too hard, or making too many commitments. Linking the plane crash dreams with upsetting times in my life helped me see that the dreams were warning me of an emotional imbalance. They were telling me that I was "flying too high"—that if I didn't slow down, I was risking a fiery crash back to earth.

HOW I LEARNED TO USE
MY TURNING POINT DREAMS

As more of my dream journals filled the shelf, I began to observe themes and symbols that were closely related to disturbing events and personal crises in my life. Shortly after moving into my first off-campus apartment as a sophomore in college, I came home to discover that I had been robbed. I had been warned that the neighborhood was not safe, but I had ignored the warnings. That night I had a terrible dream.

Snake in Paradise

I am near my hometown in Florida, walking near a citrus grove. I see a lawyer reading a book called Lawyer Talk. *I assume there are law offices nearby. I go over to pick some oranges, but I get tangled in the branches and stuck by thorns. I can't get untangled; I fall down. There is a thin green rope next to me. I think it's a snake but assume it's harmless. The lawyer somehow communicates to me that the snakes in that area are extremely dangerous. Terrified, I try frantically to untangle myself. The rope now looks like an arrow-headed poisonous snake. I toss violently as I wake up.*

I sketched the snake and the clutching arms of the thorny orange tree. The image of the snake fascinated and terrified me. In my journal, I spent a considerable amount of time writing down feelings and memories that were inspired by the dream.

As I pictured the snake, I realized that this was not my first snake dream. The very first dream I can remember was a nightmare I had several times when I was four and five years old.

Pleasing the Snake

I am submerged and swimming about peacefully in sea vegetation. A water snake begins to stalk me and I am scared to death. Panic-stricken, I try to flee but I am trapped and forced to face the vicious

*snake. My panic grows to hysterical proportions. I
think, "How can it do this to me?" I will do anything to escape death. Suddenly I try to win it over
and offer to be friends. I will do what it wants if it
will spare me.*

I knew from my studies that threatening animal images
are especially common in children's dreams. But why were
my dreams choosing the snake as a symbol for the dangerous or vulnerable times in my life?

When I discussed these dreams with friends, their re-
plies were stereotypically Freudian: "Aha, a sexual dream.
Snakes are phallic symbols." In fact, I've had other dreams
in which this explanation rang true, and I have observed clients' dreams in which snakes were linked to sexual or phallic symbolism. But for the snake dreams described above,
this explanation seemed inaccurate; the serpents in my
dreams were more terrifying. For me, they seemed to represent a primal sense of danger and vulnerability, a powerful
force that could threaten or destroy me.

Like the plane crash dreams, the snake dreams responded directly to events in my life. Observing the clear
linkages helped me understand the terrifying snakes in my
dreams. They were alerting me to vulnerable feelings in a
particular situation or relationship. I continued to have
snake dreams periodically: after a car accident, when I was
seriously ill with dysentery while traveling alone in Mexico,
after moving to California from the East Coast, and during
the breakup of an important relationship in my early twenties. They continued to serve as a warning from my unconscious that I was facing an impasse in resolving a turning
point.

Dreams also helped me come to terms with feelings of
grief over the loss of my grandfather. Immediately following
his death, I had a series of dreams that portrayed the stages

of my mourning. In the first dreams, he appeared just as I remembered him before his death from stomach cancer: gaunt and obviously mortally ill. In these dreams, I was worried about him and tried to talk with him. But either he would not be very communicative or the dream would end before I could talk to him. The painful quality of these dreams made me realize that I still had strong feelings of loss that were unresolved, and reflecting on the dreams helped me to clarify important aspects of my relationship with my grandfather. As I worked through my grief, those dreams became less frequent.

About a year after my grandfather's death, I had another dream that made it clear to me that I'd reached a resolution in my grieving.

In the Orange Grove with My Grandfather

I am walking in an orange grove and talking to my grandfather. There are many ripe oranges on the trees, and the grass and trees seem very green. My grandfather is talking with me and giving me some advice about my career, encouraging me to finish school or to pursue something. He seems rotund and healthy, and I am surprised that he is alive, but somehow it makes sense.

In this fertile orange grove my grandfather was acting like a mentor, giving me advice and encouragement as he did when he was alive. He'd been restored to a healthy appearance and no longer appeared gaunt or cancer-stricken. This image was devoid of the upsetting feelings of loss that had plagued me consciously as well as in my earlier dreams. This dream and others like it allowed me to see that I had reached a stage where the most painful mourning was over. I was no longer preoccupied with his illness and death and was more focused on remembering the positive qualities that he gave to me while he was alive.

HOW I USED MY DREAMS
TO RESOLVE A CAREER TURNING POINT

I searched for explanations that would clarify the striking patterns in the dreams I had at turning points. Through undergraduate course work, I encountered the writings of the renowned Swiss psychiatrist Carl Jung. Jung had observed that critical turning points often were accompanied by exceptionally vivid dreams that seemed to have universal themes. He called these Archetypal or Big Dreams. Inspired also by mythologist Joseph Campbell, I studied how other cultures utilized dreams and visions at turning points in the life cycle. I discovered that throughout recorded history, dreams have been a part of spiritual and healing practices and viewed as critically important during life transitions.

I became eager to use my own dreams to resolve a major life dilemma of my early twenties: the choice of a career. I was in a master's degree program in psychology and working in a psychiatric halfway house, but I wasn't sure I wanted to embark on the arduous training involved in a doctoral program in psychology. I longed for a career vision that would inspire me. With my professor and graduate advisor, the late Gordon Tappan, as my guide, I created a dream ritual based upon healing ceremonies practiced in hundreds of dream incubation temples in ancient Greece. I also drew inspiration from the vision quest of the Plains Indians of North America, who sent their teenage sons into the wilderness to seek a dream that would give them a career vision. Such dreams often defined a young man's adult role in the tribe as a hunter, warrior, healer, or leader.

Sleeping alone in a grove of redwoods in the California coastal hills, I had a series of dreams that created a significant turning point in my life. In the dreams, I faced my self-doubt and fears of growing up, of making adult commitments. From the depths of my fearful dreams of failure and emptiness came a vivid dream of tall, carved totem poles.

Sacred Totem Poles

There is a foolish man working for my guide. I wake up in the dream and suddenly the man has carved the redwoods into intricate lattice designs to an unreachable height. I am amazed. Previously my guide didn't think this man was competent, yet now he has done this beautiful work. I think I can do the same. He leaves and I fall back to sleep and envision each post as a totem pole. The one closest to me has especially vivid colored faces.

Exploring this and other dreams that I had in the redwoods helped me find a reservoir of confidence and decisiveness to counter my self-doubt. I began to gain a more clear picture of what I wanted to offer others in my career as a psychologist and teacher. In the Sacred Totem Pole dream, my guide had doubted that the foolish man was capable of creating those beautiful poles, just as in my life, I had imagined others were judging me as incapable of carving out my own artistic and professional vision.

These dreams didn't erase my self-doubt, but they did help me move more decisively forward in my career and resolve long-standing tendencies toward harsh self-judgment.

HOW I HELPED OTHERS LEARN TO USE THEIR TURNING POINT DREAMS

Since beginning my work as a psychotherapist in 1974, I have observed unique patterns in the turning point dreams of my clients. As clinical director of a psychiatric halfway house, I heard reports from schizophrenic clients about their terrifying nightmares just prior to their descent into psychosis. While working with abused children, I observed that they suffered from excruciating nightmares of monsters chasing them. Recent immigrants from Asia and Latin

America had recurring journey dreams of returning to their homeland, reflecting their struggle to adjust in a new and bewildering culture.

I began to conduct dream-sharing groups. In addition, I taught courses and workshops on dreams through community colleges and privately. Many of the individuals who took my courses and workshops were undergoing life transitions and were troubled as well as inspired by vivid dreams and nightmares. Because of my interest in dreams, many colleagues and friends also shared with me important dreams they experienced during life passages.

As I became aware of the amazing patterns in the dreams of people undergoing life transitions, I focused my dream workshops on the healing power of dreams and their potential for resolving the emotional dilemmas of life passages and crises.

I experimented with dream groups for expectant parents. Almost every expectant parent had anxiety dreams about the baby having birth defects, about the sex of the baby, about birthing kittens, puppies, or other furry mammals, and dreams in which the baby could precociously walk and talk. Surprisingly, quite a few men had as many or more pregnancy-related dreams as their wives.

Discussing their pregnancy dreams allowed the expectant parents to acknowledge their fears and to feel more secure in the knowledge that their anxieties were shared by couples experiencing a similar transition. Exploring the symbolism of the dreams was somehow safer and more rewarding than directly discussing a troubling issue, such as their doubts about whether they would be competent or nurturing parents.

The exciting response of the expectant parent dream groups led me to initiate the first formal research on the dreams of expectant fathers. In addition, I designed and conducted workshops especially tailored to individuals undergoing a variety of life passages. In 1980 I began a series of wilderness therapy workshops, which I called Dream Quests, inspired by my own use of dream incubation to resolve an impasse at an important life passage. These workshops combined individual and group dream exploration techniques with a structured wilderness backpacking journey.

During the 1980s I conducted professional seminars for psychotherapists, health professionals, and graduate students in psychology on how to utilize dreams to help clients resolve the emotional dilemmas of life transitions. I continued to sponsor research on dreams and life transitions by serving on dissertation committees of graduate students at the California School of Professional Psychology.

Throughout my work, the most effective training tool has proved to be an individual's in-depth exploration of his or her own dreams. It is a continual source of professional inspiration to see my clients, students, and colleagues learn how to explore and derive deeper meaning from their dreams.

USING DREAMS TO RESOLVE
YOUR OWN TURNING POINTS

This book is a guide to the healing power of dreams as a source of inner guidance and creative change during turning points. Its perspective is complementary to the insights of Sigmund Freud and C. G. Jung and to more contemporary approaches to dream work.

Freud emphasized the distinction between the manifest content and the latent content of dreams. According to Freud, the manifest or apparent content was a sophisticated camouflage for deeper, darker instincts (usually sexual or aggressive).

Contemporary proponents of psychoanalysis have questioned the idea that dreams have one specific latent content or bottom-line interpretation. Rather, there are numerous latent or hidden meanings—a collage of possibilities that can only be helpful when explored in a relationship with a psychotherapist trained in working with dreams.

There is great wisdom in this notion that dreams contain deeper levels of meaning that are not immediately visible. Indeed, working with a series of dreams is one of the most valuable approaches in the repertoire of an experienced psychotherapist. In this book, however, we will challenge the notion that dream exploration can only be accomplished within the inner chambers of the psychoanalytic or Jungian-oriented psychotherapist who is an expert on dreams.

There has been renewed interest in the individual and group exploration of dreams through the use of journals, creative writing, group sharing, and other artistic forms of expression, including drama, dance, photography, and music. Innovative techniques such as dream incubation and lucid dreaming gained prominence in the 1980s. Educators, scientists, even businessmen have used dreams for problem solving and inspiration.

The idea that dream work requires an expert analyst is often more of a barrier than an open door to working with dreams. This book stresses the need to develop a sense of confidence and expertise in working with your own dreams. It builds upon your current experiences of important life events rather than trying to fit your dreams or feelings into a rigid theoretical framework.

The emphasis will not be upon what I call a "cookbook approach" to the meaning of dreams, where the reader can look up prepackaged recipes for dream interpretation. Rather, this book will stress the need to use our dreams as a launching pad for active exploration of our feelings, ideas, and memories. Through examples, suggestions, and exercises, you will learn how you can search for emotional linkages between turning points you are experiencing and the people, places, activities, and feelings in your dreams. The book will also emphasize how turning point dreams can help you access important memories and conflicts from the past. These linkages to the past can provide vital clues to resolving emotional stumbling blocks in the present.

A turning point or period of stress is an ideal time to develop confidence in exploring your dreams, because the manifest content and underlying meanings are usually closely related to the emotional challenges you are facing. For example, in the weeks before marriage or the birth of a baby, or in the weeks after a serious injury or illness, your dreams will nearly always be focused on important conflicts related to the turning point that you're trying to resolve.

HOW TO USE THIS BOOK

In the following chapters we'll explore the extraordinary patterns of dreams that occur at specific life passages: falling in love, forming a committed relationship, pregnancy and birth, separation and divorce, career transitions, midlife crisis, illness, traumatic incidents, injury and illness, and loss. As we examine each turning point, we'll see how dreams provide an accurate gauge of the inner changes that occur at life transitions.

Some of these chapters may relate to a turning point you are going through or have encountered in the past. As you read the chapters on turning points that you have already experienced, use them as an opportunity to review the inner changes you experienced at the time. Reading about the dreams and fantasies, terrors and joys of a person preparing for marriage may recall memories of your own period of courtship, engagement, and adjustment to marriage. As you read the chapters that cover turning points you haven't yet experienced, imagine how you might react when you arrive at a midlife crisis or experience the death of a parent or close friend.

The 120 or so dreams you'll read about are reported exactly as told to me by the dreamers. The names and biographical details, however, have been altered to protect the confidentiality of the dreamers. The dreams were selected from those reported to me by my patients, students, workshop participants, research subjects, and people whom I interviewed while collecting material for this book. Some dreams are drawn from other sources and are so noted in the Notes at the back of the book.

Don't be concerned if your dream themes are less obvious or differ somewhat from the patterns described in this book. These examples have been selected for their vividness and clarity. Also don't be deceived by explanations that may seem obvious or simplistic. Even the greatest dream experts may be blind to obvious symbolism in their own dreams, and many of the explanations that appear simple and straightforward are a distillation of extensive exploration and discussion.

In order to discover the vital connections between the emotional challenges of a turning point and the bewildering images of our dreams, we need to devote special time and attention to our dreams and inner feelings. Many of us are intrigued or frightened by a vivid dream. Often a flash of insight will lead us to an explanation of the dream that feels satisfying. In this book, I will stress the value of persevering beyond that first flash of insight and discovering deeper layers of meaning in a dream. Continuing the process of exploring the many levels of meaning will be more valuable than finding a specific bottom-line interpretation.

Keep in mind that your own impressions about the unique images, feelings, and memories of your dreams are more important than what an expert says about their meaning. Even if your dreams are different from those described in this book, the process of comparing your own dreams with those in the book may trigger vital insights and help you grasp key psychological issues at each turning point. Seeing how others confront and resolve an emotional impasse will help you grasp the crucial patterns in the way you face similar turning points.

Before we embark on our dream journey through the turning points of the adult life cycle, I recommend the following steps to enhance your appreciation of your own dreams as you read this book.

Dream Journal. Keep a journal by your bed while you read this book or for a two-week period. Write down your dreams and the feelings and ideas that accompany them. *Consider every dream as important, even if it seems confused, fragmentary, trivial, or nonsensical.* Many dreams that don't seem "worthwhile" in the morning may bear rich treasures later in the day.

Dream Recall. Reserve a few moments in the morning, preferably while still in bed, to gather and mentally review your dreams.

Dream Sharing. Share and exchange one or more of your dreams with your spouse or partner or with a trusted friend during this two-week period. Tell your dream in the present tense and be aware of feelings and ideas you experience as you relate it. Also listen to your friend's dreams. Try not to analyze or interpret each other's dreams. Instead, take a supportive stance. Empathize with the feelings and marvel at the images.

As you read this book, you may notice a heightened receptivity to remembering your dreams. This frequently occurs for those who participate in dream classes or workshops or read books about dreams. So use the period while you are reading this book as a special time of paying attention to your dreams. Your efforts will be rewarded with insights, inspirations, and a closer sense of alignment with your own inner guidance.

If you're eager to learn or review more detailed guidelines for remembering and exploring dreams, turn to chapter 10, "Working with Turning Point Dreams: Recall, Journals, Symbolism, Groups, and Therapy." This chapter introduces the two-week Turning Point Dream Program, which provides a framework for connecting dream images to the crucial emotional issues you are facing. Experiencing the program will help you increase your recall of dreams, observe patterns in the symbols in your dreams, and enhance creative problem-solving skills.

Chapter 10 also provides details on the most effective techniques for working with dreams that I've discovered throughout fifteen years of teaching workshops and seminars on dreams, leading dream groups, conducting research on turning point dreams, and working with clients in psychotherapy. Details are also provided on remembering dreams, keeping a dream journal, creative techniques for exploring dreams, and interpreting dream symbolism.

1. *Can Dreams Change Your Life?*

HAVE YOU EVER wished for a source of guidance during times of crisis or critical change like the formation or breakup of a relationship, a career transition, an illness or loss of someone close? Have you ever hoped for a voice from within that could express your deepest feelings and needs?

During these moments of heightened pressures, our dreams offer an incredible inner resource. Every night we experience four to six cycles of dreaming. In an average lifetime this amounts to approximately 150,000 dreams, or four or more years of solid dreaming.

If we focus on our dreams during times of transition, they can change our life by opening a window to our unconscious. Dreams can give us access to hidden feelings and unexpressed needs that get bottled up. Learning to remember and explore dreams stimulates insights and enhances our ability to understand and resolve the unique emotional challenges that arise at turning points in life.

Throughout our lives, we face an inevitable series of profound changes and transitions. Many of these are predictable life passages, like leaving home, forming a relationship, having a family, changing jobs, reaching midlife, or retiring. Other turning points are unexpected or traumatic, such as contracting a serious illness, getting divorced, having a car accident, or enduring the death of a loved one.

Turning points can pave the way for dramatic personal growth. Our stable pattern of life is shattered and we are confronted with an awareness of how vulnerable we are. In this emotionally raw state, we experience an intense and sometimes bittersweet sense of the meaning of life. Our defenses are down and we feel a now-or-never sense of urgency. At these times we are more open to taking risks and making dramatic positive changes than we would be during more stable times.

Turning points, however, present emotional hazards as well as opportunities for personal growth. We may feel out of control or confused. We may say or do things that are out of character. During these sensitive times, we are also more likely to suffer from emotional distress, self-defeating behaviors, even physical ailments.

The choice is ours. If we don't resolve the emotional challenges that confront us, we may reach an impasse that prolongs or even paralyzes our ability to make healthy choices. On the other hand, by throwing us off-balance, turning points paradoxically offer an opportunity for healing old emotional wounds and achieving new levels of fulfillment in love and work.

At turning points, vivid dreams and nightmares are especially common. In addition to the universal themes that often occur in dreams, there are amazing patterns unique to each major type of turning point. Understanding these patterns and exploring the feelings, memories, and ideas that are sparked by turning point dreams can change your life.

When you remember your dreams, you remember your Self, your hidden wounds, fears, desires and joys. When you explore your dreams, you begin to make yourself whole: you take back the powerful feelings of grief, rage, and love that you've denied or avoided. When you share your dreams, you are sharing deeply personal feelings that create bonds of intimacy and help you receive the love and support needed to heal and grow at times of change.

The following example illustrates how turning point dreams can be viewed as an X-ray of our inner life. Rose is a woman in her late forties who has three grown daughters. She had recently made a decision that would profoundly affect the course of her life: after twenty-eight years of marriage, Rose had separated from her husband. She had wrestled with the decision to leave for over five years and was still plagued with doubts about whether she had done the right thing. She had the following dream after visiting her husband for the first time in five months.

Riding a Unicycle

I dream that I am riding along in a group of bicycles. All of a sudden I realize that everyone's attention is focused on the fact that I am riding a unicycle and not a regular two-wheeler bike. In the dream, I am thinking this is weird because I've never ridden a unicycle before. I'm feeling very self-conscious. I begin to ride away from the group and somehow I'm able to keep riding. I am incredibly happy that I can actually ride the unicycle.

At the time of the dream, Rose was pondering whether to follow through with the divorce and had met with her husband to try to make a final decision. As she discussed her dream with me, she realized that despite all of the attention, she was able to ride the unicycle. For Rose, riding the unicycle as opposed to the two-wheeler bike symbolized her struggle to do things on her own for the first time in her life.

Exploring this dream gave Rose a renewed sense of certainty. Pondering the striking image of the unicycle helped her focus on her newly emerging sense of independence.

She realized that being single felt like being a unicycle in a world of married "two-wheelers." Despite the fact that she felt stigmatized by her new status, Rose was able to take pride in her unique new way of getting around. Discussing this dream and others helped bolster her confidence that she could thrive on her own. This surprising realization helped to crystallize her decision to follow through with the divorce and to pursue graduate training for a career in business.

THE HEALING POWER OF
TURNING POINT DREAMS

Dreaming is a crucial part of how we recover from events that upset the sense of balance and security in our lives. When we are off-balance, the conscious mind may feel overwhelmed and out of control. Simultaneously, the unconscious, dreaming mind becomes more active, producing compelling images that respond directly to the emotional challenges we are facing.

Current research confirms that there is a dramatic upsurge in the number and intensity of dreams at life crises and transitions. Even the physiological experience of dreaming undergoes a transformation. During periods of upheaval, dreaming begins sooner in our sleep and our dreams become longer and involve more powerful brain activity.

Some of the biologically restorative and emotional healing powers of the dreaming mind occur whether we remember our dreams or not. However, when we begin to focus on remembering our dreams or keeping a written record of them, we activate their full therapeutic potential. Ideas and creative inspirations connected to a dream may occur to us spontaneously, and we may perceive insights and solutions to personal problems by the mere act of recalling and documenting a dream. However, the full potential of dreams can be tapped only if we devote more time and attention to experiencing, understanding, and following the wisdom of our inner dream oracle.

Following the wisdom of our dreams may take many forms. At times it may mean encountering and working through feelings that we have repressed or kept hidden. At other times it may lead to dramatic insights that we can test in important relationships. Dreams can even inspire us to consider making significant changes in our job situation or our habits and behavior patterns.

In this book we'll demonstrate the many ways that dreams can help us navigate a smoother course through the emotional turbulence of life's turning points. In particular we will look at how dreams can change our lives by

- Allowing us to identify and reclaim powerful hidden feelings that undermine our ability to move forward
- Showing us what stage we have reached in the slow process of adapting to a major turning point and providing us with an accurate gauge of the inner changes that are occurring
- Warning us about emotional conflicts and self-defeating behaviors that are blocking our ability to cope with change
- Helping us to identify and resolve wounds and anxieties from the past that have reemerged to plague us in the present
- Pointing to solutions to an emotional impasse and confirming our successes at resolving the challenges of a turning point
- Helping us to see the importance of reaching out to others for crucial emotional support at times of change
- Allowing us to perceive solutions to conflicts in our close relationships
- Getting us in touch with new sources of creativity in our work and inspiring new directions and projects

• Restoring a sense of meaning and instilling hope that
we can make it through troubling times

THE STAGES OF TURNING POINTS

Since the publication of Gail Sheehy's *Passages* in 1976,
many excellent books have described crucial psychological
features of adult life passages and crises. One of the most
valuable ways to understand life passages and human development in general is the idea of stages. It is clear that our
personalities continue to change and grow during adulthood, and there appear to be certain critical periods that
can lead to increased growth in our emotional development
or to stagnation.

In his influential book *The Seasons of a Man's Life*,
Daniel Levinson emphasizes that reaching certain crucial
age brackets, especially around the age of forty, provokes intense changes in almost all aspects of life (see chapter 5).
Psychoanalyst Roger Gould also stresses stages in his book
Transformations: Growth and Change in Adult Life. At
each new stage, illusions of security and parental protection
(which Gould calls "childhood consciousness") are dis-
pelled, and we experience a phase of grief and confusion
that can create an opportunity for greater fulfillment and
control over our lives.

In his book *Transitions*, William Bridges emphasizes
that all turning points have three stages: an ending, a period
of disorientation, and finally a resolution or new beginning.
Every turning point begins with an ending: the end of being a
single person, the end of a job or a marriage, the death of a
loved one. The ending stage disrupts our sense of security
and stability. At the same time, the disruption prepares us to
accept new circumstances. It is important not to skip over
the sense of loss that emerges in the beginning stage of a
turning point.

The second stage of a transition is often a period of disorientation. During this middle stage, old familiar ways of being have been jarred loose but a new solution has not emerged. For example, a physically active person who becomes disabled with a chronic back injury may experience an extended period of depression or anger. A woman whose husband abandoned her with two children may be so filled with resentment that she is unable to begin the arduous work of rebuilding her life.

People in this stage may not be ready to let go of the way things were. Nor can they face their grief for what's been lost or their fear of unknown circumstances ahead. They may succumb to the instinctive human tendency to cling to the old way of being and doing things even when it's no longer appropriate for the current situation. For example, the teenager who had demanded independence may secretly long for the protected security of the parental nest when leaving for college. A man or woman who enters marriage joyfully may secretly grieve over the loss of independence as a single person. People may choose divorce, yet regret the loss of some features of their former married life. Those who are unable to accept the necessary losses of the first stage may linger in the emotional twilight zone of this middle stage of a turning point.

In the final stage of a transition, painful feelings and confusion begin to subside. There has been a metamorphosis. Our identities, the roles we play in relation to others, and our feelings have all changed. In this stage, a divorcing woman may begin to feel pride in her independence and accomplishments. She may be much more hopeful about life's prospects and willing to risk forming a new love relationship. New friendships and new career directions seem more feasible.

The final stage of a transition may lead the person back to her previous level of adjustment or allow her to reach a new level of fulfillment in love and work. When we reemerge from the stages of a turning point, we often enter a new period of stability that lasts until the next turning point arrives.

THE SIGNS OF A TURNING POINT IMPASSE

A turning point impasse results when you are unable to progress through the stages of a turning point and begin to suffer from persistent signs of emotional and/or physical distress. There is often pronounced avoidance of the very issues that need to be resolved. In addition to dreams and nightmares, a variety of symptoms of distress may signal that you have reached a turning point impasse. For example, in the transition of and after a stressful or traumatic event, you may find yourself:

dreams.The dreaming mind has an uncanny ability to shine the spotlight of awareness on the emotional issues that are most challenging to us. We cannot shield ourselves from life's inevitable changes, but our dreams offer a way to overcome the hidden barriers of life's turning points. They are direct signals from the unconscious about what's really going on inside us.

RESOLVING TURNING POINTS

Be patient. There is no way to rush yourself through the emotional stages of a turning point. The emotional effects of changing careers, facing the death of a parent, or watching your last child leave for college do not disappear after a few weeks. They come and go in waves. The cycle may continue for months as you overcome your resistance to change and gradually gather strength to confront the core of your feelings.

Keep in mind that even so-called positive turning points that we feel happy about consciously, such as having a child, getting married, or receiving a promotion, are filled with hidden stresses. Because we feel we are supposed to show a happy face during these times, it is hard to admit any worries.

Many people feel deeply ashamed that they're still troubled by feelings left over from an unresolved turning point. They feel that they should have worked out all the changes and gotten back to normal. However, long after friends and family members stop inquiring about their distress, they may have lingering feelings of grief, anger, or doubt.

Different kinds of turning points will be more devastating to one person than to another. After a divorce one person may be well on the road to recovery after a few weeks. A year or more later, another person may still be seriously depressed and showing signs of an impasse. If your thoughts and feelings continue to be dominated by a turning point or if you are experiencing symptoms of turning point impasse, you probably need more time and some assistance to get through it.

Ask for help. The best antidote to the hazards of a turning point is to seek extra emotional support from others. At times when they need it the most, many people tend to withdraw from others or to neglect valuable sources of support in their life. At turning points, supportive friends and family members may be your best medicine. It's important to set aside the shame or doubts you may feel and reach out to others at a moment of need. Seeking support often triggers other constructive actions that will move you in the direction of a healthy resolution. If you are experiencing the signs of a turning point impasse, you may also want to consider professional help from a psychotherapist, support group, or clergy person.

Try not to judge the nature of your emotional reactions or measure the timetable of your recovery. Keep in mind that we all resist changes and are subject to psychological defenses such as denial and repression—for example, denying the emotional impact of a turning point or unwittingly forcing an idea, feeling, or memory out of our conscious awareness. These defenses date from childhood and were initially a way of protecting ourselves from overwhelming emotions or stimulation.

When our defense mechanisms persist, blocking our ability to respond emotionally, we may have difficulty adapting to change. Remember, however, that our defensiveness and slow response time at turning points are not evidence of moral weakness or laziness. They reflect our struggle to deal with profoundly upsetting changes in our identity, relationships, and life circumstances.

Finally, use your dreams. They offer a sensitive gauge of conflicts that may be bogging you down. By tapping into your inner reservoir, you can navigate the emotional perils of a turning point and chart a new, healthier life course.

DRAMATIC DREAM PATTERNS AT LIFE PASSAGES

During the 1970s and 1980s, a growing body of research established the presence of dramatic patterns in the content of turning point dreams. Research has included studies of expectant mothers' and fathers' dreams; dreams around the time of marriage and divorce; dreams about coping with cancer, AIDS, and other serious illnesses; dreams of elderly people and those facing imminent death; dreams of depressed and suicidal individuals; and dreams of individuals recovering from traumatic accidents and losses.

This research has helped us understand recurrent dream themes that are common to most individuals who undergo similar transitions. For example, brides and grooms-to-be often dream about disastrous events at their weddings, liaisons with old lovers, or their partners suddenly showing ghastly characteristics that were previously concealed. Recent widows or widowers may be visited by images of their departed spouses beckoning to them or disappearing and abandoning them. People with grave illnesses may dream about time running out and clocks breaking. Immigrants often have recurrent journey dreams about returning to their homeland.

Pregnancy is a turning point that is fertile for dreams as well as for the growing fetus. Pregnant women may dream about fears of birth defects, nurturing furry puppies and sea otters, and whether the baby will be a boy or girl. Expectant fathers are also prolific dreamers. An especially common turning point dream for them is what I call Fetal Identification dreams. In these dreams, the father-to-be unconsciously expresses the power of his prenatal bond with his child by taking on a role that is directly parallel to the experience of the fetus in the womb. Late in pregnancy, it is not uncommon for men to dream of popping out of caves or emerging from underwater bubbles.

Daniel, thirty-two, who worked in public relations, had a classic Fetal Identification dream. Daniel was enthusiastic about the birth of his child. Prior to telling me his dream, he expressed strong views about the decision he and his wife had made to have a home birth attended by a midwife and labor coach. The dream he related to me went as follows.

Winning the Race

I was in a swimming pool and there was going to be a race. I was swimming very fast. Our labor coach was on the side of the pool cheering me on. I was winning the race but it felt like I was swimming downhill. Suddenly I am in the locker room. It seems like I won the race and I am being wrapped in a towel by a woman, maybe our midwife.

Despite the transparent symbolism of identification with the fetus traveling and emerging from the waters of the birth canal, when I asked Daniel what feelings or ideas occurred to him, he indicated that the only thing he could get from the dream was that perhaps he should swim more. He said he hadn't been getting much exercise recently and needed to get back into his swimming routine. When I pointed out the dream's possible connection to the birthing process, he was a little embarrassed but very excited, as if something he had been searching for but couldn't quite grasp had been confirmed.

Prior to exploring this dream, he had felt uncertain about his role in the pregnancy and nervous about his impending fatherhood. Discussing his dream helped Daniel understand the strength of his psychological identification with his child.

For men, awareness of dreaming about the pregnancy and their child-to-be provides a visual, sensory, and emotional connection to their baby. Remembering and discussing his dreams can help a man to more fully acknowledge the magnitude of his emotional response to pregnancy and the importance of taking a collaborative role in the preparation for parenting.

This book draws upon our growing knowledge about the special wisdom of the dreaming mind. As we embark on a guided tour of the passages and crises of adulthood, you'll see a theme emerging. During each turning point, our dreams tell the inner story of our deepest feelings. These include hidden feelings of grief, confusion, anger, even joy and fulfillment—feelings that we are unaware of, not ready to face, or that we fear may leave us devastated.

BREAKING THE SPELL OF NIGHTMARES

Nightmares are more frequent at turning points than at more stable times. They are an indication of the inner turmoil that accompanies momentous passages, even supposedly positive ones such as marriage, pregnancy, and graduation.

Nightmares are fearful dreams that overwhelm us and often cause us to awaken. Psychoanalyst and eminent nightmare researcher Ernest Hartmann defines nightmares as simply "something from inside that awakens a person with a scared feeling." Because nightmares awaken us and waking up is necessary for remembering dreams, we recall a larger proportion of our nightmares. Especially at turning points, it may seem that the world of dreams is a realm of nightmares. As painful as nightmares feel, they are one of the most direct sources of self-knowledge. They give us a raw, uncensored view of the very issues that are most upsetting to us.

At turning points, just when you're most vulnerable and really need those precious hours of sleep, nightmares may invade your psyche like terrifying marauders that torture you and leave you shaken upon awakening. There are many variations on the basic nightmare theme of being overwhelmed by powerful forces. You may dream that you're being chased by crack dealers with Uzis, or that your car is going out control but your foot is paralyzed so you can't hit the brakes, or that a giant earthquake destroys your home and you don't know if your family was inside. Such nightmares are common at turning points.

Nightmares often involve profound anxiety and a threat to our physical safety or survival. In our nightmares, we commit, witness, or are threatened by acts of violence and immorality. The most common themes include being chased, paralyzed, violently attacked, abandoned or rejected, imprisoned or kidnapped, and subject to disasters such as tidal waves, earthquakes, fire, or nuclear contamination.

Nightmares are the reason many people prefer to forget their dreams. Like a child who can't distinguish dream from reality, the awesome emotional power of a nightmare may leave us in a state of confusion. Will we be arrested for the murder we committed? Will our spouse file for divorce after that flagrant affair?

How can such painful experiences help us to resolve the emotional challenges of a turning point? If we can learn to break the painful spell of our turning point nightmares, we can begin to decode the vital messages they bring us.

To break that spell, it is important to understand that nightmares increase at turning points and exaggerate our deepest fears. Becoming familiar with the recurring themes in our nightmares can be reassuring. As we begin to explore the themes of our nightmares, searching for patterns, their terrifying grip will loosen. As soon as we remember, write down, share, or explore a nightmare, we are beginning to break that spell and see our nightmares as a source of awareness rather than a nightly stint in a torture chamber.

For example, a series of nightmares about being pursued by armed terrorists becomes less daunting when you realize that the lead terrorist reminds you of your boss and the dreams are related to your reactions to unfair demands he's imposing. The aftermath of a nightmare is less upsetting if you can understand how it relates to unresolved issues in your life.

Furthermore, nightmares are not necessarily a sign of a turning point impasse. Remembering a nightmare may even be a sign that we are beginning to master the emotional challenges of a turning point. In a study of pregnant women, those who remembered more dreams with threatening and hostile themes actually had shorter labors and fewer complications.

Each nightmare offers us a vital message, even a warning about issues and relationships that we've been unable to resolve. By bringing our hidden fears into the light of day, nightmares can become a potent resource for healing. Nightmares, like all dreams, clarify exactly what's troubling us and open up opportunities for growth.

2. Relationship Dreams
Working Out Fears
of Commitment
before Marriage

And yet there was no objective truth to the dreams, since Sarah was ahead of schedule in arranging practical details of the wedding. In fact, both the rings and the wedding dress had already been purchased. Was her unconscious telling her she should call off the wedding? Sarah *was* unprepared— emotionally. It was hard for her to admit to herself or anyone else that she was intensely ashamed about being uncertain as she approached her wedding. Until she faced the fears that were causing her uncertainty about the marriage, Sarah's nightmares continued. In the section of this chapter titled Dreams of Losing Valuables, I will present one more of Sarah's nightmares and describe how exploring dreams helped her to acknowledge her ambivalence about marriage and take constructive steps to resolve her anxieties.

DREAMS REVEAL THE AGONY AND ECSTASY OF PREPARING FOR MARRIAGE

At each stage of the courtship process and with each successive level of emotional commitment, new themes emerge in our dreams. And when we decide to tie the proverbial knot, wedding-related themes dominate our dreams during the last three months before marriage. In fact, the innovative research of psychologist Dale Westbrook, Ph.D., has shown that 40 percent of all dreams in this prenuptial period contain direct or slightly disguised references to the wedding ceremony, the spouse-to-be, and the marriage in general.

The tears of joy often shed by a bride or groom on their wedding day may express the profound emotional commitment they are publicly declaring. But this apparent bliss shouldn't give the illusion that getting ready for marriage is easy. In reality, like other major turning points, such as having a first child or beginning a planned retirement, marriage requires extensive and often stressful preparations.

After the marriage plans are set and deposits for the caterer, florist, photographer, and dress are paid, a claustrophobic feeling may set in. It feels like there is no escape. Almost everyone experiences one or more bouts of panic about the magnitude of the commitment.

Under the pressure of the final days, some people head for the exit sign. In fact, over a fifty-year period in New York City, a steady 5 percent of those who take out marriage licenses do not get married within the required sixty-day period.

For the large majority who go ahead with marriage, there is an obstacle course of worries during the final days of being single. Although premarital anxieties are common and in most cases a healthy sign of adjustment, there is a persistent tendency to deny them.

One of the most prevalent feelings that couples try to avoid is doubt. Most of us hate to admit that we're worried about doing the right thing. After all, aren't we supposed to be totally certain when we take that marriage vow committing ourselves for life? It's hard to admit that we're feeling ambivalent, especially in the last few weeks when plans are set and invitations have already gone out. Yet, is it really abnormal to worry when the divorce rate is over 50 percent? Is it pathological to be concerned about whether your spouse will be a loving parent to your children? Is it strange to be apprehensive about repeating your parents' pattern of endless bickering and emotional alienation?

Many couples focus their energies and anxieties on the external demands of organizing the wedding and neglect the profound inner transformation that is taking place. They're so busy planning the huge expenses and ritualistic events that they may not look deeply at their feelings. Besides that, they may have two families breathing down their necks with endless expectations and advice.

Before the wedding, our dreams act like an inner radar, exaggerating the very feelings that are most difficult to admit or accept. When we allow our dream radar to alert us to hidden fears and deeper dimensions of our feelings, we may harvest subtle yet important insights. We may even be inspired to make changes in marriage plans and preparations that express our true needs and feelings. Occasionally, a dream or series of dreams will even stimulate a person to delay or cancel an engagement or wedding.

In this chapter, we'll explore the most common prewedding dreams and learn how they can help you to cope with the inner experience of marriage. We will see how sharing and exploring dreams can offer an antidote to your anxieties by helping you to

- Recognize and communicate your feeling and needs to your fiancé over issues such as conflicts over the details of the wedding, performance anxieties about the wedding day, and tension with family and in-laws
- Deal with fears of intimacy and commitment, such as the sense of panic about whether you are choosing the right person (is there someone more suited to you, or will your prince turn out to be a frog in disguise?), the grief of losing the personal and sexual freedom of being single, and fears of repeating unhealthy patterns from your parents' or your own past relationships
- Resolve anxieties about changes in identity and roles, including changes in name, relationships, religious orientation, and status in the community
- Savor the joy and the spiritual dimension of the marriage preparation and ritual

Ceremonial Disaster Dreams. Dreams about mishaps and misfortunes at the ceremony and reception recur frequently during the period just before the marriage. These Ceremonial Disaster dreams are a direct reflection of the most common conscious anxieties about planning a wedding. They portray every imaginable calamity that could spoil our enjoyment of the event.

For example, Robin, twenty-five, had been working with her mother to plan an elegantly catered affair. They'd been having many stormy arguments because Robin didn't want the wedding to be as formal as her mother did. She was resentful, moreover, of her mother's attempts to control every detail of the wedding but at the same time secretly worried about pleasing her.

Tacky Food at My Wedding

We're sitting at the head table at the reception and I notice that the waiters are serving canned spaghetti directly from the cans. I'm horrified and I don't know what to do.

Robin woke with a feeling of humiliation and panic. After all the planning and verbal battles, would they really end up with canned spaghetti? Would she be mortified in front of her family and friends and disappoint her mother?

Robin's panicky feeling began to subside when she told her dream to her fiancé, who laughed out loud when he heard it. Life would be easier, he said, if they *could* just serve canned spaghetti at the reception. He also reminded her that when they went on their first camping trip the summer they met, she had brought along canned spaghetti, and they had enjoyed it. In discussing the dream further with her fiancé, she realized that she wanted her wedding to be more down to earth with an emphasis on sharing the emotional experience rather than obsessing over expensive and showy material details.

The absurdity of the spaghetti banquet made Robin aware of how much tension had built up between her and her mother. As long as she could remember, her mother had been nervous about how the food would turn out at any party she was throwing. Robin realized that she too had succumbed to her mother's emphasis on how things look and what other people would think.

Robin's dream also stimulated her to think about the deeper changes that were occurring beneath the conscious conflicts in her relationship with her mother. Robin had desperately wanted her mother's approval of her marriage plans, but her mother had initially been critical and said Robin was too young. Robin realized now that her mother was having a difficult time accepting the marriage because it represented a separation. Financing and planning the wedding was a way for her mother to reassert the control over Robin she feared she was losing.

In any case, Robin began to insist on toning down some of the expenses and formalities of her wedding reception. This initially led to further arguments, but Robin was gradually feeling more sure of what she wanted. Ultimately her mother acceded to Robin's demands and they were able to work collaboratively, with Robin taking more of the lead.

Understanding her dream helped Robin become assertive in a new way, a way that changed her relationship with her mother. She felt that she was no longer just her mother's daughter but would be on more equal footing, with a husband and eventually a family of her own.

Ceremonial Disaster dreams take many forms. Forgetting one's lines during the ceremony is another common theme. Prior to my own wedding, I had a series of dreams that depicted variations on this theme.

Forgetting My Lines
The wedding is beginning and everyone is watching us. I begin to panic because I realize that we have never rehearsed and we forgot to even write our vows. I don't know what to do or say next.

At that point in our wedding planning, we had in fact neither rehearsed nor written our vows. Soon afterward, we spent a weekend in Yosemite, writing our vows and planning the final details of the ceremony. Even this didn't cure me of my wedding anxiety dreams. I continued to have dreams about forgetting to rehearse and forgetting my lines. I was becoming increasingly nervous and impatient.

A final variation occurred twice within two weeks of the wedding. In these dreams, the ceremony seemed to be flowing well and I knew my lines, but something was missing. I felt that I should be having stronger feelings. I didn't feel ready. At this point my optimism was shaky. Was I doing the right thing? Finally, during the last week before the wedding, a resolution of these fears appeared.

Finding My Lines

The wedding ceremony is beginning. It isn't at the hotel. It is outside near the ocean. Everyone is surrounding us in a circular formation. I'm worried because I forgot to bring our vows and the Ketubbah (the Jewish wedding contract). As I speak, I am ad-libbing, making up new lines and new vows to Tracy that seem more meaningful and more emotional than what we had written. I feel incredibly excited and that everything is working out perfectly.

This dream begins with the fears that had been plaguing my dreams for weeks—forgetting my lines and performing poorly in front of family and friends. But then at the crucial moment, I find my inner voice and declare my love for my wife in a more heartfelt and highly original way. This dream was consistent with a lifting of anxiety in the days preceding our wedding. Our material and emotional preparations had helped me to feel ready for the marriage ritual.

Finding my voice in this dream left a glow of confidence that carried me to the joyful day itself. The dream represented an emotional breakthrough for me. It was parallel to my Sacred Totem Poles dream (see Introduction), through which I discovered a reservoir of confidence and creativity at a moment of self-doubt.

If you have a Ceremonial Disaster dream, it may appear at first glance to be nothing more than an inner reminder to memorize your lines, pick up the rings, make sure you are on time, and so on. Closer examination, however, often reveals that these dreams are only the tip of the iceberg. Lurking just below the surface is an underworld of upsetting feelings. These include anxieties about how you will "perform" in the new cycle of life, and about fears of being judged by family and friends, as well about your loss of independence, and for some, a perplexing sense of now being ready for the finality and permanence of marriage.

identity as a married man. When I began to talk about these fears with my fiancée and close friends, I began "finding my lines" in my dreams.

Sexual Adventure Dreams. Many infidelities and erotic adventures occur in the dreams that precede marriage. Sexual Adventure dreams feature sensual or directly sexual liaisons, often with partners other than your intended spouse. These may involve old flames, unknown or anonymous partners, friends, relatives, or even colleagues.

Julia was only eight days away from her marriage to Bruce when she had the following dream.

The Kiss

There is a muscular-looking man who is with me in my office at work. He looks sort of like Tony, an associate at my company, but he seems much more attractive. We are kissing and at first it seems strange because we work together. But somehow that doesn't matter. He is kissing me with his tongue and it seems like we are in a bedroom. His kiss is incredibly pleasurable and seems to go on for a long time. Right in the middle of this sexy interlude, the scene changes and I hear the phone ringing and I think it is Bruce on the line but it's all static and I can't hear his voice well. I wake up saying out loud: "Is that you, Bruce?" (and coincidentally the phone is ringing when I wake up and it really is Bruce on the line).

Julia experienced the first part of the dream as surprisingly pleasurable, though Tony was a man she had rejected in the past. In fact, Tony had tried to take advantage of their professional relationship by making sexual advances. Although Tony's macho tendencies were repugnant to her in waking life, she found herself consenting to his advances in her dream.

Julia wondered why she was making love in this dream with her work associate and not her fiancé. She felt no conscious desire to be sexually intimate with Tony or any other man except Bruce. In fact, she remembered that she had recently told Bruce that her working relationship with Tony had improved considerably since she had announced their engagement.

At times, overtly sexual dreams may symbolize non-erotic themes. This dream mirrors the rapprochement that Julia had achieved with Tony in their working relationship, but there was something more in the dream that had to do with her sexual relationship with Bruce. In the past, Julia had become sexually involved with men who were brusque and not very open emotionally, like Tony. Bruce was dramatically different, more emotionally expressive and caring. Julia felt that the dream was telling her that she had begun to escape her old pattern of picking macho men. The sexual pleasure in the dream was more like the new kind of erotic warmth she was feeling with Bruce, a feeling she never had in any previous sexual relationships. After exploring her dream, Julia concluded that it was not so much about Tony, as about breakthroughs in her ability to be intimate with Bruce.

Fear and anxieties about the meaning of loyalty are common stumbling blocks on the road to marital commitment. As the wedding date approaches, themes of sexual fidelity and infidelity abound in the dreams of both men and women. A frequent theme is of a spontaneous erotic encounter interrupted by an awareness that you are now engaged or married, making such behavior taboo.

Dennis' premarital Sexual Adventure dream featured an anonymous younger woman. Dennis awoke with feelings of guilt and anxiety three weeks before his wedding.

I Can't; I'm an Engaged Man

A young attractive woman comes up to me and makes seductive overtures and we engage in some making out and light petting. I feel anxious because I know it isn't right for an engaged man to be making out with someone else. I am suspicious of the young woman's motives, call it off, and she leaves.

Dennis worried that he would still be attracted to old lovers and wouldn't be able to maintain his loyalty after so many years of being single. Would he be tempted in real life to taste the forbidden fruit and engage in sexual infidelity?

One way to understand this type of dream is as a form of unconscious rehearsal for maintaining self-control in an exclusive sexual relationship. As we enter into a marriage, our dreams frequently remind us of our newly formed commitment by contrasting our impending vows of fidelity with images of infidelity.

If you have a blissful or warm Sexual Adventure dream with your fiancé or in any important new relationship, it may be reflective of a period of sexual passion that you are enjoying. But even during a passionate period in your sexual relationship, you may have dreams of other sexual partners. This nocturnal wanderlust is not necessarily a sign that your partner can't satisfy you. It may be a way of representing the depth, variety, and newness of your current sexual relationship.

There are other issues to keep in mind as you explore your own Sexual Adventure dreams. Just as symbols in dreams may have camouflaged sexual meaning, overtly sexual dreams may have hidden meanings that relate to issues other than sex. For Julia, her dream affair with her colleague reflected changes in her waking relationship with Tony, but more profoundly it was evidence of a new emotional openness with a man. The wonderful sensuality of her dream kiss gave Julia confidence that she had chosen a man who would treat her well.

Sexual Rejection Dreams. Six weeks prior to his wedding, thirty-four-year-old Brian began to have a series of vivid dreams about sexual encounters with old girlfriends. When I met with him to discuss his dream series, he was ashamed about his persistent dream infidelities. He was not only feeling guilty, but he had been experiencing signs of depression such as disturbed sleep, loss of appetite, irritability, and persistent sadness. He was beginning to feel that his dreams and his depression were telling him that the marriage was not right.

As he shared his dream series with me I noticed that his initial dreams involved liaisons with women with whom he had been involved just prior to his engagement. Subsequent dreams portrayed earlier girlfriends of his twenties, and he even dreamt of reunions with girlfriends from high school and junior high.

Back with My High School Girlfriend

I'm back in my hometown visiting Andrea, my high school girlfriend. She wants to make love and tells me she has loved me all these years. "Aren't you still married?" I ask her. She doesn't answer but I have a feeling that she has left her husband.

Brian was especially troubled by these dreams and wondered whether they were telling him that he still had wild oats to sow or that he wasn't ready for the commitment of marriage.

A series of repetitive dreams usually reveals unresolved emotional issues. As Brian reread more than a dozen of these dreams in his journal, he began to see a pattern. In over half the related dreams, his sexual partner would reject him toward the end, becoming cold or appearing with another man. In one dream, Brian was seduced and then scorned by Arlene, a woman he had lived with in college. Their relationship had ended when she left him for another man.

Jilted Again

I am back living with Arlene in our old apartment in New York. I can see her naked body. She still looks young, as if she hasn't aged at all. I feel very sexual. Maybe we have just made love or are about to. She suddenly says that she has to leave and starts to get dressed. I ask her if there is another man. She is reluctant but finally says yes as she is about to leave. I feel incredibly sad.

In waking life, Brian's sexual relationship with his fiancée was still passionate. He wondered what could be causing his mind to focus on old lovers and especially on being rejected. Brian had always feared rejection. In two previous serious relationships, he had experienced rejection when the woman decided to end the relationship. As the middle child in his family, in fact, he had always secretly felt that his older sister and younger brother had gotten more of his parents' love. Consequently he had always felt insecure in close relationships.

As he explored this series of dreams, Brian realized that they weren't really expressing desires for sexual infidelity, nor were they literal predictions that he would face rejection if he went through with the marriage. Rather, his guided tour of being teased and rejected by old flames was a persistent message about his fear of rejection. On the threshold of making a lifelong commitment, deep fears of abandonment were surfacing.

Sharing and exploring his Sexual Rejection dreams helped Brian understand how his deeply rooted fears of abandonment were blocking him from being able to accept the emotional commitment of marriage. By acknowledging his fears and seeking emotional support, Brian was able to restore his optimism about the wedding and alleviate his depression.

As you explore your own Sexual Rejection dreams, you may discover that you are still vulnerable to old wounds of being rejected or abandoned. These emotional wounds may come from adult experiences of being rejected in love, or they may date back to childhood traumas, such as the birth of a younger sibling or separation from a parent or other significant relative due to divorce or death. They may also relate to lingering Oedipal conflicts. According to Freud, such conflicts occur when a child's normal feelings of attraction toward the opposite-sex parent and rivalry with the same-sex parent are not adequately resolved.

Dreams of Losing Valuables. Sarah had been looking forward to her marriage with David and to the long-cherished hope of having a child. They had been getting along well and both families approved of the match. They decided to move in together after getting engaged three months earlier. As her wedding date approached, however, Sarah became preoccupied with an uneasiness that she couldn't explain. Her dreams, which had initially been joyful, gave way to a series of troubling nightmares. Two of Sarah's Ceremonial Disaster dreams are described at the beginning of this chapter.

She tried to suppress her anxieties. She felt ashamed about getting cold feet at this late date. But as much as she tried to deny her doubts about the marriage, the nightmares kept increasing. She began to have a recurrent dream, which was always followed by a feeling of helplessness and depression.

Losing My Purse

I want to go out to do something by myself. I realize I can't find my purse anywhere. I look frantically for it but can't find it. Suddenly, I remember that I left it in the trunk of David's car. I won't be able to go anywhere until he gets home. I feel trapped.

Sarah discussed her dreams with her fiancé. He became quite worried that she had changed her mind about the wedding. After confiding in her friends, she decided to seek guidance from a psychotherapist and came to see me.

The meaning of her repetitive nightmares did not seem obvious at first. I encouraged Sarah to brainstorm about what the dream was telling her. Her first thought was that David was very possessive about his car and didn't like her to drive it. Then she said she couldn't remember losing a purse or leaving anything in his trunk. She decided to focus in a general way on what else she might be losing. Before the word "losing" could roll off her tongue, her mind began to click on a number of possibilities.

Sarah had been secretly upset about giving up her apartment of seven years and moving in with David. Her old apartment had been decorated with souvenirs from trips she had taken to Europe and Asia. David said he would allow her to redecorate parts of his house with her artifacts, but so far they had never had the time to do so. In fact, she had even been reluctant to unpack her belongings. She felt as if she was losing the strong identity of her old home and with it a hard-earned sense of independence and separateness.

Discussing the dream also allowed Sarah to become aware of mixed feelings about the religious aspects of the wedding. She had agreed to be married in the Catholic church where all of David's family were members. Sarah realized that David and his family were overwhelming her. She felt as if she was losing her connection to her own familiar religious and cultural traditions.

"Talking about these dreams made me realize that I was afraid of losing my independence and being dominated by David and his family. When I finally put my finger on what was bothering me, I knew I could at least try to do something about it," she said.

The dream of losing a purse or wallet is one of the most common themes worldwide. A purse or wallet is something that you keep with you and protect. It contains identification, valuables, and photos of important people in your life. Dreaming that you lose your wallet or purse often symbolizes fears about changes in your identity or losing a connection to religious, moral, or cultural values that may be important to you.

Sarah did not call off the wedding. She did, however, take a more assertive stance with David and his family. She insisted that David help her begin redecorating the house with some of her belongings and that they spend less time visiting his family on weekends. She also took a stronger stance with David's mother on planning the wedding reception. These actions did not completely resolve Sarah's fears of being dominated by David and his family, but they did make her feel hopeful that she could maintain her sense of independence and work out issues in the future. Sarah's depression improved substantially and her nightmares subsided as the result of confronting these issues.

If you have dreams of losing valuables such as wallets, purses, money, jewels, or other precious possessions, you may want to consider what emotional losses you are experiencing. The types of losses may vary at different turning points, but fears about losing one's identity and independence are especially common prior to marriage.

Bride of Frankenstein Dreams. Dreams exaggerate our fears and doubts about the marriage partner. A common expression of these fears is dreams that portray the fiancé with some previously unknown, unacceptable—even grotesque—quality. These dreams often have more to do with the dreamer than with the marriage partner. For example, a woman named Diane had the following dream.

Blue Suede Suit

My fiancé shows up dressed in a horrible blue suede patchwork jacket and announces he is getting married. He feels that if he married me he couldn't be wild. I think this is odd, since before he arrived, I'd been flying through the air, convertible.

air in convertibles and wear wild and crazy clothes. Reflecting on this dream helped Diane to better understand her own ambivalence about losing her independence as a single person.

In her study of women's dreams, Patricia Garfield describes an attractive woman who dreamed that her fiancé announced he wasn't going to marry her because she was ugly. He then turned into a terrifying monster. In the dream she thought she'd have to cancel the wedding but was horrified at the prospect.

In some instances, this kind of dream could be considered as a warning that some unknown attribute of the marriage partner may prove disastrous for the success of the marriage. In this case, however, the dream was not a premonition of her fiancé becoming a verbally abusive or rejecting husband; Garfield reported that the couple was happy three years after their wedding.

Knowing the happy outcome, we can speculate that this dream was rather a reflection of wounds the woman suffered earlier in her life. On the threshold of commitment, fears of reliving harsh parental criticism, abandonment, or even physical abuse may surface and limit the bride or groom's ability to be intimate. This bride was able to identify and overcome her fears. Until they are acknowledged, however, such fears can exert a hidden influence that may limit our emotional readiness for marriage.

In a related dream analysis, Carl Jung writes of a university student who developed a severe difficulty in swallowing after becoming engaged to a girl from a good family. He was also unable to study for his final exams. Jung requested that the man remember and report his dreams in an effort to discover the source of the physical symptoms. When he related his dreams to Jung, he was stunned to observe that his fiancée frequently appeared as a prostitute or in other unflattering circumstances.

In this case, Jung had an intuition that the dreams contained a kernel of truth. Although the patient strenuously objected to the suggestion that his dreams were based on fact, an investigation of the woman by a private detective revealed that the dreams were accurate. According to Jung, the "shock of the unpleasant discovery did not kill the patient but on the contrary, cured him of his neurosis and also of his bride."

Even a dream that has an objective basis should be considered on a more subjective level. In the book *Dreams, A Portal to the Source*, Jungian analysts Edward Whitmont and Sylvia Perera discuss this same patient further. In their view, his dream may have revealed what his heart had known but was unable to admit. They speculate that the dreamer may have unconsciously chosen a partner lacking in integrity or commitment because he was unable to face those very attributes in himself. Or perhaps he had been prostituting himself by engaging in marriage plans for some expected financial or social gain.

Bride of Frankenstein dreams present grotesque and even humorous caricatures of the prospective partner. When you have a dream of this nature, consider whether it is about some upsetting feature of your partner or whether it may be a parody of some unexplored aspect of your own character.

Clothing and Nudity Dreams. Clothing or the lack of it is a frequent theme in prenuptial dreams. A woman may have fantasized for many years about how she will look in her wedding gown. Consequently, anxiety about being improperly dressed or in some state of nakedness is common. One woman dreamed she looked down during the ceremony and noticed that she was wearing one blue shoe and one white shoe. Another woman dreamed that she had completely forgotten to hem her dress, which had ragged edges.

Another dreamed that while putting on her wedding dress she noticed that it looked like a huge, very unflattering padded bra.

Dreams such as these are a variation on the Ceremonial Disaster dream. A focus on clothing, new hairstyles, or improper attire appears frequently in dreams of people who are going through transformations in their identity. Changing clothing often symbolizes an inner rehearsal of new roles. These dream rehearsals don't usually proceed smoothly. As in the dreams above, there is often an anxious moment of awareness. An appearance or a role that we thought we could fit into suddenly seems impossible.

Appearing naked in public is another theme common to many cultures. Although the meaning may differ for each dreamer, this type of imaginary embarrassment often occurs when the dreamer is afraid of exposing some emotional vulnerability in waking life. Frequently associated with a feeling of being unprepared, it is another variant of the performance anxiety theme of Ceremonial Disaster dreams. A common premarital variation is dreams that feature the bride or groom in underwear, being exposed or partly naked at the wedding ceremony, or in other compromising circumstances.

Dream researcher Dale Westbrook examined the issue of clothing dreams in her 1989 study of the premarital dreams of men and women over the age of thirty-five marrying for the first time. The grooms-to-be had clothing references in 28 percent of their dreams, as compared to only 2 percent for a matched control group. Phrases such as "feeling well-suited" and trying to "fit in" to new clothes were typical.

Andrew, a thirty-nine-year-old man in Westbrook's study, had two dreams in the same week that related to changing roles and identities. Andrew had been rebellious in his twenties and thirties, refusing to conform to the social norms he perceived to be a part of mainstream society. He had refused to work in a traditional career or to dress in a conventional manner.

In Andrew's first dream he found himself with his fiancée, Nancy, in a neighborhood of older homes.

Naked in a World of Traditional Values
I'm naked. At first this is OK. Then I realize how easily I could be spotted on the street. I ask Nancy to go to the headquarters of the enemy and sneak out clothes for me. She could try this because they wouldn't have to suspect she was helping me.

In this dream, Andrew has no secure role within the world of mainstream commitments. He is oblivious at first, but suddenly experiences fear at his nakedness. To resolve his sense of vulnerability, he uses his fiancée as an infiltrator in the world of his former enemy: traditional values.

Later that week, Andrew had the second dream in this series.

Designing My New Uniform
I have been given a promotion at my job. I'm designing a new uniform for the position. It will consist of yellow tennis shoes with black soles and laces, yellow pants, yellow shirt, a pleated coat/ shirt that is black on the outside and yellow on the inside. I don't know if the tie is to be yellow or black.

Andrew felt "excitement and preoccupation" as he described his new uniform. He had not actually received a new job or promotion, but felt that this dream symbolized his efforts to fit into social norms. Andrew's yellow uniform is a far cry from a pinstripe suit, and he is clearly not ready to adopt a totally traditional lifestyle. But his dream does suggest that he is engaged in an inner struggle to develop a new look, a new way of appearing to others and experiencing himself in the world.

The necktie is another recurrent symbol of "tying the knot" for men who are entering into marital commitments. One groom dreamed he was struggling to tie a yellow tie. Another dreamed his tie was too tight. In reality, he ultimately broke off the engagement.

Clothing and Nudity dreams are common throughout the life cycle. At turning points that require us to take on new roles, such as marriage, clothing dreams often represent explorations of new appearances. Nudity dreams in general are suggestive of a feeling of being exposed or psychologically vulnerable. They also correlate with a sense of openness and sincerity.

Dreams of Physical Danger. A common focus of anxiety in prewedding dreams is fear of physical danger to oneself or one's fiancé. Dreaming of physical danger may relate to actual fears for the safety of the partner. A spouse who works in a dangerous occupation—a police officer, for example— may inspire this kind of dream. More often dreams of danger have a symbolic meaning that has to do with perceived emotional threats to oneself or to the relationship.

In the following example cited by Westbrook, Allison, a thirty-five-year-old woman, was coordinating the arrangements for her $10,000 wedding and feeling happy about her upcoming marriage. Consequently, her dream about needing heart surgery came as a shock.

Operation of the Heart
I was scheduled for heart surgery. The nurse had a piece of paper that she asked me to sign saying, "Do you want the doctors to do everything they

can regardless of cost?" The paper stated that they would spend up to $10,000 to prolong my life, but no more than that (in case something went wrong). If they did use all means to prolong life, I would be billed. I really struggled with what to do, even not to have the surgery. I had already been anesthetized and was getting very sleepy, yet struggling to stay awake to tell them I wasn't sure whether I wanted the surgery.

Allison was upset after this dream and at first wondered whether she might be facing a serious illness or perhaps surgery. As she was writing in her journal, she stared at the words "heart surgery." Suddenly it occurred to her: "Of course, my wedding is an operation of the heart, and it's going to cost $10,000."

This flash of insight revealed the key metaphor of her dream. As she discussed its possible meanings, she was struck by her ambivalence to this "heart surgery." Could she afford it emotionally? Would the surgeons damage her heart?

Then Allison remembered her father's bypass surgery two years earlier. She had been terrified about the outcome. Getting married, however, didn't seem like a life-or-death situation. The dream was exaggerating a physical danger to make her aware of the emotional risks. Worrying about planning the details had been like the anesthesia, keeping her from awareness of fears related to the wedding.

Allison's anxiety dreams did not cause her to question her marriage. They did motivate her to take time out from the planning to focus on her feelings and share them with her fiancé.

Getting married represents an emotional transformation, a permanent change in loyalties of the heart. Even in well-matched couples who enjoy a happy marital adjustment, dreams often show fears about the emotional commitment and a sense of loss of identity as a single person.

Dreams of physical danger offer an opportunity to examine whether there are physical dangers to you or your loved ones. When realistic physical danger or illness are not present concerns, your dreams are probably indicating a perception of danger to your emotional well-being.

Culture Clash Dreams. Mixed marriages have become increasingly commonplace. Many couples of different ethnic or religious backgrounds establish a family life that integrates important rituals and wisdom from both cultures. In order to forge a blend of cultures, couples must take time to communicate their expectations and be willing to compromise.

Many couples underestimate the conflicts they may encounter. They hope that if they behave in a low-key manner or try to avoid religious or ethnic confrontations, everything will work out. But cultural differences do not easily evaporate. Strong preferences often assert themselves at turning points.

These issues cannot necessarily be solved before marriage. They tend to simmer underneath the surface as the wedding approaches. Dreams can reveal these issues and point out emotional sore spots that require discussion and resolution.

Roger, a Presbyterian, was about to marry Sandy, a Jew. Roger played down their cultural and religious differences. He had agreed to be married by a rabbi; because "neither of us is very religious," he didn't expect any problems to arise. But one month before the wedding, he had an unsettling dream.

Middle Eastern Invaders Move into Our House
A group of dark-looking people from a country in
the Middle East come to stay at my house. They say

*they are moving in and are going to take over my
house and live there. I try to talk to my fiancée, but
she doesn't seem to be able to help me get them out.
They may have even captured her in some way so
she is loyal to them.*

When Roger was asked to free-associate about the image of the Middle Eastern invaders, his first thoughts were of his fiancée's parents, whom they had recently visited. His future in-laws had shown him a treasured photo album of their numerous trips to Israel, including visits to relatives who were Holocaust survivors. Although Sandy's family was not dark-skinned, many of the photographs were of deeply suntanned Israelis.

The invading Middle Eastern family was an exaggeration of Roger's unconscious concerns. Would Sandy's family's cultural traditions dominate their family life? Would she be loyal to him on crucial issues or would she side with her family? Discussing this dream helped Roger to see that his differences with Sandy were not trivial. He did feel a little unsettled about being married by a rabbi, and he had been touchy about some of the wedding plans. As a result of examining this dream, Roger became more open about his concerns. Subsequently, Sandy agreed to have further discussions about the wedding ceremony and about Roger's general feelings on religion and childrearing.

Not all cultural differences are a source of anxiety or alienation. In some instances the cultural differences may be part of the attraction. A cross-cultural marriage may bring a sense of warmth and acceptance that a person may not have in his or her own family of origin.

For example, Bob, an Anglo man, was about to be married to Yolanda, whose family was from Nicaragua. Bob's dream helped confirm the feelings of warmth he had experienced with Yolanda's family.

The Hopi Indians Welcome Us

Yolanda and I are on the Hopi Indian reservation. The Indians we meet are helpful and warm. I think to myself they have accepted us. Yolanda and I discuss this with excitement. Several men and women help us. They treat us as if we are part of their tribe.

Both of Bob's parents had been alcoholics. His father had been physically abusive and his mother was often depressed. Bob had participated in groups for Adult Children of Alcoholics and realized that his previous reluctance to make a commitment had been related to fears about aggravating the wounds suffered in childhood. He also worried about the possibility of inflicting similar damage on his children.

For Bob, the Hopis symbolized the warmth and acceptance of his new in-laws. The dream bolstered his confidence in his decision to marry Yolanda and left him feeling excited and positive about the wedding.

Culture Clash dreams are common in people who are about to marry someone from an ethnic, religious, or economic strata different from their own family's. They may occur even in marriages that are not mixed, symbolizing the emotional or physical difference between the two families.

Couples who spend time openly discussing and learning about the differences in their backgrounds will be better prepared to resolve the inevitable conflicts. Culture Clash dreams provide us an opportunity to appreciate the richness of our own and our spouse's cultural identity. In so doing we can forge a healthier identity for our marriage and our children.

HOW TO USE WEDDING AND
RELATIONSHIP DREAMS

We tend to put on a happy face when we make the commitment to marry, throughout the wedding preparations, honeymoon, and aftermath. It's hard, therefore, to admit the normal and expectable anxieties that we inevitably experience. It's important to keep in mind that upsetting dreams and even occasional nightmares are normal. They may even be a positive sign that we're actively wrestling with important feelings that need to be worked out.

Examining patterns in wedding and relationship dreams reminds us that making a commitment is not an easy task. We often feel passion, intense joy, and fulfillment. But, we may also experience ambivalence, fears about intimacy, struggles for power and control, stress over assuming new roles with family and friends, and grief over the loss of the single life.

Nightmares and recurring anxiety dreams are an SOS from the unconscious. They emphasize feelings that we have been unaware of or are denying. In most cases, the feelings are appropriate and normal and can be worked through as part of the preparation for commitment. Occasionally, a series of dreams or nightmares will help us discover unrecognized feelings that suggest that a delay or cancellation of marriage plans may be prudent.

Because of the predominance of anxiety dreams prior to and during a turning point and because of the tendency for dreams to be exaggerated and distorted, it would be unwise to base any rash decisions about your commitment to marriage or a relationship on a single dream. A Ceremonial Disaster dream should not be taken as an accurate psychic prediction that your wedding ceremony will turn into a fiasco. Nor does a Bride of Frankenstein dream mean that your groom will awaken one night transformed into a monster.

To appreciate the hidden meaning of relationship and prewedding dreams, you need to look behind the obvious and conscious anxieties and see if your own dreams reveal symbols, distortions, reversals, and disguises for your deeper feelings and needs. A dream about sexual adventure may reveal ambivalence about sexual fidelity or a fear of abandonment; the shock of dreaming of being naked at your wedding may expose a performance anxiety or other vulnerability; when your fiancé turns in a dream from Dr. Jekyll to Mr. Hyde, it may illuminate your own fears of commitment and not his.

To reveal the deeper meaning of your prewedding dreams, try to devote some time to remembering, communicating, and exploring them. For couples preparing for marriage, remembering and sharing dreams provides a special forum for expressing feelings.

Positive dreams remind both partners about the emotional and spiritual depth of the marriage commitment. Anxious dreams and nightmares are also a vital source of information. Sharing anxious dreams and other upsetting feelings can bring about a sense of empathy and collaboration that will form the basis for successful problem solving and a resilient marriage in future years together. Helping each other to understand your dreams may even guide you to take new approaches to planning your wedding and honeymoon, dealing with your families, or planning when to have your own family.

A vast amount of time, energy, and financial resources is devoted to preparing for a set of marriage rituals that last for a few hours. Much less time is set aside for emotional preparation for a marriage commitment that is meant to last a lifetime. Exploring dreams with your partner can help both of you to work through the profound changes that you are experiencing and to establish a solid foundation for your marriage.

3. *From Conception to Birth*
Dreams of Expectant Mothers and Fathers

PREGNANCY IS A turning point in life that's likely to be filled with compelling dreams. Because of their prevalence, the vivid themes of pregnancy dreams have been studied in more depth than those of any other turning point. In this chapter we'll examine the remarkable patterns in the dreams of expectant mothers and fathers and demonstrate how awareness and exploration of these dreams can enhance our emotional preparation for parenting.

The first two dreams we will look at were collected from women in the final stage of their first pregnancies. Although almost 100 years apart, both have elements that are common to the dreams of late pregnancy: the presence of water and the arrival of furry mammals. The first dream is taken from Sigmund Freud's *The Interpretation of Dreams* and was probably the dream of a Viennese woman at the turn of the twentieth century.

The Trapdoor Seal
A subterranean channel led directly into the water from a place in the floor of her room. She raised a trapdoor in the floor and a creature dressed in brown fur, very much resembling a seal, presently appeared.

In the briefly reported associations to this dream, Freud noted that the "creature turned out to be her younger brother to whom she had always been like a mother." Freud did not elaborate at length on this dream, except to note also that the subterranean channel and the water represented the birth canal and the amniotic fluid.

The second dream, from the mid-1980s, is Jennifer's, a San Francisco nurse in her eighth month of pregnancy.

The Smooth Skin of the Otter
I'm in labor and I am lying on a beach. The tide is coming in and big waves are washing up onto shore. I keep calling for my husband. I know he's there, but I can't see him. The waves are getting bigger and more dangerous. Just when the waves seem like they are going to drown me, I see a little sea otter next to me. I know it was supposed to be my baby, but I am confused that it looks like an otter. I touch its skin and it is incredibly smooth.

Jennifer worried that her dream might signify something abnormal about her baby; perhaps a premonition of some malformation. But as she told her dream at one of my workshops for nurses and childbirth educators on the psychology of pregnancy, there were many looks of recognition on the faces of the other women in the class. They quickly volunteered that they, too, had frightening dreams during their pregnancies. As Jennifer listened to the other women discuss the details of their anxiety dreams, she was reassured. She saw the dream as representing not danger, but joyful expectation of holding her baby and touching its wonderful soft skin.

Jennifer's dream contains a number of other themes common to women in their last trimester of pregnancy. The imminence of labor is often represented by waves, earth tremors, other powerful movements, and a feeling of losing control.

During the second and third trimester of pregnancy, many women also have heightened fears about the well-being of their spouse. In Jennifer's dream, her husband's presence is sensed, but he is unable to arrive soon enough to protect her from the dangerous waves of labor.

Dreams also focus on anxieties that haunt both men and women even during a healthy pregnancy. These include themes that exaggerate the dangers of labor and delivery, and fears about birth defects. Dreams also express marital tensions, feelings of rejection, and fears about being an incompetent parent.

For example, early in his wife's pregnancy, one man who was in the process of wallpapering a room for his child-to-be had a nightmare that he entered the room and saw his baby stuck to the wall with glue. Another woman nearing her delivery date was horrified by a dream that a little boy ran away from his mother and fell off a cliff into a turbulent ocean.

These and other pregnancy nightmares do not necessarily predict disaster. In fact, remembering a disturbing dream may be a positive sign that the dreamer is actively coping with the emotional challenges of becoming a parent. As horrifying as they may feel, anxiety dreams and nightmares during pregnancy provide us with an early warning system that alerts us to the fears and concerns that we need to work out.

You may feel reassured to know that women who have more frequent dreams involving anxiety or threat had shorter labors and healthier deliveries with fewer complications. A 1972 study of seventy women, by researchers Carolyn Winget and Frederic Kapp at the University of Cincinnati, concluded that troubling dreams may be evidence of important conflicts that were being resolved. When fewer distressing dreams were remembered, women tended to have longer labors and more complications. Those women who recalled more troubling dreams had shorter labors with fewer complications. Their dreams appeared to have helped them work out the normal anxieties that accompany the final stage of pregnancy.

Medical breakthroughs have given us the technology to diagnose and treat risk factors during pregnancy and delivery. With amniocentesis we can read the genetic code of the fetus. With electronic enhancement we can listen to our baby's heartbeat very early in the pregnancy. With ultrasound we can actually look into the womb to see our baby.

Technological advances, however, are not the only resources we have for understanding what's going on with us during pregnancy. We can also use our dreams as an emotional ultrasound. They provide a way to look into the unconscious and see how we're responding to the changes in our identity, our marriage, our relationships with family and friends, and our newly forming attachment to our unborn child.

In the sections that follow, we'll explore how remembering, sharing, and exploring dreams can help expectant parents to

- Understand and enhance the powerful prenatal attachment to the unborn child
- Recognize unique patterns in dreams during the three stages of pregnancy and become aware of how

they relate to the emotional stages of becoming a
parent
- Understand the similarities and differences between
  men's and women's psychological conflicts and fulfillments
- Generate mutual understanding and empathy for
  emotional reactions to pregnancy and rekindle communication on issues that often create tension and
  confusion
- Explore patterns in the erotic dream adventures and
  misadventures of expectant parents, and to use these
  dreams to help resolve confusion and misunder-
  standings that may arise in the couple's sexual relationship
- Recognize how identity changes and new roles linked
  to parenthood will cause the parents to experience
  themselves in new and unaccustomed ways with family and friends

DREAMS OF CONCEPTION, PREGNANCY, AND BIRTH

Pregnancy is a major turning point in the lives of both the
mother and the father-to-be. Consequently, each night during pregnancy, a kaleidoscope of images dance in front of
the sleeping eyes of expectant parents. As the fetus grows, a
new psychological relationship is growing, a powerful attachment that is vividly pictured in turning point dreams.

Many dreams make direct references to pregnancy,
childbirth, the appearance of the baby, and the roles of parents. Others are symbolic of the fetus, its experience in the
womb and the birth canal. Themes of fertility, virility,
dances, and other celebrations express the joy and pride
that accompany parenthood.

There are distinct differences between the dreams of early pregnancy and those closer to delivery. Dream images closely parallel the biological milestones of pregnancy. When a woman misses her period or feels the first signs of pregnancy, when she senses the first movements of the baby in the womb, when her body grows progressively larger, or when the contractions of labor are felt, the unconscious minds of the expectant mother and father generate dreams that tell the story of their varied responses.

Fetal Identification Dreams. Some dreams tend to occur more frequently at certain stages of pregnancy. Others happen throughout pregnancy, but their form changes as the pregnancy progresses. An example of the latter is what I call Fetal Identification dreams, which are common for both men and women throughout pregnancy. In these dreams, the dreamer experiences a fantasy version of what the fetus might be undergoing.

Early-pregnancy Fetal Identification dreams may focus on a quiescent fetus lolling about in a fertile womb. For example, one father-to-be during the first trimester of pregnancy described a dream in which he was floating in an enclosed body of water with fertile vegetation and rose colors at the horizon. On the other hand, late-pregnancy Fetal Identification dreams focus on the dangers of the journey down and out of the birth canal. Third-trimester examples include dreams of being trapped or suffocated in small spaces, perilous escapes from caves, and swimming downhill.

Pregnancy Identification Dreams. In addition to Fetal Identification dreams, both men and women have Pregnancy Identification dreams, which begin around the time of conception and continue unabated until birth. These dreams feature references to every aspect of the biology of pregnancy. Some of these dreams are realistic depictions; others are cloaked in exotic or even humorous symbolism.

Conception Dreams. For most people, the beginning of pregnancy unleashes a wave of fantasies and dreams after the confirming test. It can be fascinating to reread your dream journal on the dates around the time of conception. Many women have noted themes related to impregnation at this time. Fish or amphibious animals swimming up narrow channels and objects or people merging together are common themes at the time of conception.

Around the time of conceiving our daughter, Zoe, my wife, Tracy, had a dream that evoked a powerful feeling that she had indeed conceived a child.

Embryonic Journey
I am in the ocean and have to swim down this channel to get to the shore. As I swim down the channel, whales and big boats pass me. I am bodysurfing on three-foot waves which are very scary. When I get tired of bodysurfing and want to get out of the water, I get really scared because the waves are very high and are crashing up against the shore.

When Tracy awoke, she was anxious but quite exhilarated to have escaped the water. This feeling was similar to how she felt after getting off a roller coaster. Two weeks later, after confirming that she was pregnant, Tracy reviewed her dream journal. Her Embryonic Journey dream had occurred on the day after she thought she had ovulated. She felt that the imagery of that dream symbolized the perilous journey of the egg down the fallopian tube. As in the Fetal Identification dreams discussed above, she experienced the uterine environment in a personal way.

Fertility Dreams. In the first trimester of pregnancy, the excitement and sense of creativity are often evident in dreams. For women and sometimes for men, dreams of incredible fertility appear without direct reference to the fetus. One woman whom I interviewed dreamed that while swimming, she saw a beautifully pruned pear tree with gorgeous fruit that appeared to be shaped like a uterus.

In Dr. Myra Leifer's excellent book on first pregnancy, *The Psychological Effects of Motherhood*, she describes the following fertility dream.

My Breasts Are Blossoming

I dreamed about my breasts having all these big, bright flowers flowing out of them. It was just beautiful. I was in a swimming pool and I must have taken myself for a water lily and these flowers were blooming from my breast. Then I came out and everyone, men, women, and children were looking with great admiration at my flowers.

Fertility dreams symbolize the body's creative powers during a period of rapid growth of the fetus. In Arthur and Libby Colman's groundbreaking book, *Pregnancy: The Psychological Experience*, they assert that acceptance of the reality of the pregnancy is the most important psychological task of the first trimester. Remembering and sharing fertility dreams with your loved one can enhance your mutual positive feelings about the pregnancy and hasten the process of accepting its reality.

Aquatic Dreams. There are no droughts in pregnancy dreams. Water is everywhere: tidal waves, coursing streams, warm amniotic fluids, swimming pools, and one of the most common water dreams—the washing machine dream.

The washing machine is of course useful to have for the diapers and extra laundry of infancy. But why would the unconscious mind of so many expectant parents focus on an appliance? Because the watery inner space of a washing machine is a symbol of the pregnant womb.

With the advent of high-tech methods of observing the fetus, washing machine dreams may coincide with ultrasound diagnosis. For example, prior to an appointment for an ultrasound exam, Kathy, a thirty-year-old teacher, dreamed that she was looking inside an old-fashioned glass washing machine and saw a boy waving at her.

Joel, a computer programmer in a large urban hospital, had a humorous version of a washing machine dream.

A Wild Ride on Our Washing Machine
My wife and I are at an amusement park full of household items that are giant-sized. We are riding a giant washing machine agitator. My wife is trying to hang on. She laughs and says that she used to do this as a child.

Joel was amused by the dream. His first association was how both he and his wife enjoy the rides at Disneyland and go there every year. The dream brought back positive memories of visits there with his own parents and stimulated fantasies about how wonderful it would be to share the fun with his own child.

As he continued to explore this dream, Joel remarked that he and his wife were experiencing what it must be like for their child in the womb. The agitator arm made him aware that the pregnancy was bringing some agitation. At times, as in the dream, it felt hard to hold on and stay above water emotionally.

Female Body Image Dreams. While some dreams are filled with disguised symbolism of pregnancy and birth, other dreams make direct reference to pregnancy. Despite reassurances from others, many women feel that their changing bodies are unattractive.

One woman dreamed that she was accused by her mother of gaining too much weight during pregnancy. Another dreamed that she looked in the mirror and saw herself as incredibly bloated, like the fat woman she had seen in a circus.

Toby, an attorney, had not yet announced her pregnancy to her co-workers because she wanted to wait until all dangers of miscarriage were over. At twelve weeks, many of her clothes were already too tight and she was beginning to feel dowdy, dressing in more loosely fitting clothes. She had two upsetting dreams about her mother criticizing her for being too fat. She woke up from the following dream in tears.

Nothing to Wear

My husband, Andrew, is telling me that we are invited to a dinner party at an elegant restaurant with his business associates. I see him changing into a tuxedo, and I suddenly see the other women as we are arriving at the restaurant. They are all wearing very fancy dresses with velvet and sequins. My outfit feels old and frumpy in comparison, and my stomach is sticking out even though I know I am only a few weeks pregnant. I burst out crying and run sobbing to the bathroom.

Toby was agitated and tearful as she told this dream to Andrew. She could not stop thinking about feeling physically unattractive. Andrew tried to reassure her about her attractiveness and pointed out how exaggerated the contrast was between her frumpy old clothes and the elegant gowns of the other women.

As Toby calmed down, she began to realize how hard it was to accept the physical changes that accompanied being pregnant. As we observed in prewedding dreams, changes in clothing may represent changes in identity.

The lack of social acknowledgment may have hampered Toby's ability to accept the changes in her pregnant body. After discussing this dream, Toby and Andrew decided it was time to inform her co-workers about her pregnancy and to buy or borrow some attractive maternity clothes.

Because of our nearly universal standard of being slim and fit, many women are ashamed to be gaining weight, even during pregnancy when it is essential for the health of the child. Exploring dreams that exaggerate the physical changes of pregnancy can help a woman accept not only her own altered body image but the psychological reality of the pregnancy. By sharing dreams related to weight gain, a woman can receive reassurance that these worries are a normal part of adjusting to the physical changes that occur during pregnancy.

For women who have had mild or serious problems with anorexia or bulimia, dreams that emphasize the issues of weight and body image are especially important. Eating disorders may get stirred up during pregnancy, so these dreams emphasize the need to work out responses to the physical changes of pregnancy. If dreams and anxieties about eating or body changes persist, it may be important to seek professional support.

Labor and Delivery Dreams. As the due date approaches, women's and men's dreams begin to focus on the symbolism of labor, traveling through the birth canal, and giving birth. Whereas early-pregnancy dreams of floating and swimming are more tranquil, late-pregnancy dreams portray the powerful contractions of labor, including themes of earthquakes, powerful tides, and overwhelming waves. Experiences of loss of control may be seen in dreams of falling, cars going out of control, or drowning. These dreams may be a direct anticipation of labor but may also give us a warning that we are feeling emotionally overwhelmed.

Dreams depicting physical danger or actual pain or injury to the mother or child increase in late pregnancy. Dreams of damaged buildings and other architectural features symbolize the structural damage that is feared in the birth process.

Traveling in and emerging from narrow passageways is the late-pregnancy version of the Fetal Identification dream. Caves, tunnels, and interior hallways represent the birth canal. Many swimming dreams and narrow-passage dreams feature downhill motions that parallel the downward journey of the fetus through the birth canal.

Two weeks before her due date, Maureen had a frightening dream that she did not immediately associate to pregnancy.

Escape from the Jungle Gym

I am playing on top of a jungle gym with a friend from elementary school whom I haven't seen for years. Even though I am very pregnant, I'm still able to climb up and around. Suddenly I start to lose my grip and fall through the bars. I am all tangled in the bars and can't seem to get out. I slowly work my way downward on the bars till I come out of a larger hole near the bottom that someone had pulled apart. I am incredibly tired from the exercise and from how scared I was about falling.

Maureen associated the anxiety in the dream to her fears about something going wrong at the birth, such as needing a cesarean section or having a prolonged labor. As she told her dream a second time, however, she began to see the emergence from the jungle gym as an image of what it must be like for her baby to make its way out of the labyrinth of the womb.

Maureen was puzzled about why she dreamed about a jungle gym and a friend she hadn't seen for so long. As she allowed her mind to associate, she remembered that she had fallen off of a jungle gym in elementary school, chipping a tooth and suffering a mild concussion. After that she had developed a phobia about jungle gyms and other similar playground equipment.

Maureen's dream had drawn an image of danger from her long-term memory banks and associated it with birthing. Acknowledging the nature of her fears did not make them evaporate, because she knew there is real danger at the time of birth. A certain level of fear is normal and helps to mobilize us to action when we are facing a difficult situation. Maureen felt that exploring her dream helped her to ventilate her feelings, reduced her level of fear, and helped her become more prepared for the birth.

DREAMS ABOUT BABIES AND CHILDREN

A vital part of the process of forming an emotional bond with the child occurs during pregnancy. In dreams and in waking fantasy, we are preoccupied with images of how our baby will look and what our relationship with our child will be. In daydreams we may dwell upon feeding or brushing hair or playing ball in the park. At night, our dreams continue where our conscious fantasies leave off.

In fact, babies are featured in up to 40 percent of pregnant women's dreams, versus only 1 percent in a comparative study of other young women. My own research revealed that 21 percent of expectant fathers had dreams about babies during a two-week journal-keeping period.

Animal Dreams. Studies of pregnant women's dreams have shown that 17 percent contain animals, more than twice as many as in a nonpregnant group. Dreams of giving birth to

furry mammals such as puppies, kittens, and seals are common in pregnancy. The endearing creatures symbolize the
vulnerable newborn who will soon be needing the tender
care of the parents. These dreams reveal an inner rehearsal
that prepares the dreamer for a new or renewed role as a
parent.

In addition to cute furry mammals, a wide variety of
other dream creatures may appear. Fish and amphibious
creatures tend to represent the water-dwelling fetus that
eventually makes its way to land. Common farm animals
such as chickens and pigs may represent an exaggerated image of fertility, as we often picture them teeming with off-
spring. Injured or defective animals represent fears about
birth defects.

Animal dreams, like most common pregnancy dreams,
change over the course of the pregnancy. For some women
they may even follow a course similar to the evolution of
species, which began in water and gradually moved onto
land. Early in pregnancy, dream animals tend to be smaller.
Aquatic animals such as fish and tadpoles are common. In-
sects such as spiders, which are known to have multiple
births, also appear. As the fetus grows and begins to move
around in the middle of pregnancy, dream animals grow
larger, too. As the due date approaches, larger species such
as seals and monkeys and other large mammals are more
common.

In my research, I found that men do not have more frequent animal dreams during their wives' pregnancies. The
animal dreams they do have, however, relate directly to fantasies about the child and the birth process. Neal, an archi-
tect and oldest of four children, had the following dream late
in his wife's pregnancy.

The Old Dog Under the Sea
*I am fishing at the beach with Will, my younger
brother. Out of a bubble comes a "boo" sound,*

*which startles me. Then as I pull in my line, I feel
no resistance. There is a white, fluffy, ripply thing
attached to the end. Then I get it up on the beach,
and I see it's a very old dog. It is alive. I have a feeling that it lived in the ocean to be protected so no
one knew that it was alive.*

Although there is no specific mention of children or
birth, Neal's dream is filled with images of pregnancy and
birthing. It portrays the mysterious arrival of an animal,
barely alive, that was hidden under water for protection.
Emerging from a placentalike bubble with a shout, Neal's
dream dog is clearly a symbolic vision of his child's coming
arrival.

Like many expectant fathers, Neal was puzzled by what
his dream might be telling him. He did not immediately connect the dream to his feelings about the pregnancy. When I
explained that animals often serve as symbols of the baby
during pregnancy, Neal became quite animated. The whole
dream seemed to make sense to him, and he was pleased
that he had had a dream related to the birth of his child.

The presence in the dream of his younger brother reminded Neal of the actual birth of his brother when he was
four. His mother's return from the hospital with Will was one
of his first memories. According to his parents, Neal did not
adjust easily to his brother; he was frequently angry and
threw tantrums.

Discussing this dream helped Neal realize that he was
harboring hidden fears about the impending arrival of his
child. Although he very much wanted to be a father, he discovered that he was also afraid of being emotionally displaced by a baby, which is what he experienced after the
birth of his brothers.

Neal talked to his wife about his fears and his positive
sense of being touched by the pregnancy. She was sympathetic and in fact admitted to him that she had been so busy

dealing with her own reactions that she hadn't stopped to think about his. Finally, in an attempt to follow through on the message of the dream, he enlisted the help of his mother to review how he had reacted when his brother was born.

Some animal dreams are unpleasant or nightmarish. In *Pregnancy: The Psychological Experience*, the Colmans reported a pregnant woman's dream that depicted a cat leaping up to claw the dreamer. In retaliation, the dreamer flung the vicious cat against the wall.

Dreams of violence or injury toward an animal may represent fears of injury of the baby. They also may represent feelings of aggression toward the child. Despite our positive feelings about pregnancy, we also have mixed feelings about the upsetting physical and emotional changes that the pregnancy is causing and about how the baby may intrude upon the stability of our relationships and career, not to mention sleep.

Animal dreams during pregnancy are closely related to feelings about the fetus and the pregnancy. Even when such dreams are troubling, they are directing the expectant parent to focus on preparing for the new relationship.

Dreams of Forgetting the Baby. One of the most troubling types of pregnancy dreams typically culminates with the shocking realization that you've left your baby somewhere, unattended or in dangerous circumstances. Frequently the dreamer has gone on to some other activity, oblivious of the fact that she is now a parent.

Anna, thirty-six, a junior high school principal, had been married for less than a year when she became pregnant. Although her pregnancy was planned and both she and her husband were looking forward to the arrival of their daughter (the sex confirmed by amniocentesis), Anna had been troubled by fears about how she was going to balance her successful career with the demands of parenthood. She had been granted a six-month maternity leave but wasn't sure it would be enough time to establish a relationship with her daughter. She didn't see how she could handle a demanding job, which often required overtime, and care for her child as well.

In her ninth month of pregnancy she had a nightmare that left her anxious and shaken for days. It occurred three weeks before her due date, on her last day at work before her maternity leave.

The Abandoned Baby

I am walking along the waterfront pushing a stroller with my baby in it. I think it is a girl. A brightly lit yacht pulls up nearby and a woman in a professional suit offers me a ride on the boat and a luxury trip to Hawaii. I accept and am suddenly on board, sailing in the open sea. All of a sudden, I realize that I left my baby alone on the dock. I panic and start shouting, trying desperately to get the boat to turn around, but no one will listen. I wake up crying and feeling incredibly guilty.

Anna was worried and occasionally tearful for days after she had this dream. Although she saw herself as a responsible person, something about the dream touched off irrational fears that were haunting her. She was desperately afraid that she would act in life the way she did in the dream: like a hedonistic woman who would recklessly abandon her baby. She was afraid to share her fears with anyone, including her husband, and was beginning to wonder if she had made a mistake by getting pregnant.

In a dream workshop, as Anna visualized the first part of her dream, where she was tempted onto the Hawaiian cruise boat, she was reminded about a number of trips she had taken during school vacations. On a couple of occasions she had spontaneously embarked on a trip to Hawaii at the last minute with a group of friends. As she continued to recount some of the travel adventures of her younger days, Anna realized that this part of the dream was reminding her that she would no longer have the freedom to travel spontaneously.

The most compelling moment in the dream, however, was her sense of panic when she realized that she had left her baby on the dock and was screaming, trying to get back. As she explored the image of forgetting her baby, Anna began to see the dream as an exaggeration of her fears about being a responsible parent and not a prediction that she would be a negligent mother.

Starting with her role as the oldest of four children, Anna had always been efficient at caring for others' needs. On the other hand, she found it hard to ask for help for herself at work or with friends. Discussing this dream and her fears about being an inadequate parent and about balancing work and mothering helped Anna realize that she needed emotional support.

Because Anna had been busy at work prior to her leave, she had not had time to read books on parenting or talk at length to friends who were parents of young children. She understood now that she needed to spend much more time talking with her husband and with other parents. Although she was on the phone with her mother more frequently, her family lived 2,000 miles away. Because she lacked good contacts with friends or relatives with small children, I encouraged Anna to seek out a support group for new parents. As a result of discussing this dream, Anna also resolved to extend her maternity leave, then work part-time in her present job and seek other related work that did not require a lot of overtime.

Dreams of Forgetting the Baby exaggerate our worst fears about being inadequate parents. At the same time, they can provide us with a stimulus to become more prepared by seeking emotional support and guidance from others.

Dreams of Losing Valuables. Dreams of finding, carrying, and losing valuables are especially common among pregnant women. In most cases the valuable item has womblike attributes—purses, pouches, and suitcases, for example.

Dreaming of losing or sustaining damage to a precious item is thematically similar to dreams of Forgetting the Baby and to Endangered Baby dreams (see below). Generally this kind of dream can be linked to anxieties about the responsibilities of carrying such a precious inner cargo. Many dreams of this type feature the loss of precious items, and some depict dangerous quests to retrieve them. For some people, repetitive dreams of losing or missing valuables can be a sign that grief about past losses is bottled up, jeopardizing the psychological well-being of the mother and the physical well-being of mother and child.

While working as a psychological consultant to a high-risk maternity clinic, I was asked to consult with Denise, who was seven months pregnant and suffering extreme anxiety and depression. In talking to her obstetrician, I learned that her first child had been born without kidneys and had lived only for ten days. In a stroke of cruel irony, Denise's second child was scheduled to be delivered by cesarean section on the first anniversary of her first baby's death.

Denise refused to talk about her first child but was frequently tearful. According to her family, she had made no preparations for the arrival of the baby, was eating poorly, and had been forced to quit her part-time secretarial job because she was so preoccupied. Her doctor was concerned about her health and the well-being of her baby. She repeatedly refused to speak with a psychologist or social worker, insisting that she wasn't crazy and didn't need to talk to a "shrink." As her condition worsened, she began to have repetitive nightmares. When she learned that I was a "dream expert," she requested a meeting with me.

With little introduction, she tearfully told me the nightmare. Almost every night she would wake up sweating and crying, unable to sleep after the dream.

My Suitcase Is Missing Something

It is almost time to go to the hospital, and I search for my suitcase to prepare to leave. As I desperately throw things into the suitcase and try to push it shut, I panic because it is time to leave and there is something missing.

Through her tears, Denise pleaded with me to help her with her terrible nightmare. I suggested to her that if it were my dream, I would feel there was something I wasn't ready for. Upon hearing my words, Denise launched into an emotional description of her fears about the upcoming birth of her child. She tearfully confessed that she didn't feel ready. She knew that her family and her husband were worried, but she didn't know what to do to prepare herself.

Talking about her dream allowed Denise to access her grief and guilt. I asked her how she would feel if something was missing from her suitcase. She spontaneously realized that the suitcase with the missing item represented the baby who had died. She was finally able to talk about her guilt. For months she had blamed herself for her baby's death even though the doctors had assured her it was not her fault. She was terrified that her second child would also die and that it would again be her fault. Over the next hour, as Denise poured out her feelings, her mood and demeanor visibly lifted.

Exploring the elements of her dream allowed Denise to feel more secure about discussing vital feelings that had terrified her. She was increasingly receptive to talking with the nurses in the clinic and with her family about her guilt and grief. The date of her cesarean was changed, and she gave birth to a healthy child. Although Denise was resistant to ongoing counseling, sharing and working on her dream allowed her to break out of the mire of a turning point impasse and move toward forming a healthy connection with her new baby.

Deformed and Endangered Baby Dreams. Even to those who don't consider themselves superstitious, having a dream about a deformed or injured baby is likely to induce a feeling of worry or panic. Although these dreams are quite common and usually not a danger sign, nightmares about endangered babies can leave an emotional residue of anxiety and even depression.

Joel, whose washing machine dream we discussed above, had listened to his wife talk about her fears of giving birth to a Down's syndrome child. Joel was sympathetic but didn't pay much attention. He figured that at thirty-one, she wasn't at risk according to the statistics he had read. Joel was finding it difficult, however, to watch the eleven o'clock news, especially stories of children injured in auto accidents. When a special documentary came on TV about premature babies, he was surprised at how quickly he wanted to change the channel.

Early in the second trimester of his wife's pregnancy, Joel had the following dream.

The Clinic for Retarded Children
I am in a medical clinic where everyone speaks Spanish. I am on a lengthy tour of the place and am being shown new techniques to deal with mentally retarded children. I am saddened but very relieved that our own baby, who is now a year old, was born normal. I want to get out of the place, but

the director drones on and on and I don't want to offend him.

Joel's dream helped him to accept the fact that he, too, was fearful about something being wrong with the baby. Although Joel's Deformed Baby dream appears to be reassuring him that his baby will be normal, it also clearly shows his anxiety.

As in many pregnancy dreams of both men and women, Joel's baby is not a newborn. Seeing your child as a few months or even a few years old in pregnancy dreams is usually associated with an attempt to skip the anxiety danger of labor, as well as the fears about adjusting to the early weeks of parenting a newborn.

Joel was perplexed about why everyone was speaking Spanish. He realized it had something to do with the way he felt about pregnancy. He felt out of place when he and his wife took a tour of the maternity ward and when they went to the obstetrician's office. He felt like an outsider in a foreign country.

This dream helped Joel acknowledge his fears and his feeling of being an outsider. By being consciously aware of these issues, Joel became more assertive about being involved as the pregnancy progressed. He insisted on going to all of the doctor visits. He went to the classes at the hospital, and he talked more to friends who were fathers.

Paying careful attention to dreams about deformed or endangered babies can help us identify fears we find difficult to admit consciously. It can be deeply reassuring to know that the fears and nightmares that afflict us are part of a normal process of psychological preparation for parenthood. When we stop denying the stresses of having a baby, we can turn our attention to seeking the extra support that is essential during pregnancy.

Psychoanalyst Robert Gillman's 1968 study of pregnant women's dreams found that one in eight women dreamed of deformed babies. Dreams of endangered babies appear to be even more common. These dreams are profoundly disturbing to expectant parents. No matter how much we try to tell ourselves that "it's only a dream," we have a powerful tendency to believe that our nighttime visions are predictive of real disaster.

Breaking the spell of these nightmares can help us understand our fears and motivate us to prepare more thoroughly by monitoring our nutrition and seeking medical, educational and psychological support to reduce the chances of endangering the health of our baby.

Dreams About the Baby's Name and Gender. Many baby dreams focus on the identity of the baby. This includes dreams about naming the baby or about a physical or emotional characteristic of the baby. Whenever I speak to groups about dreams and the psychology of pregnancy, one of the most frequent topics raised is whether dreams can predict gender. Every culture and every family seems to have its own criteria for determining the baby's gender, and dreams are often part of the formula.

Dreams that identify the baby's gender are very common. A 1986 study found a 50 percent accuracy rate for pregnant women who dreamed about the sex of their unborn. Gillman's study showed a much lower accuracy rate. In that study, women's baby gender dreams disproportionately featured male children by a ratio of two to one.

Of course, those of us whose dreams correctly identify the sex of the baby are convinced that the dream was a precise predictor. Those whose dreams turn out wrong aren't so sure. In my experience, the value of these dreams is not their predictive accuracy. The deeper meaning has to do with the formation of a prenatal bond with the child and the parent's ability to accept and relate to a male or female child.

Despite her desire to have a girl, Linda had repeated anxious dreams of giving birth to a boy who was extremely active and hard to discipline. In one of her upsetting dreams, the rowdy boy had a name that puzzled her.

A Brat Named Island

My baby looks like he is almost two years old. It doesn't seem like I know him very well. My neighbor is there looking very angry. He says that Island broke some things at his house. Then he yells at me for having such a bratty kid and not controlling him. I'm very upset, confused, and don't know how this happened.

Linda was disturbed by the bratty boy in her dream. Although she didn't believe in precognitive dreams, she had become preoccupied with wondering whether the dream was predicting not only the sex but the temperament of her child. The offbeat name Island seemed very odd to Linda; she and her husband had been considering traditional names such as James and Ellen.

As she thought about the name Island, she linked it to Ireland, the place of origin of her father's family. This association helped her clarify the nature of the dream's meaning. Linda's father had been abusive to her mother and had gone on occasional drinking and womanizing binges. He left the family when Linda was fourteen and rarely saw them after that. She feared that a male child would somehow be like her father, uncontrollably violent and destructive.

Understanding this dream stimulated her to talk more about her relationship with her father and the pain he'd caused her. She even contacted him after five years of not being in touch. Although he wasn't very warm, he expressed interest in seeing her and her baby. Although her father hadn't changed much, the experience of focusing on her relationship helped Linda resolve some of the grief and anger she had harbored toward him.

Because of the repetitive nature of her dreams, Linda

was surprised when she had a girl. Although she was very pleased with her daughter, she felt that focusing on her dreams had helped her work out conflicts related to having a male child. She now felt that she would like her second child to be a boy.

For expectant fathers or mothers who have a strong preference for either a boy or girl, dreams about the name and gender can serve a vital purpose. They call our attention to the unconscious reasons we may prefer one sex over the other. Exploring these dreams often unearths strong feelings about our own identity as a man or woman and how we feel about our parents and siblings; for example, "My father had a violent temper and he (like other males) can't be trusted," or "My mother (like other females) was domineering and never left me room to breathe or to be myself." Feelings, ideas, and memories like these, along with cultural conditioning, create strong gender preferences in some people.

Whether we admit it or not, we all have distinct feelings about what it would mean to have a male or female child. These feelings are influenced by the nature of our early relationships with our parents and siblings. Our dreams reveal our preferences and can help us prepare to accept and establish a strong relationship with a baby of the less preferred sex.

Dreams about the baby's name and gender are connected with our growing images of what it will be like to relate to our child. Exploring these dreams can reveal positive aspects of a growing prenatal bond. They can also alert us to potential conflicts in our ability to form a healthy attachment with our child.

DREAMS AND THE SECRET LIFE
OF THE EXPECTANT FATHER

The strength of men's emotional experience of pregnancy has only recently come to light. Beginning with the confirmation of pregnancy, powerful feelings and dreams emerge. Some of these responses are similar to those of women. Others are unique to men.

Awareness and discussion of these dreams can help transform what frequently is a sense of alienation for expectant fathers. Dreams are a resource for helping men to feel more secure about their role in pregnancy and to forge a closer bond with both wife and child.

In 1981 I began the first systematic study of the patterns in expectant fathers' dreams. When I compared expectant fathers' dreams with the dreams of a matched group of married men who were not fathers and not expecting, there were striking differences. From the earliest days of the pregnancy, the expectant fathers' dreams were replete with vivid imagery of pregnancy, birth, and babies. Dreams of rejection and exclusion were especially prominent throughout pregnancy, as well as many graphic sexual and homosexual encounters and dreams of wild celebratory birthday parties.

This finding challenges the notion that the expectant father faces no significant emotional upheaval until later in the pregnancy or after the birth. In reality, throughout the pregnancy a father's dreams are intimately related to his role as a father, his changing relationship with his wife, and his newly forming relationship with his child-to-be.

Left-out Dreams. One of the most common issues in expectant fathers' dreams is the theme of feeling left out, misunderstood, deprived, or threatened in other ways. These dreams reveal old wounds and sensitivities to rejection that are reopened by fears about being displaced by the arrival of the baby.

Joel, whose dreams we discussed above, had increased his hours at work to try to make more money to pay for the expenses of his child. When Joel's wife was five months pregnant, he had a troubling dream that took place during a baseball game at Candlestick Park in San Francisco.

Banished to the Back of the Stadium

In the middle of the game, I get up to get some beer.
When I return, I can't find my seat. I look around
for a new one, but many of the women in the
stands are pregnant, and they are taking up two
seats. I have to go to the back of the stadium and
stand. I am very annoyed.

Joel was upset and puzzled by this dream. He wasn't
much of a sports fan, and he generally avoided alcohol because his father had a drinking problem. "The feeling I have
in this dream is that of being left out. There is no room for
me with all these huge pregnant women." Joel was able to
laugh at the absurdity of a stadium full of pregnant women
crowding him out. Even in the generally male domain of
beer and baseball, he felt like an outcast, rejected and
forced to the back of the stadium.

Exploring this dream helped Joel to understand that he
was having a strong emotional reaction to his wife's pregnancy. Despite his positive conscious reaction to becoming
a father, he was feeling excluded by his wife, which is a painful phase of pregnancy that many men suffer through. The
message of the dream was not about baseball; it was about
Joel's sense of exclusion and his need to find more ways to
be involved in the pregnancy and planning for the baby. After discussing this dream, Joel was able to express his left-
out feelings more directly with his wife. They decided that
he would cut back on overtime hours at work so that he
could spend more time with her and be more involved in
preparations for the baby's arrival.

Male Pregnancy Dreams. Dreams of actually being pregnant or giving birth are dramatic evidence of men's psychological involvement in pregnancy. Until the 1970s, male symptoms of pregnancy were generally viewed as pathological,
as womb-envy as opposed to a wish to share and be involved

in the pregnancy. Men were not expected to have any unique or strong feelings, especially early in pregnancy.

Many men experience what is known as the couvade syndrome, which is a cluster of physical and psychological symptoms mimicking a woman's experience of pregnancy. Studies by Jacqueline Clinton, a professor of nursing at the University of Wisconsin, have shown that over 90 percent of expectant fathers experience one of the signs of couvade, such as weight gain, nausea, stomach bloating, food cravings, fatigue, and irritability. Pronounced cases of couvade syndrome involve multiple symptoms and occur in approximately 10 to 30 percent of expectant fathers. These symptoms are considered to be characteristic of the pregnant female, yet some men have more of them than their wives.

Anthropologists who study primitive cultures have found widespread evidence of couvade rituals, in which expectant fathers engage in elaborate dietary and behavioral practices that mimic aspects of pregnancy. In some cases the men go into huts and simulate the pain of labor. These rituals are thought to be a form of sympathetic magic, a way of distracting and fooling evil spirits and thus protecting the wife. In addition, couvade rituals establish that the man is indeed the father and give him an important role to play in the pregnancy and birth.

In our culture, we have few roles or rites of passage to help men understand and integrate the experience of becoming a father. Without couvade rituals, it appears that men's unfulfilled wishes for involvement are converted into an unconscious male version of pregnancy.

In some men, couvade dreams take the form of actual pregnancy or giving birth. Alex, a thirty-three-year-old engineer, felt he was having difficulty accepting the reality of the pregnancy. Even after the baby began to move, he did not feel that the pregnancy had made much of an impact on him. Late in the second trimester he had the following dream.

It's My Baby

*I am standing on a street corner carrying my baby
fetus under my shirt against my chest. I have my
hands cupped over the fetus to protect it. It is moving and people ask what it is. I say it's my baby!
Someone tries to smash the fetus by hitting my
chest. I become enraged at the person and pick him
up and throw him into the street.*

The powerful feeling of protectiveness in this dream occurs in many expectant fathers' dreams. Alex is not only
pregnant out in public, he is ready to defend fiercely his baby
against threats. Alex did not ordinarily remember his
dreams. He was surprised by the intensity of his protective
feelings and by the fact that he was pregnant in the dream.
After exploring his feelings, Alex realized that he might have
been denying some of his reactions to the pregnancy because he felt that he should be the strong one to help out his
wife while she was nauseous.

I have collected many other dreams with direct pregnancy references in which men show strong feelings of protectiveness toward their wives and unborn children. These
dreams, which I call Magical Protection dreams, often portray creative and sometimes amusing solutions to the fears
of pregnancy.

In the first trimester, the danger of miscarriage is high.
Don, whose wife had experienced a previous miscarriage,
had three dreams in a two-week period that suggested magical solutions to his fears about the progress of the pregnancy. In one dream he was advised by a neighbor to find a
doctor willing to make home visits in case his wife was too
tired to go to the office. In another, he fashioned a wooden
bowl that would provide protection for his child inside his
wife's growing belly. His final dream is an early version of an
Endangered Baby dream.

Miscarriage Prevention
My wife is telling me that she has been using a tampon every day. She doesn't explain it, but it makes sense to me as a way of making sure that there's not a premature birth.

When Don looked over his dream journal entries, he was shocked at how many different ways he was trying to protect his wife and baby. Seeing the persistent pattern in his dreams was irrefutable evidence that he was involved in the pregnancy. Knowing this helped Don to convert his dream protectiveness into more conscious protection and support for his wife in the early months of the pregnancy.

Many men may be unaware that they are having symptoms directly related to pregnancy. Because their experience is not socially validated by women or by the medical establishment, their fierce feelings of protectiveness and their actual physical symptoms of pregnancy may go unnoticed. On the other hand, when a man's protective fantasies are acknowledged, he is likely to feel gratified by becoming consciously aware of his protective instincts and may be more inclined to express his involvement in waking activities. Discussion of dreams can help a man acknowledge his unconscious preoccupation with pregnancy and convert it into more active conscious involvement with his wife and child.

Sexual Adventure Dreams. Sexual experiences appear frequently in the dreams of both men and women during pregnancy. They may experience exquisite sensuality, award-winning orgasms, and animal passions in their dreams— with their spouse, old lovers, colleagues, or friends.

The biological necessity for sexual relations is fulfilled once conception occurs. However, the psychological importance and influence of our sexual feelings do not subside during pregnancy. Judging by the increase in dreams and fantasies with sexual themes, a massive alteration of our sexual identity and appetites occurs as pregnancy progresses.

Many couples have achieved an equilibrium in their sexual and emotional intimacy prior to pregnancy if they have been together for a long time. In early pregnancy, the joyful news of conception often fuels the erotic flames of the marriage. Experimentation, increased closeness, and enhanced communication may grow out of the excitement of pregnancy.

My study of expectant fathers revealed some exotic Sexual Adventure dreams, including a ménage à trois after-hours at Disneyland, necking furiously with a young blonde on a spaceship, and a hooker offering a full range of services.

When your dream amour is not your spouse, pangs of guilt may afflict you when you awake. One expectant father, Frank, who had experienced extended couvade symptoms of nausea, food cravings, and stomach bloating during the first trimester, also was having wild erotic fantasies in daydreams and at night. In one second-trimester dream he experienced an awareness within the dream that his desires were adulterous.

The Alarm in My Wedding Ring

I am being approached by a voluptuous woman. I can tell she wants to seduce me and I am very tempted. All of a sudden, I know I am in trouble. An alarm goes off and I think it's my watch, but when I look I realize the alarm is on my wedding ring and I have to get home to my wife.

When Frank's wedding ring alarm goes off, he is torn between powerful desires and a sense of loyalty to his wife. For weeks he had been preoccupied with his own sexual fantasies and physical symptoms set off by the pregnancy. At the same time, he was anxious about his increased responsibilities as a nurturer and provider for his wife and child.

Frank's Sexual Adventure dreams did not inspire him to pursue extramarital sex. Rather, Frank felt that his sexual dreams were related to a feeling of sexual neediness on his part. He recognized that in the past an increase in sexual fantasies had been related to a need to be taken care of and given attention. He felt that his wife had been preoccupied with other aspects of the pregnancy and had rejected him sexually during the first trimester when they had both been feeling ill.

Frank came to see that the alarm was meant to wake him out of his own neediness, his physical and sexual preoccupations, and to focus on improving his marriage so that they could be prepared for the arrival of the baby. When he shared his dreams and fantasies with his wife, she was able to understand what he'd been going through and they were able to reestablish a greater feeling of closeness that they had both been missing.

Virility and Impotence Dreams. For many men, the general decrease in sexual relations during pregnancy may result in conflicts that linger on, dampening the intimacy of the marriage. The balance of intimacy shifts when nausea and other physical changes affect the woman (or even the man, if he suffers from couvade syndrome). Confusion and feelings of rejection may surface. Sometimes sexual inhibitions and hang-ups that the man thought had been set aside years earlier reappear.

Expectant fathers' dreams and fantasies reveal sexual preoccupations that often focus on pride or doubts about their sexual powers. Especially in early pregnancy, men have dreams that express their concerns about their changing masculinity. Over 40 percent of the expectant fathers who participated in my study during early pregnancy had what I call Macho dreams. These dreams feature heroic acts by famous football coaches such as Bill Walsh and actors such as John Wayne. In a typical Macho dream sequence, Burt Reynolds crashes a hang glider but emerges unscathed and chipper.

During pregnancy, a man's masculine identity goes through a reorganization as he struggles to integrate more nurturing, feminine feelings into his sense of self and to create a new identity as a father. Many men are unaware of the emotional crisis taking place inside them. In behavior as in dreams, they attempt to seek refuge in being macho to compensate for fears of being unmanly, impotent, or homosexual.

Mixed in with dreams of virility, sexual prowess, and macho heroics are dreams that feature sexual inferiority, impotence, and homosexuality. A sampling of homosexual dream themes in the expectant fathers I studied included the following: soliciting a man for oral sex; being accused of being gay and attacked for it; watching a gay doctor dancing in a tutu; and being accused of perverting a group of children.

One man dreamed that his penis was shorter and less experienced than another man's.

Penis Contest

I am lying down and looking down at my naked body. I can see another naked man whose penis is larger than mine in spite of perspective. He is taking some course on human sexuality and as a result his penis is longer.

At a concrete level, these dreams are linked to the changing nature of marital sex during pregnancy. The predominance of dreams of virility and impotence suggests a deeper change, a confusion about sexual and masculine identity and a struggle to create a new identity as a man who is less stereotypically macho and more able to nurture connections with his child and his wife.

Despite the so-called sexual revolution, the women's movement, and other forms of consciousness raising, many of us still find it difficult to talk about our sexual feelings. Even though we understand intellectually that pregnancy and parenting call for sacrifices, we may still feel hurt if our partner is less sexual or can't be aroused in the same old ways.

Tracking your sexual dreams, exploring them in a dream journal, and sharing them with your partner can help you to express your confused and hurt feelings before they turn into bitterness and alienation. If you have ever had tendencies to feel rejected or jealous, these tendencies may surface during pregnancy. It's vital to set aside extra time to communicate, work out hurt feelings, and discover new ways to be intimate at this crucial turning point in your marriage.

Celebration Dreams. A dramatic feature of expectant fathers' dreams throughout pregnancy is the appearance of parties, celebrations, and what appear to be initiation ceremonies related to pregnancy and childbirth. Over half the expectant fathers in my study had a Party and Celebration dream, contrasted with only one incidence of this kind of dream in my comparison group. These were slightly more common earlier in the pregnancy.

An especially notable feature of Party and Celebration dreams is that many of them feature *birth*day parties. These dreams also depicted elaborate food preparation, eating and drinking, water imagery, and relationships with masculine or macho figures. Some of these dreams were associated with the completion of a creative project, such as a man who dreamed about a big party to celebrate a writing project he had just completed.

One man dreamed about a big circle dance in a Chinese restaurant, which suddenly switched to a hospital labor room. Another man, Gavin, had a dream that had the quality of a ritual designed to initiate him into the role of fatherhood.

Birth Dance

I am watching people all around me dance and play. I am not seen or heard. A group comes near me and all play ceases. This group seems to have control over all. I like them. Their energy is high and has a calming effect on me. They come to me, surround me. One of the them comes over to me and gives me a bundle. It is a baby.

At first Gavin felt left out. The part of the dream when he was not seen or heard made him remember painful feelings of exclusion earlier in the pregnancy, as well as other times in his life when he had felt excluded from groups or other relationships.

Gavin was the middle child in a family of ten. As he explored the dream, he wondered if it related in some way to memories of the birth of his four younger siblings. For Gavin, this dream may be an example of an early-childhood birth fantasy. If this were true, the dream would represent an attempt to understand and identify with the experience of childbirth, while at the same time working out early memories of being confused and displaced by the arrival of new siblings.

At the end of the dream, Gavin is surrounded in womblike fashion and is given a baby. He felt that this part of the dream was telling him that he had worked out earlier feelings of alienation from his wife and the pregnancy. At this point, he was feeling extremely excited and ready to take on the role of father.

The lack of adequate roles and rituals to confirm their inclusion and importance causes expectant fathers to feel anxious about where they fit in. Parties are associated with important turning points such as birthdays, graduations, weddings, and accomplishments. They usually involve a sense of specialness or sacredness apart from mundane routines. The preponderance of Party and Celebration dreams reflects an unconscious awareness of the specialness and importance of becoming a father. In their Party and Celebration dreams, most men create unconscious rites of passage to express the excitement of becoming a father.

HOW TO USE PREGNANCY DREAMS

Dreams exaggerate our anxieties about harm coming to a spouse, child, and ourselves during pregnancy. Sharing and exploring anxiety dreams (such as Deformed and Endangered Baby dreams, Forgetting the Baby dreams, and Losing Valuables dreams) helps to make us more aware of our fears. When we can articulate what we fear, we have a chance to understand how appropriate and necessary our fears are. When we can share what troubles us with our spouse, family, and friends, we have the chance to feel reassured, to understand and resolve our changing emotional needs.

Awareness of dreams also can help men to convert their unconscious emotional reactions and fears of being excluded into an energetic involvement with the events of the pregnancy and the preparations for nurturing the baby. It is especially important that men be encouraged to participate in prenatal classes, obstetric visits, genetic counseling and amniocentesis, shopping for the baby's needs, and baby showers and other celebratory events.

An invisible drama unfolds in the dreams of expectant parents. When we make this drama visible, by remembering and sharing dreams together, we can nurture the marital relationship and prepare for our new role as parents.

Just as proper nutrition and medical care will enhance the physical growth of the fetus, extra communication and emotional support enhance the parents' psychological readiness. Using our dreams to explore hidden conflicts, feelings, anxieties, and joys can be of tremendous value to couples as they prepare to make the crucial adjustment to parenthood.

4. *Separation and Divorce Dreams*
Breaking Up, Recovering, and Moving On

FOR MONTHS AFTER her husband walked out on her, Nora was emotionally paralyzed, afraid to let go of the marriage yet unable to find a new identity. After ten years of being married, she was faced with the need to support her two daughters and start a new life. Her shame about the divorce caused her to withdraw from many of her friends, especially her married friends whom she thought were unsympathetic.

Ten months after her separation, she began to have a series of vivid dreams that helped her to break free from the depths of her depression. Initially, all of the dreams were terrifying and unresolved: nightmares of thieves robbing her and threatening her with knives; of being paralyzed and unable to scream for help. On three occasions she had terrifying dreams about the brakes locking on her car. In the first two dreams, nothing would stop the car, not the hand brake, not downshifting, not steering. During the third dream, she grasped the hand brake and it finally worked.

As Nora made notes in her dream journal, she realized this was the first dream since her separation that had a resolution. Maybe something was beginning to change, she thought. Soon after, Nora had another series of dreams that felt very important to her. They took place at the museum where she had been a docent.

The Art Heist, I

I am outside the art museum dressed completely in black. Even my face is blackened. I have a bag of equipment for the job. My challenge is to scale the wall, cut through the skylight, drop down, avoid the sensor, and pick up a Pieter Bruegel painting called Peasant Wedding, *and then escape. The alarms will bring the police in fifteen to twenty minutes. My goal is just to see if it can be done, not to steal the art. The dream ends as I successfully scale down the wall to get into the museum.*

Nora was puzzled by this dream. She felt a strange sense of physical exhilaration when she awoke, a feeling of having accomplished something important. In her journal she wrote: "I had to depend entirely on myself, know my limitations and succeed." The physical challenge of the dream was related to facing the emotional task of overcoming her depression.

Nora was surprised when two nights later she had a similar dream.

The Art Heist, II

Breaking into the museum again. The same as before, although this time my face isn't blackened. I secretly know, with one other friend who volunteers at the museum, that this is a test of the security system. The museum director and secur-

*ity chief don't know it is a test. This time, I not
only go in and get the Bruegel but also descend on
the museum and crack the safe for the master
drawings and get the most valuable of the collection. The director and security chief are furious
when they find out.*

The following night, Nora had a third and final version
of this dream. This time she is even bolder in her efforts to
steal the paintings despite the fact that some people see her.
She scales the wall and gets away in the nick of time.

By this time, Nora was beginning to see that these
dreams were telling her something about how she was finally making a breakthrough in her recovery from divorce.
As we talked about the elements of her dream, Nora commented on how striking was the image of her blackened
face. It reminded her at first of pictures of coal miners in Ap-
palachia. She also thought wearing black had to do with
mourning the loss of her marriage as she succumbed to the
bleakness of depression. Nora felt that her blackness represented the state of prolonged grief she had endured, a period
in which she had been hiding from her friends and the world.
From that darkness, she found that she had a bag of tools,
resources that were now becoming accessible to her. She
also had a challenging job to do—recovering and building a
new life.

But why was she trying to steal a sixteenth-century
Flemish painting of a wedding scene? She recalled that in
her undergraduate studies she had written a term paper
on Pieter Bruegel and had discussed that very painting,
Peasant Wedding. When she traveled in Europe after college,
she made a special point of visiting the museum in Vienna
where it was displayed. She recalled from her college research paper that *Peasant Wedding* portrayed a superficial
appearance of joyful and prosperous village life. A closer

examination of the painting, however, reveals an emphasis on guzzling alcohol and overeating. Critics considered the painting to be a social commentary on the vices of drunkenness and gluttony.

Remembering her interest in that painting set off a chain of associations related to the alcoholism of her father and her husband. To the outside world her family had appeared to be a perfect 1950s family. In reality, the illusion was shattered by her mother's depression and passive acceptance of her father's verbal abuse, late nights out at bars, and occasional gambling binges.

Nora's marriage was also considered ideal. Unknown to their friends, however, Nora's ex-husband, Jack, was a heavy drinker, even on the job. A workaholic building contractor, he had become more successful but progressively more distant from Nora and their children. Although she was devastated when he ran off with his secretary, she was now seeing how empty their marriage had become.

Brazenly stealing the Bruegel painting had a number of important meanings for Nora. The fact that the painting portrayed a wedding scene was especially significant. Capturing the painting related to exposing the hypocrisy and alcoholism of her own marriage and that of her parents. She was the child and ex-wife of an alcoholic. She could no longer mask the emotional damage that had occurred. She had to face the role she had played in colluding with her husband's alcoholism and be careful not to choose another partner who would be as emotionally cold.

Nora saw her Art Heist dreams as a turning point in her recovery, related to recapturing the inner creativity that had been dormant in her marriage. Exploring the dreams gave her hope that she had reached a new stage in recovering from her divorce. She was beginning to move out of the blackness of her months of depression. She could risk breaking out of the security system of her old fears and recapture the precious resources of her strength and creativity.

SEPARATION AND DIVORCE AS A TURNING POINT

The way in which we cope with the end of a marriage or an important love relationship can alter the course of our lives. When we emerge from the turmoil of divorce or final separation, we face a perilous moment of opportunity. We may discover creative possibilities and establish a more fulfilling relationship. Or we may wallow in depression, psychosomatic illnesses, and a bitterness that paralyzes our emotional growth and psychologically poisons our children.

Statistics show that more than half of us will undergo one or more divorces in a lifetime. Many more who are not legally married will undergo the end of long-term relationships. Children born in the mid-1980s have a 38 percent chance of enduring one or more parental divorces before the age of eighteen, not to mention the risk of experiencing divorce in their own marriages.

By the time separation occurs, the handwriting usually has been on the wall for some time. The seeds for a separation are sown long before the formal papers are filed. Often the roots of a breakup reach back to our relationships with our parents and even to their relationships with previous generations.

Just as the decision to break up a marriage or long-term partnership takes time to incubate, the period of recovery also can take months or years. Although each of us is unique, experts suggest that the period of intense crisis may last from several weeks to several months. This phase of being in shock is followed by a gradual period of readjustment that may take the better part of a year. For some, recovery may take one or more years.

During the turbulent weeks and months of rebuilding our lives, dreams can provide insights, inner guidance, and confirmation of our feelings. Remembering and exploring separation and divorce dreams offers us

- Warnings about emotional impasses we are facing at the end of a relationship or beginning of a separation

- Insights about issues from the past that are hampering our ability to accept the reality of the loss
- Clarification of strong feelings such as grief, anger, and guilt, which we need to express and resolve
- Awareness of our progress through the stages of grieving, emotional resolution, and rebuilding
- Renewed hope and confidence by highlighting breakthroughs we are achieving in our recovery from the separation

THE STAGES OF RECOVERY FROM
SEPARATION AND DIVORCE

Psychotherapists generally view recovery from divorce and separation as progressing through stages similar to those encountered in facing death or grieving the death of a loved one. The sequence of the stages may vary, but the psychological tasks that go with them are considered necessary for full recovery. Since four out of five divorced persons will remarry, it is essential to come to terms with the lessons of previous relationships, or risk repeating the same mistakes.

The process of the recovery from divorce and separation can be seen as unfolding in three stages.

Stage 1: The first stage is one of shock and denial. It often begins before we make the actual separation and continues until after the break. During this time, it's crucial for us to overcome a powerful tendency to hang onto the marriage and fantasize about a reconciliation instead of accepting the reality of the separation.

Dreams in this period may include themes of being stuck, such as imprisonment and paralysis. Dreams of natural disasters such as earthquakes or tidal waves may occur, symbolizing the disastrous impact of the change. Other dream themes may include out-of-control events such as falling, cars going off the road, or losing valuables like a wallet or purse.

Stage 2: The second stage of the recovery process is one of anger, depression, and despair. Our culture tells us to be brave, to put aside our feelings and return to productive activities, so dealing with anger is an especially tricky dilemma. We feel hurt and abandoned and fear that we are unlovable. Blaming our villainous ex-spouse or assuming the victim role obscures our ability to resolve the emotional crisis of separation. We need to reach the point where we can express our anger nondestructively and take responsibility for our own shortcomings in the relationship.

Dreams in the second stage of transition may include themes of betrayal or rejection such as Sexual Rejection dreams or Left-out dreams. They may also include dreams associated with depression in which we find ourselves feeling inadequate, self-destructive, or unable to cope with threatening forces. Other themes may include nakedness, symbolizing our vulnerability, or new clothing dreams related to the letting go of old roles. Dreams of anger or revenge are also likely to appear at this stage.

Stage 3: The final stage of recovery is one of hope and renewal. A new identity is forming. We reclaim our independence and rediscover the voice within us that goes back to the time before we were married, even to our childhood. In this final stage, we need to be able to overcome our insecurity and self-doubt and take risks to build a new life.

As we move back into the world, we renew old ties and establish new friendships and interests. In this period we have what Judith Wallerstein and Sandra Blakeslee call a "second chance": a window of opportunity to exorcise ghosts from childhood, achieve a more fulfilling marriage, and find deeper meaning in work and friendships.

In this last stage, dreams of threat and struggle still occur but tend to end with greater resolution, like Nora's three dreams. In our dreams at this point we may choose new outfits, find new rooms in houses, and discover unexpected val-

uables as we establish new roles and develop new parts of
our personality. Unresolved issues from childhood or earlier relationships may also come to the surface and achieve
resolution. We are beginning to thrive in the role of a single
individual, and this is reflected in our dreams.

DREAMS FORESHADOWING SEPARATION

The stresses of balancing two careers, caring for children,
and maintaining a household are enormous. A serious illness or death in the family, financial troubles, moving, pressures from in-laws, or traumatic events may tip the balance
in a negative direction for a married couple.

The idea to separate or divorce may be brewing in the
mind of one or both partners for months or even years prior
to the actual breakup. As the emotional knots tighten and
hope dwindles, it is vitally important to decide whether the
marriage is worth saving. For most of us this is an agonizing
decision, especially if children are involved or our religious
beliefs are strong.

Many people wait too long before seeking help when
problems arise in their relationship. They are unable or un-
willing to take advantage of family or friends who can provide support and guidance. Even if the necessity for professional help becomes clear, denial often causes couples to
wait until the differences between them have escalated
beyond repair.

Remembering and exploring dreams can help us to
overcome denial and gain a crucial understanding of our unconscious reactions to a relationship impasse. Through our
dreams we can gain a better understanding of what isn't
working and be in a better position to seek help in repairing
the marriage or in making the decision to leave a marriage
that is emotionally destructive.

Adam, a successful bookstore owner, did not want
to admit that things were not working in his second mar-

riage, to Bev. His first marriage had ended unhappily seven years earlier. Because his first wife complained of feeling squelched, Adam was careful the second time around to choose someone who had her own professional identity. From the beginning, Adam had admired Bev's growing creativity and self-confidence as she became more successful as a fashion designer. As a result, however, she was working longer hours and traveling more frequently.

At forty, Adam was eager to have more children. He had wanted to be closer to his children in a way that had been impossible in his first marriage. At thirty-four, Bev didn't feel ready to have children. She felt her career was just getting launched. In fact, she was feeling less sure that she wanted children at all. After a series of bitter fights, Adam had a dream that he feels changed the course of his life.

The Fallen Idol
I am encouraging Bev to climb up on a stand that is something like a pedestal for a statue. She doesn't really want to but she complies. I keep asking her to raise her arm higher, like the Statue of Liberty raising her torch. Suddenly she begins to teeter and fall off. I am terrified that she might get hurt or killed, but I'm paralyzed and can't do anything to stop her from falling.

As Adam related his dream to an old friend, he realized that he had put Bev on a pedestal. He had idealized her so much that he had been blinded to who she really was. Yes, she was creative, assertive, and successful, but she had been giving him a clear message for over a year: her career was more important than having a family or deepening their marriage. To his dismay, his idol had fallen.

The more Adam talked about his marital problems, the more he realized Bev had been telling him the marriage wasn't working. She had withdrawn from him and invested herself in her career. Adam realized that if he really did want to have more children, he would have to leave her and find someone who shared his vision of family life.

Following this discussion, Adam sought individual psychotherapy. He realized he needed to work out his tendency to idealize women and his fears of intimacy before he could achieve a successful marriage. Although he may have been on the verge of deciding to leave the marriage anyway, Adam credits his dream for initiating the process that led him to separate from Bev.

When we are at an impasse in our relationship, dreams can help us understand where we are blocked. Knowing this, we can make a realistic decision about whether to repair the relationship or end it. In addition, dreams foreshadowing a separation give us clues to repetitive patterns in relationships, such as Adam's tendency to idealize women. Understanding these tendencies can help us avoid repeating the same mistakes in future relationships.

ABANDONMENT AND
SEXUAL REJECTIONS DREAMS

Early adjustment to divorce is influenced by whether one is the person who leaves or the person who is left. The person who initiates a divorce generally feels more in control and suffers less distress in the immediate aftermath. The person who leaves may feel guilty but is less likely in the early stages of a divorce to feel the pain of abandonment and depression.

In the weeks following a marital separation, Sexual Rejection dreams are common, especially for the person who has been left. A person who has experienced painful rejections and losses earlier in life is especially vulnerable to dreams of abandonment or betrayal. When one spouse is sexually unfaithful or leaves the marriage to be with another person, there is an even higher likelihood of feelings of abandonment taking the form of Sexual Rejection dreams.

For Sabina, the discovery of her husband's affair led to the breakup of their three-year marriage. The more she asked around, the more she discovered about Bob's philandering.

Sabina had repetitive Sexual Rejection dreams for months after their separation. In the first weeks many of her dreams had unresolved endings and, according to Sabina, distinct patterns. In some, she would feel lonely or longing for Bob. In others, he would either directly mention that he had been with another woman or she would find out the upsetting news from a friend. In the final pattern, she would be making love with him and he would spitefully reject her plea for a committed relationship. One of Sabina's dreams combined all three of these themes into a series of degrading and enraging rebuffs from her ex-husband.

Multiple Rejections

I run into Bob at his office. He is telling me about a boating regatta that was going to happen. I want him to invite me but he doesn't. Then it seems like it is the next day at work and one of my supervisors is telling me she saw Bob in the building. I think he came to talk to me but he goes around a corner without looking at me. Somehow, I hear that he is dating someone at the office. I go into the bathroom and there she is—wearing a bright yellow dress like one I used to have. I ask her point-blank if she is seeing him. She says she has been seeing him since October, which is before we broke up. I'm extremely upset that he would date someone so stupid. I'm looking for him again and catch a glimpse of him walking away, but he is gone. I go outside, furious. I start hitting cars with a baseball bat. I want to find him and tell him off, but he's nowhere to be seen.

Sabina's dream mirrors her inability to overcome her feeling of being deceived and abandoned. In this dream, she is rejected by the elusive Bob and his latest flame, but is still desperately seeking him.

Sabina's dreams indicate that she was bogged down in the shock and denial stage of adjustment to separation. Although the dream suggests rage and frustration in the final image of smashing cars with a baseball bat, she could not consciously accept her anger at Bob. Not only was she unable to banish him from her mind and go on with her life, but in reality she continued to seek him out for more inevitable rejections.

For Seth and Martha, there were no incidents of infidelity associated with their breakup. They had lived together for four years, then became engaged. Just before the invitations were to be sent, Martha got cold feet and called off the wedding. Increasingly she became moody, found fault with Seth's behavior, and began to pick fights over minor issues. When pressed, Martha admitted not being sure why she was alienating Seth. But she was increasingly convinced that they should split up.

After Martha left, Seth had great difficulty sleeping. Almost every night, he had nightmares of Martha rejecting him, going out with other guys and flaunting it. He was beginning to lose weight and found it hard to function at work.

Two weeks after Martha left, Seth had the following dream.

The Baby That Will Never Be
Martha and I have had a baby. It's two weeks old but we haven't named it. We are distant. Martha

*seems especially aloof. I come home and it seems
like we have three houses. One isn't even fur-
nished yet. She will be taking over one of them
when we break up. I look all around to see where
she is. I want to see the baby. When I see Martha, I
tell myself I'm no longer sexually attracted to her.
But then I become nostalgic and do feel very attracted to her and start to touch her breasts in a
sexual way. She responds but in a mechanical
way, and I can see that she is no longer attracted to
me or wanting to make love with me. The dream
ends while I am wondering what to name the
baby.*

Seth awoke tearful. He had registered for a workshop
on dreams and was eager to explore the meaning of his repetitive dreams of rejection. After describing his dream, he
began to have a flood of associations. He felt that the two-
week-old baby was more than just the baby that he would
never have with Martha. It represented exactly the amount
of time since they had broken up. *He* was the baby, and his
dream represented his vulnerable new sense of self in the
postseparation period. The fact that the baby was unnamed
indicated that the separation was so new that he did not
know yet who he was without Martha.

Seth wasn't sure about the meaning of the three houses,
but another group member suggested that they symbolized
the new house Martha had moved to, the house that Seth and
Martha had lived in, and that same house (where Seth continued to live) in the post-Martha period. Seth remembered
that he had been rearranging the furniture the previous day
to make the house feel more his own. Seth also felt that the
dream was telling him that he hadn't yet been able to detach
himself from Martha. He tried to resist her but ended up
making a sexual advance, only to be rejected.

When asked whether the dream reminded him of any events from the past, Seth recalled one of his earliest memories: his mother bringing home his baby sister when he was almost three years old. He remembered feeling upset that everyone was paying so much attention to the baby. His parents confirmed that he had had a bad case of jealousy of his sister and would tease her a lot when she was young.

Seth felt that discussing his dream helped him to understand the roots of his feelings of rejection that lay in his childhood and to lessen his preoccupation with feeling like a victim. Seth continued to keep careful records of his dreams. Although he had other Sexual Rejection dreams in the ensuing weeks, they became less frequent and less disturbing. Gradually his dreams changed. Occasionally, he would reject Martha in his dreams or meet other women who would accept his sexual advances. As time passed, the rejection theme became less frequent in his dreams as he recovered from the separation.

DREAMS, SEPARATION, AND DEPRESSION

Rosalind Cartwright, Ph.D., has been studying the relationship of waking life events to dreams for nearly thirty years. As chair of the Department of Psychology and Social Sciences at Rush Medical College, Dr. Cartwright has undertaken an ambitious study of 300 men and women in Chicago who had filed for divorce. She has interviewed them, psychologically tested them, monitored their sleep, and collected their dreams during a three-night stay in a sleep laboratory. This was done immediately following separation and again at a one year follow-up. Her results show that divorce has much in common with other turning points. Dreams connected to divorce can help us gain a deeper understanding of how people cope with profound change.

One of the most important aspects of Cartwright's work is her analysis of the dreams of people who experienced severe depression after separation. Such dreamers had themes of drowning, having depleted resources such as a gas tank that couldn't be filled up, being totally alone or abandoned, or being taken advantage of or threatened. In fact, 39 percent of the women and 24 percent of the men were undergoing a severe depression at the time of separation, a percentage many times higher than that of depression in the general population. According to Cartwright, many of the more seriously depressed people appeared to embody an intensely self-blaming attitude that "everything has gone wrong, and it is all my fault."

Upsetting dreams may be a prerequisite to emotional resolution of a turning point. Repressing upsetting feelings and dreams may create an impasse in the necessary emotional tumult of working through a separation. Anxiety, victimization, masochism, and abandonment themes are common in the dreams of many people in the early period following marital separation. Cartwright found that people who experienced normal grief, but not depression, had more disturbing dreams compared to those who were stuck in their depression.

In fact, the nondepressed women had more anxiety dreams than did the depressed women. Although such dreams were very upsetting, the anxious and threatening elements were more often directed at others and not at themselves, compared to the dreams of women suffering from depression. The recovering women had dreams that hearkened back to the past but also seemed directly connected to solving problems in the present and future. In other words, the problem-solving function of dreaming appeared to be working in the recovering women and failing in the depressed women.

Cartwright uncovered extraordinary patterns in the dream biology as well as the dream content of her subjects. She found that the dreamers who were not depressed, plus a large portion of those who were depressed but recovered quickly, had dreaming patterns that appeared to be linked to a healthy response to the trauma of separation. Physiologically, the nondepressed and recovering dreamers began to dream very early in the nightly cycle of sleep and had more dense bursts of the rapid eye movements that are characteristic of dreaming sleep. In other words, the recovering dreamers seemed to be having a more powerful and insistent physiological dream response.

Upsetting dreams and intensified dream physiology are evidence of facing conflicts related to emotional upheaval of separation. This pattern is characteristic of a healthier emotional response to a turning point. However, unchanging, unresolved dreams that dwell upon the past and unrelentingly portray the dreamer as a victim are likely to be those of a depressed person who is frozen in unresolved grief and anger.

One of Cartwright's subjects, Marj, had been married for ten years and was the mother of two. Although she had a master's degree in education, she had been a housewife in her unhappy marriage. After enduring repeated physical abuse from her alcoholic husband, she finally left him. She had been suffering from depression for months with frequent crying spells, weight loss, and sleep disturbance. Marj was at an impasse in working through her depression, and her dreams reflected this emotional block.

Some turning point dreams only show us where we are; they don't illuminate the way out of an impasse. During one night of being monitored in Cartwright's sleep lab, Marj had a series of dreams related to her depression about the separation. Her first dream of the evening revealed her sense of vulnerability.

Ambushed

Someone was after me. I was in a street by myself walking from a parking lot. Someone jumped out from between parked cars. It was very frightening.

The parking lot reminded her of the trailer park where she used to live with her husband during a period when he assaulted her frequently. The dream was highlighting the terrifying situation in which she had been living, the constant danger of unprovoked physical attack.

In another dream of the same night, the theme of eating emerges, and Marj is shocked by what she finds when she bites into a hot dog.

A Mouthful of Yukky Cat Hair
I was eating some cat hair by mistake. It was in the cafeteria. There was a white counter that had condiments and two cats on it. I got half of one of the two cats instead of the condiments and put it in my mouth with my hot dog. I said, yuk! The cats were sleeping. Their heads were down in a curled position.

This dream was associated with an oral sex act that was disgusting to her. It was linked to her continuing tendency to get involved in degrading and unpalatable sexual relationships. She did not appear to be getting the nourishment she needed from either food or sex.

In the final dream of the evening, Marj gets cheated out of her place by two policemen who steal her place in line to remove the electrodes from her head in the dream lab. One of them has a car like her ex-husband's. References to her ex-husband's car and the trailer park indicate that she is still struggling to overcome her sense of being abused by unfair and insensitive men. In the entire series of dreams, she is plagued by her status as a victim with no resources to combat her continuing victimization.

Some separation dreams can inspire us to investigate new avenues for resolving an impasse. Sabina, whose Sexual Rejection dream is mentioned above, had new insights through the following dream about her role as a victim in relationships. Two months after separating from Bob, she continued to fantasize about getting back with him and was unable to resolve her grief.

Please Help Me Find My Old Dog

I'm back in college studying hard for a final exam that I'm worried about. Then I am going to the exam with my old dog, Amber. Amber suddenly turns into a scraggly dog contrary to what she was really like, and she runs away. Then my college boyfriend comes up to me. He was the one I was going out with when we got the dog. I ask him to help me find Amber. He refuses and is cold to me. I run out crying and upset.

Sabina explained that her dog, Amber, had died of old age one year earlier. At the time, Bob refused to go to the veterinarian's office when Amber had to be put to sleep. Sabina was very depressed after Amber's death and felt Bob was unsupportive and insensitive. When she explored her dream, Sabina wondered why Amber had looked so scraggly and why her boyfriend had been so cruel and rejecting. She guessed that her old boyfriend represented Bob's cruelty to her.

For Sabina, the pathetic ghost of her dog represented her emotionally weary self. Being with Amber may have had to do with comforting her own depletion and depression. At first, Amber is a soothing presence during Sabina's big exam. The exam is probably symbolic of the emotional test she is undergoing in facing the marital separation. As the dream progresses she loses touch with Amber, and her boyfriend coldly rejects her, paying no attention to her sense of loss or neediness.

Discussing her dream helped Sabina realize how deeply she had sunk into her role as a victim and how her longing for Bob to become a loving partner was a false hope.

It wasn't until weeks later that Sabina was able to see how her fruitless longings for a disinterested man were repeating a pattern from childhood with her father. (See her Caught in the Act dream below.)

If your dreams are filled with conflicts related to grief, anger, and rejection, and if over time these conflicts begin to show signs of gradual resolution, you are probably on the road to a healthy recovery even if your dreams are still upsetting or even nightmarish. On the other hand, if your dreams never achieve resolution and relentlessly portray you as a victim, or if they are bland and don't seem to focus at all on the separation, you may be at an impasse. It is vital to seek help from friends, family, or a psychotherapist as soon as you sense that your recovery may be stuck in the early stages of separation.

CLOTHING AND NUDITY DREAMS

Many familiar roles are shed during a separation. For some this may feel like a relief, the necessary molting of an old, shriveled skin. For many others the change is more excruciating, like being stripped bare or having one's flesh torn away.

As old roles fall aside, we go through a period of flux and begin to experiment with new roles. Clothing and Nudity dreams may represent the phase of loss of identity, the naked sense of vulnerability and experimentation with new roles and identities.

Rose's Clothing and Nudity dream occurred shortly after her Riding a Unicycle dream, which is mentioned at the beginning of chapter 1. After a long period of contemplating the move, Rose left her husband of twenty-seven years and moved across the country to a city they had lived in ten years earlier.

Rose's unicycle dream took place just after her first meeting with her estranged husband, Leo, after five months of separation. In that dream she rides a unicycle, symbolic of the single life, when everyone around her is riding two-wheeler bikes, symbolic of married life. Although she feels alienated and clumsy, she is able to succeed and feel pride. The unicycle dream occurred just as she was beginning to shake the deep depression that had afflicted her prior to and immediately following the separation.

The following dream occurred two nights after her unicycle dream and one week after her meeting with Leo. The dream focuses on her own attire or lack of it, and is further evidence of the awkwardness of the role changes that occur with divorce. As in the unicycle dream, Rose is beginning to achieve resolution about the identity change she was undergoing.

Dressed in an Old Towel at the Cocktail Party

I am at a cocktail party like the ones I used to go to for my husband's company. Everyone is dressed to the nines in furs and jewels. I realize that all I have on is a bath towel. It is kind of strange but I don't really feel that weird. People start to look at me funny as if they are questioning or condemning what I was wearing. I can sense that all the people around me are not comfortable.

As she told her dream, I asked Rose to focus on the strongest feelings she was experiencing. She focused on the sense of being alienated from people. She said, "I have always felt that way a little bit, but my sense of not fitting in was especially strong with Leo and his business-oriented dinners and parties. The party in the dream reminds me of any number of real parties I used to go to in my other life with my husband. I hated those parties. They were so superficial, just like Leo. I never felt that I fit in."

The estrangement Rose feels in her dream is characteristic of the unconscious and conscious experiences of the newly separated person. Rose's dream related to her sense of humiliation about being divorced, as well as to the financial hardships of separation.

In dreams, we often discover that details that seem trivial or mundane at first turn out to be rich with associations and meanings. For Rose the old bath towel was such an object. The towel reminded her of a set of towels she had bought years ago before she married Leo. She smiled as she thought about them. Leo's mother had always hated them when she visited, but Rose kept them until they were torn and ratty. She realized they were a symbol of the brief period of independence she had before marriage.

In this dream, Rose is beginning to recover from her depression. One indication of this is that she's not alone and desolate in her dream. Although she is feeling inadequate, she is determined and able to weather the scorn of others at the party. In Cartwright's study, 74 percent of depressed divorcing women had one or more dreams with no other person in them, as compared to 42 percent of the nondepressed divorcing women.

Learning to accept loss or change in key relationships and adapting to the new status of being independent are crucial variables in getting over divorce or separation. Clothing and Nudity dreams are among the ways our dreams express our reactions to our changing identity. Exploring these dreams can help us to clarify whether we are moving forward toward establishing a postseparation identity.

CONFRONTING ISSUES FROM THE PAST

Separation and divorce afford an opportunity to create a more healthy relationship with a new partner. In order to move forward and avoid repeating past mistakes in relationships, it's vital that we learn from our own relationship history. We risk making the same or even worse choices if we fly forward into a new relationship without understanding our contribution to the demise of the one that just ended.

At turning points such as divorce, our dreams have an uncanny way of spotlighting issues and relationships from the past that are blocking us. A year after her separation from Leo, Rose had a dream that helped her understand the roots of her difficulty in escaping her marriage. This dream, like the others, came around the time of a brief visit with him. She had only seen him twice since their separation, and she feared that the visit would make her revert back into depression. Although she was only planning to have lunch with him to discuss minor details of their final settlement, Rose was on the verge of canceling the meeting when she had the following dream.

The Boathouse Party

I am in the boathouse down by the lake where we used to spend summers when I was a kid. Instead of my father owning it, it seems to be my older brother's house. There is a big family party and somehow the boathouse is different, larger. I am in a part of the house that had been added on. The house begins to undulate as if it wasn't stable. I keep struggling back to where the ground is more stable, and he reassures me not to worry. The ground is still swaying dangerously under me. I wake up and am just able to struggle back to solid ground.

A year after her separation, Rose's dream was taking her farther back into her past, beyond Leo and back to her relationships with her father and brother. Rose recalled that the boathouse was not a place of happy summer memories. During the family's summer visits there, her father would drink and become verbally and occasionally physically abusive to her three brothers. There were few other children in the neighborhood, and her older brother would tease her mercilessly.

Her dream of returning to the boathouse helped Rose see how she was still under the spell of the abuse she received there. She associated her brother's reassurances in the dream with his denial of ever harassing her. She remembered that whenever she complained about the vicious teasing, her mother did nothing. The lack of acknowledgment and protection by her family had infused Rose with self-doubt and a self-defeating tendency that had influenced her whole life.

As she discussed her boathouse dream in therapy, Rose began to understand the incredible emotional parallels between her relationships with her father, her brother, and her husband. Leo had been unexpressive and frequently criticized her. On three occasions he had undermined her attempts to go back to school and begin a career. He seemed to want a loyal business wife who accepted her place.

For years, she told herself she was staying for the kids. But after they both went to college, it was another year before she could bring herself to leave. Through therapy and her own self-exploration, she understood that she had thought she deserved Leo's abuse and his constant sabotage of her autonomy.

The shaking of the ground under the boathouse symbolized the unstable period she had been going through. The dream helped her see that there could be no reassurance from her brother, her family, or Leo. She had to weather the earthquake she was experiencing and struggle back to solid ground through her own efforts.

In the dream Rose discovers a new part of the boathouse. Dreams of discovering a new room in a house and related images often occur at moments of personal growth when new aspects of our personality are emerging. Rose felt that she was trying to remake or rework her childhood, to find a room that would support her growing self-confidence and movements toward autonomy. Although the earth is swaying dangerously, the dream ends with Rose achieving a degree of resolution.

By discussing this dream in therapy and with two close friends, Rose resolved to go ahead with the visit with Leo. She kept it brief and emerged from the meeting with a renewed confidence that Leo's spell on her—and that of her father and her brother—had been broken.

For Sabina, a dream five months after her separation shows that earlier conflicts with her father and mother remain unresolved and are still blocking her recovery.

Caught in the Act

I'm in my bedroom in my parents' home where I grew up. I can see the familiar yellow color of the walls. Suddenly I see Bob coming in through the window. He wants to come in my bed and have sex with me. I want to, but I'm afraid that my parents will find out. I go into the bathroom to put my diaphragm on. It is all wet in there and it seems like my dad just finished taking a shower. Bob becomes impatient, so we start making love. A nun comes in ranting: "This is disgusting!" Then my mom comes in angry because of the nun screaming and because I'm in bed with Bob. I'm angry now also. I think they should get out and respect the fact that I had the door closed. I want to continue to make love with Bob but all the interruptions seem to have ruined it and I'm disappointed.

In the dream, we again see Sabina's continuing desperation to be reunited sexually with Bob under any circumstance. The other elements of the dream made Sabina especially curious. As she recounted her dream, she was shocked by the graphic depiction of the sexual scene in her bedroom in her family home. It reminded her of constant fights she used to have with her parents when she was a teenager. They would yell at her and try to restrict her, but she was rebellious, shouting back and often defying them by going on dates with older guys.

Sabina thought the cameo appearance by the screaming nun was "weird." She wasn't Catholic. Why should a nun show up in her dream? At first she was sure that it related to her parents, especially her mother. When I suggested that the raging nun might represent a part of herself, Sabina became silent, and a sad look came over her face. Although she had been sexually active at an early age and had always prided herself on being liberated, maybe she did have fears and inhibitions after all. It would certainly make sense, given how negative her parents were about sex. Sabina guessed that some of her early sexual activity was the only way she could find of getting love and attention.

Sabina became tearful as she thought more about how much mistreatment she had been willing to put up with when she was with Bob, yet how much urgency she still felt to win him back sexually. Her friends had been telling her that he was unkind and that she should give up on him. She knew they were right, but the advice just didn't sink in.

As she reviewed the dream, I asked her about the part in which she sensed that her father had just taken a shower. At first she remembered that her family only had one bathroom and that her father would take long showers, blocking anyone else from using the bathroom. As she thought more about this memory, she remembered that he was incredibly insensitive in other ways. "He was always critical. He never gave a compliment." Sabina remembered that in the period before her parents' divorce, when she was sixteen, her mother and father used to have shouting matches and he would say incredibly nasty things to Sabina's mother.

Sabina began to make a link between the wet bathroom, her father, and her desperate need to make love to

Bob at all costs. She had a strong sense that her difficulty in letting go of Bob concerned unresolved issues with her father. Bob was like her father in many ways, capable of being charming at times but often selfish and temperamental.

Sabina's dream helped her to understand more about the addictive quality of her continuing preoccupation with Bob. Although her dream indicates that she is still at an impasse, her exploration of the dream helped her recognize her masochistic pattern with men and how it was connected to her unfulfilling relationship with her father.

DREAMS AND RECOVERY AFTER SEPARATION

Dreams provide a compass to navigate through the difficult passage of separation and divorce. Through our dreams we can understand where we are in our journey from being part of a couple to being a single person who may want to reconnect with a new partner.

In the early stages of breaking up, dreams and nightmares provide a gauge for viewing our confusion and our powerful feelings of grief, rage, and abandonment. Our dreams show us feeling out of control, threatened, exposed, and inadequate. At that stage our dreams can help us overcome our powerful tendency toward denial, bitterness, or clinging to the past.

Exploring our dreams also helps us to understand issues from the past that have contributed to the failure of our marriage and may also block intimacy in the future. During the crisis of separation, our dreams review events when we faced a similar loss or separation. Through dreams, the unconscious mind searches for times in the past when we solved a parallel emotional challenge. Our dreams can help us by picturing our crisis from many different angles and exaggerating it. We need to be able to see our predicament in a new way to make a change.

Rose's unicycle dream and Nora's art heists show us how dreams are like rehearsals for crucial new behaviors and attitudes. Just as dreams of the expectant parent show a rehearsal of nurturing, divorcing people's dreams show a rehearsal of roles associated with a single life separate from a former spouse. If we are open to the messages of our dreams, we can use them to repair old wounds that prevent us from creating a fulfilling relationship.

5. *Work Dreams*
Resolving Career Conflicts and Finding a Meaningful Job

ERICA, THIRTY-NINE, had returned to graduate school after ten years of working as a waitress. She had completed her undergraduate degree at a top university with honors and was about to complete an MBA. At last she was ready to begin her career.

In her final round of job interviews, she began to experience bouts of anxiety. First she procrastinated in setting up the interviews. Then, although she performed reasonably well, she was terrified that her insecurity would be detected and she would not only be denied a job but would not make it in her new profession. During this period she had the following dream.

Leap of Faith
I am on top of a mountain, being forced to jump from my mountain to the top of another mountain. There is a steep valley below so it is very dangerous. I know I have to take a chance. I imagine

*that I'm jumping and finally take a great leap and
make it. I am aware of all my movements and how
I'm breathing as I land.*

Erica felt relieved when she awoke, as if a burden had
been lifted. As she explored the elements of her dream, her
first association was to her fear of heights. She was surprised that she would have climbed so high, because in waking life she would have avoided such a mountain precipice.

The image of being on the top of the mountain also triggered associations for Erica about her career status. She
was about to reach new heights in her career and was nervous about making the transition from graduate school to
the business world. The image of the valley in her dream
symbolized the lesser job she had worked in and the fact
that she had come from a family of lower means.

Although it reminded her of dangers ahead, Erica's
dream also gave her an image of confidence. In the dream
she is able to jump from mountain to mountain, and she
does make her final great leap. Remembering this part of the
dream gave her a sense of confidence that she felt could help
her persevere and succeed in her career transition.

During this same period Erica had another anxiety
dream that she'd had many times before while working as a
waitress. After years of repetition, the dream took a more resolved form, again presenting a symbolic solution to her
performance anxieties.

A New Way of Taking Orders
*I am waiting on tables at my restaurant. I am
very nervous about confusing or forgetting the
orders. I decide that I am going to try something
new and I give everyone a piece of paper to write
their orders. That way I don't have to risk getting*

*their order wrong, I won't forget them, and I can
correct them before I give them to the chef. I try it
and it seems to work.*

For years, the dream had not included a new method of
taking orders. It had been a pure anxiety dream about ruin-
ing orders or being scolded by the customers or the chef for
poor performance. The new ending provided a solution indicating a sense of confidence that Erica could contain her
anxiety and enjoy her work. In retrospect, Erica saw that she
never had complaints from the chef and rarely from customers, because her anxiety caused her to be overly meticu-
lous in her duties. Erica's dream solution paralleled a lessening of the anxiety she felt in her job as a waitress. It also
heralded a growing sense of esteem that allowed her to feel
confident about returning to school and changing careers.

CAREER CHANGE AS A TURNING POINT

In this chapter we'll examine how our dreams can guide us
to find meaningful work that moves us closer to fulfilling
our emotional, spiritual, and material needs. We'll see how
dreams can help us navigate the many crises and transitions
of our career. We'll explore dreams at each stage of the career cycle, focusing on the psychological issues and stages
related to making a career transition.

During our thirty to fifty years of working, we face
many turning points, some anticipated and manageable, others sudden and devastating. Most people can expect a number of job changes and one or more career changes. Even
apparently positive events, such as receiving a promotion
or a new job or getting an award, may cause serious work-
related stress.

Virtually everyone experiences minor career conflicts
and crises. Every so often, however, we experience profound
career turning points that can alter our economic and

social stability and even endanger our physical and emotional health. Turning points in the career cycle can be caused by external factors, internal psychological factors, or an interplay of the two.

External situations that may precipitate turning points include being abused by insensitive supervisors or management; suffering a work-related injury; topping out or losing out on promotions; being demoted or losing a job; having to learn unfamiliar skills; dealing with boring, meaningless, or unrewarding tasks; lacking educational opportunities; and being subject to discrimination because of race, gender, age, disabilities, or sexual orientation.

Common internal factors that contribute to career turning points include burnout, depression, authority conflicts, performance anxieties, fears of commitment, fears of success, reactions to stresses unrelated to work, and general dissatisfaction and loss of incentive.

There are distinct phases to the career cycle. As early as childhood we may begin to explore visions of our future work identity, idealizing our parents or movie stars, athletes, or teachers. This exploration phase may lead us to change majors in college or experiment with different jobs to find ourselves. For some, experimentation may be brief and decisive. For others, it may take them well into their twenties or even thirties and involve job changes and more schooling before they can settle on one path.

Disengagement from a career or job comes inevitably at retirement. We may also face the need to leave a job when dissatisfaction or adverse events make our work unbearable. At that point we need to decide whether to change jobs and start the career cycle again or find some way of adapting to our present job. Whether we change careers or revitalize our present job, we undergo a phase of exploration that can lead to breakthroughs in self-awareness.

Remembering and exploring our dreams can help us clarify internal and external factors that set off career turning points. Dreams can help us to

- Understand where we are in the stages of exploring, launching, establishing, reevaluating, revitalizing, or disengaging from a job or career
- Acknowledge and clarify hidden emotional patterns and symptoms that get in the way of resolving externally and internally induced career crises
- Master work anxieties and enhance our ability to learn and adapt to new challenges on the job
- Discover new insights, inspirations, directions, and solutions to conflicts and impasses in maintaining or changing careers
- Renew a sense of meaning in our current job or seek a vision of a new path toward meaningful work

LAUNCHING A CAREER

When we begin working as a young adult and later when we make a career change, dreams can help us find inspiration to choose a form of work that will be meaningful. Occasionally dreams will present specific ideas. More often our dreams help us focus on finding a way to express our talents and emotional needs through our work.

Kelly's dream inspired an unexpected career choice. She had come from a poor family but won a scholarship at an exclusive women's college and was finishing her sophomore year. Her parents, who both did clerical work, strongly encouraged her toward pre-law or pre-med studies. Kelly was debating between majoring in creative writing and psychology, but none of the courses inspired her. Although she was making above-average grades, she wondered where she was going and wanted to find out who she really was. While taking a course on psychology that referred to Freud and Jung, Kelly had a vivid dream that set off an amazing chain of events.

If I Were a Carpenter

I'm back in Louisiana where I used to spend my summers at my grandmother's house. I am out on a wooden pier on the river like the ones that were there. I am building a new section of the pier, hammering and doing all the work. I've got a leather belt with tools hooked on it and I am working away. My older sister, Lucy, comes over and I am talking to her about her relationship with her husband. It's almost as if I am counseling her about her marriage. I felt really at ease listening to her.

When she awoke from her dream, Kelly had a sense of confidence that she'd rarely had before in her life. The dream stayed alive and active in her mind. Two days later when Kelly was at her work-study job at the school switchboard, someone told her about opportunities for women in trades. She needed a summer job, and decided to enroll in a new pre-apprenticeship program for young women.

Within one week of her dream, she had taken a six-month leave from school and enrolled in the training program. She never returned to college. By age twenty-six she had become a licensed contractor with a thriving cabinet-making and remodeling business, one of a small number of women contractors in the early 1980s.

As Kelly recounted her dream to me ten years later, it was still as vivid as the day she had it. She wanted to understand how the dream had inspired such an unlikely career. She confided that prior to beginning her carpentry training, she had never built anything and her parents were not the fix-it type.

As she explored the imagery in her dream, Kelly focused on the setting, which felt especially important to her. The summers she had spent with her grandmother were "the happiest memories of my life. We played on the pier and would go fishing in the river in small wooden boats." She remembered how relaxed and cooperative the small community was. There were shared meals with fresh garden vegetables and fish. She remembered how the neighbors had collectively built her grandmother's pier. The summer world of her grandmother was earthy and had a joie de vivre that the rest of her life with her parents lacked.

Kelly's parents were stern, unemotional, conservative, and restrictive. They often discouraged her more independent ideas. Her closest sibling was eight years older, and Kelly was shy, isolated, and filled with self-doubt as a child and teenager. Getting the scholarship and leaving for college had been her first taste of freedom.

The part of the dream where she was counseling Lucy, her older sister, made Kelly think of how much like her mother Lucy was. It was almost like counseling her mother about her parents' marriage. Thinking about it in this way reminded Kelly of how much her father dominated her mother and never let her express her opinions openly or pursue her interests. This had infuriated Kelly for as long as she could remember. Perhaps the dream was part of her dawning awareness that she could become what her mother was never able to be—a woman who was competent and expressive, both physically and verbally.

Although Kelly didn't fully understand the meaning of her dream at the time she had it, carpentry gave her an immediate sense of physical strength and emotional confidence that was an antidote to the restrictive life her parents imposed. Being able to work for herself and create things reminded her of the freedom she'd felt during those precious summers she spent with her grandmother.

Not all dreams provide such a specific direction as Kelly's did. However, if we explore our dreams while we are searching for a career direction, we are likely to encounter feelings and ideas that will make our search more fruitful.

RECOGNIZING A CAREER IMPASSE

When your work is filled with emotional conflicts, interpersonal tensions, or tasks that no longer bring you personal or financial satisfactions, your dreams can be a source of insight. Exploring dreams can help you recognize when you have reached an impasse in your career and inspire you to begin a process of change to correct the imbalances in your work.

Lisa, thirty-five, had given up a promising career in marketing in a large corporation to start a small restaurant. Using her training in marketing, Lisa had created an appealing environment for customers. Through strategic advertising, she had become moderately successful. Despite her success, Lisa was dissatisfied with her business. She'd developed an ulcer and frequent migraine headaches. Although everything looked good on paper, she was increasingly unhappy with her business and was thinking about selling out. She had already begun to take courses in counseling to consider whether she wanted to change careers.

Although Lisa had rarely remembered her dreams, while she was participating in a course on the psychology of dreams she found it easy to remember them. When asked to review all of the dreams she had recorded during a two-week period, Lisa was shocked to discover that all five dreams she had written in her journal included angry encounters between herself and her employees. In most of them she was victimized by her employees, who alternately stole from the cash register, screamed, and threw food at her. In two of the dreams she screamed back at her employees, but it didn't seem to have any affect on them.

Too Many Cooks Spoil the Job

I am talking to the chef at my restaurant. I want to ask him about making some changes in the menu. He's cooking something that looks strange, like a weird fish stew with live sea creatures in it. He's using a large old rounded pot that's rusty. I try to ask him politely what he is doing because it looks very unappetizing. He starts screaming at me in front of all my employees and even threatens to throw the soup at me.

Lisa had, in fact, been having difficulty confronting her chef. She tried unsuccessfully to work around his stubborn, opinionated style. The dream was a caricature of her relationship with him. He wasn't doing the kind of work of which she approved; she was being overly polite to him while he was somewhat abusive in return.

As she thought about the fish stew, it reminded her at first of a special dish the chef had created that hadn't turned out well. She had wanted to discontinue it immediately, but he insisted on trying it again. She didn't like it the second time, but he still wouldn't give up the idea of including it on the menu.

Further reflection made Lisa think of her ulcer. The rust in the pot made her think of the doctor's description of how the ulcer was eating away at the lining of her stomach. Although the ulcer was diagnosed before the present chef was hired, it had worsened since. She became angry when she thought that his cooking and the way he was behaving were making her ulcer worse.

Lisa hadn't realized how much anger had built up over the situation at work. She had prided herself on her easygoing management style and been overly tolerant of poor performance from the chef and some of her other employees. Her dream series gave her undeniable evidence that she was not being assertive enough in setting and maintaining performance standards for her employees.

In some cases the symbolic language of our dreams gives us a visual image that will clarify a career impasse. Malcolm, fifty-five, a dream workshop participant, complained of feeling directionless. His business as a real estate agent had been declining and he was feeling disenchanted. Malcolm described a repetitive dream he had been having.

Spinning My Wheels

I'm in my car but it's my old red '65 Buick Riviera, the one I drove a long time ago. I put my keys in the car and start the engine. At first nothing happens and I am getting frustrated. Then it seems to start but all I can hear are the wheels spinning. The car won't move. I keep trying the key over and over. I am very upset and feel powerless.

Malcolm was drawn to the image of the red Riviera. This was a car he had bought during a period when he was highly successful. It was a fashion statement at the time, as he had normally purchased more conservative-looking cars. The frustration of not being able to start the car was easy to link to waking feelings. He had been feeling low-energy and powerless.

When asked what he thought about spinning his wheels, he smiled. He hadn't caught the pun that was contained in his dream. He felt slightly embarrassed, but the phrase clicked for him. "I *am* spinning my wheels. I'm stuck and I keep trying to turn the key in the same old way to get things started."

Malcolm began to talk about how he was stuck. The youngest of his four daughters had gone off to college two years earlier, and his wife had returned to work full-time managing a clothing store. He felt more lonely and less important now that he was no longer the primary breadwinner. In part Malcolm was a male victim of the empty-nest syndrome.

At work, his younger colleagues seemed to get all the new business and many of them had surpassed him in sales. He hadn't been attending many of the clubs and civic organizations where he had drummed up business in the past. As his career was waning, his wife's was on the rise.

The image of revving that old Riviera and going nowhere both amused and fascinated Malcolm. He had lost the success of his thirties and forties. His car was no longer snazzy; he couldn't even get it running. The dream gave visual form to his career impasse. He couldn't keep turning the key in the same way. He had to try something new.

Inspired by this discussion, Malcolm decided to see his doctor to determine if depression or any other health problem was depleting his energy and drive. Malcolm's wife was sympathetic to his new ideas and confided to him that she had been concerned about his depression for months. With her encouragement, he planned to rejoin some of the civic and church groups that had formerly been a source of social contact and business referrals.

In some cases dreams can help us discover or clarify inner resources that may be important in gaining the confidence needed to seek training in a new field. Psychologist Susan Knapp cites the case of a woman, whom we shall call Alexandra, who consistently worked in occupations that were far below her intellectual potential. She had always acted self-assured and nonchalant about her jobs, but this facade concealed a terror of failure that kept her from trying out new career possibilities.

Alexandra began preparing for the Graduate Record Exam to apply to graduate school. Both she and her husband dwelt on the emotionally catastrophic consequences of her failing to get in. Her husband went so far as to try to talk her out of taking the exam and applying altogether. After discussing her husband's attempts to block her career aspirations, she had the following dream.

Finding My Wisdom Teeth
I dreamed that my teeth were falling out. Then the support system beneath them, which was made out of toothpicks, also fell out. But then underneath both the old teeth and the toothpicks was a perfectly good set of new teeth.

A dream of losing teeth is a universal theme and often symbolizes physical or emotional injury, maturing, growing older, or a loss of power or potency. In Alexandra's case, she appears to be losing her potency, which had been artificially propped up. This part of the dream probably refers to her fear of being powerless or failing. But the dream shows an unusual twist. Rather than experiencing the upsetting, disfiguring loss of a whole set of teeth, she realizes that what she is losing is the false teeth that had covered her real molars. The new set of teeth represented the sense of power that she and her husband had conspired to ignore. This dream allowed Alexandra to understand the powerful resources that she had long denied and to move ahead with her career exploration.

Abby, thirty, knew she wanted out of her job. She and her husband, Sandy, had both reached an impasse in their careers. They were commodity options traders at the Chicago exchange. There had been a period when they were flush with two incomes of six figures, but Sandy had lost his job and suffered serious financial losses resulting in a huge debt. Now Abby was on the verge of quitting but was forced to continue working for a few more months to begin to pay off their debts while Sandy got established in another job.

Abby didn't think she could endure another day of aggressive male commodity traders screaming deals in her face on the floor of the exchange. They treated each other terribly and treated women even worse. She was sure the job wasn't worth the money. But as she prepared for the day when she would be able to give up her job, she found herself at a loss. She didn't know what else would interest her. She knew that she wanted something that was more rewarding and would be compatible with having children.

She considered teaching, counseling, landscape architecture. She dabbled in some workshops but couldn't get an inspiration. When her mother and younger sister came to visit her for a week, she noticed that she felt very childish. She realized that she wanted her mother to give her some definitive motherly advice. But what her mother offered was familiar rewarmed advice and lots of criticism of Abby and her husband. That night Abby had a nightmare.

Family Killer

Wendy, my oldest hometown friend, is telling me a terrible story. She seems very upset. She said that she and her husband Todd went camping and the family in the campsite next door had five bratty kids that were screaming and getting in trouble and running out of control. Wendy just heard they had all been brutally murdered. She was getting very upset, and then we both realized that the murderer could still be nearby and might be listening to us. It's very dark in the forest and we are running away from the murderer, who is now chasing us. He is about to kill us. We are desperately running away but he is gaining on us.

Abby was haunted by the brutality of the murderer and the image of him threatening her. She rarely had nightmares, and this one was difficult to shake. As she thought about her dream, she connected it to the miserable time she'd been having at work. When I asked her if it was linked to any recent events, she immediately recalled her mother's visit and the neediness and indecisiveness she'd felt at that time.

She wondered why Wendy was in her dream. Although Wendy had been her best friend in childhood, they had drifted apart, and Abby only saw her on yearly visits back to her hometown in New York. As we talked more about what Wendy was like, Abby described her as someone who never broke away from the influence of her mother and her family. She married a local man, who went into business with her father. In fact, Wendy was now friends with Abby's mother.

Abby began to have more insights about the meaning of her dream. Although she had moved far away and had many fights with her mother in her teens and twenties, maybe she hadn't really broken away. Maybe she was, like Wendy, still psychologically close and dependent. Perhaps that dependence on her mother was keeping her from being able to make up her mind about a career change. At some level, she realized, she not only wanted her mother's approval but wanted her mother to tell her what to do.

Abby became animated as she thought about the murdered family and realized there were five children in her family. Perhaps Wendy and her husband represented Abby and her husband or even Abby's parents. It was like her own family being murdered.

Abby felt that one way to look at the dream was that she was experiencing the death of some kind of psychological connection to her family. She longed for a closeness with her mother, the kind of closeness Wendy or her younger sister had. But when she tried to be dependent on her mother, all she got was criticism and a deaf ear to her distress.

She felt that the dream had given her a clue to what was blocking her ability to be more decisive in choosing a new career direction. She hadn't established the ability to make independent decisions and was still locked into a cycle of needing her mother's direct advice and approval. Although Abby wasn't yet sure of her career direction, she felt that working on her Family Killer dream had clarified an important impasse that was holding her back.

A subsequent dream portrayed Abby feeling excited about moving to a smaller house with her husband. It was empty and was going to need a lot of work to fix up, but she was looking forward to the process. With that dream, Abby felt that she had turned a corner. Her unconscious was beginning to picture a new identity, one that had not been defined but would provide a workable challenge.

EXPLORING OPTIONS FOR CHANGING CAREERS

Donald was exploring options for a career change. As an attorney he had been highly successful in his work for a large law firm. Although he would have been a candidate to become a partner in two years, the seventy-hour work weeks and the adversarial battles in the courtroom had gotten to him. He wanted out. He took a leave of absence but knew in his heart that he could never return to a job like that.

Donald spent the summer traveling in Asia. In the back of his mind he was considering going into international law or a business that would allow him to travel and not be confined to the law library and an office. When he returned from his travels he began doing free-lance legal work and decided to take an intensive course to become a travel agent and tour leader. He would be able to travel and meet interesting people and have a career that was more varied and relaxed.

Near the end of his travel course, Donald had an interview with a premier tour agency. They paid a high salary, gave in-depth training to their leaders, and had an outstanding reputation. The day of the interview, Donald noticed that he was uncharacteristically forgetful. Not only did he neglect to bring his resume, he arrived late because he had forgotten the exact address. Despite those glitches, the interview went well and he was offered a job leading his first tour in three weeks.

Donald was shocked at the speed of the process and requested the weekend to think it over. That night he had a dream.

If You Travel You Will Unravel

I am thinking about going traveling. I'm not sure if it's for work or pleasure. I am torn about going, and then it feels like some kind of legal argument with someone about the meaning of the word travel. I can't tell if it's travel or travail. I can't justify which it is because travel would be for fun but travail is work. As I wake up I hear a poem or a song with a silly tune saying over and over: If you travel you will unravel.

Donald was amused by his dream ditty. He knew it was connected to making a decision about taking the job but wasn't sure what to make of the dream. He was drawn first to the distinction between "travel" and "travail." He had always enjoyed knowing the meaning and etymology of words, but this argument seemed picayune. He wasn't even sure he was arguing with anyone, because there was no one else present in the dream.

The obsessive quality of the wordplay reminded him of how indecisive and obsessive he had been in debating every aspect of his career change. He could never make up his mind, and he always seemed to focus so much on details that he lost the big picture of what would be best for him emotionally.

In thinking about the dream song, his first thought was that unraveling meant being irresponsible. This puzzled him and he was uncertain how to interpret it. Maybe he needed to be a little more irresponsible and a little less obsessive; a little more like someone who would sing silly songs instead of someone who would argue and ruminate on the meaning of a word.

Exploring his dream helped him see more clearly than before that he needed to balance his serious, obsessive side with a more fun-loving, relaxed side. He had thought that becoming a tour guide would accomplish that.

As he continued to contemplate his dream, however, he also realized that the final weeks of his travel course had given him an inkling that being a tour guide might not be so much fun. It could be a lot of travail—being available twenty-four hours a day, answering inane questions, and fretting over travel connections for a whole group. The word "unravel" had other associations for him as well. If he led tours, his authority and identity as a lawyer might disintegrate. He feared that loss of identity.

Through discussing his dream, Donald decided not to accept the plum job as a tour leader. He hadn't completely given up the idea of being a travel guide, but he was feeling more encouraged about searching for a position as a lawyer that might be less remunerative than his old job, but also less stressful and more emotionally rewarding. The real issue, he concluded, was changing and revitalizing his attitude, not starting a brand-new career.

Occasionally, vivid dreams help to crystallize a decision to change careers. For Shauna, two dreams were strongly linked to her decision to move and change careers. As a vocational rehabilitation counselor, she had her own business helping clients who suffered from industrial injuries. But Shauna was feeling burned-out and depressed. Over the last two years she'd become disillusioned with her work. Many of her clients were severely disabled and had great difficulty finding work. Others got unfairly low settlements from big employers. She was losing her idealism and enthusiasm. On top of that, a long-term relationship that she'd hoped would lead to marriage had broken up painfully.

In the midst of this period, she had the first of two intensely vivid dreams that motivated her to change her life.

The Hills Are Alive

I am lying on a ledge or a cliff somewhere in the coastal hills of California. It's the end of summer and the hills are all brown with grasses waving in the breeze. As I look at the hills they suddenly begin to sprout and they turn into mountain peaks that look like the mountains near Santa Fe, New Mexico. It is intensely alive and colorful.

Shauna was excited by this dream. She emphasized how real and compelling the image of the mountains was. Her brother and his family lived in New Mexico. They were the only relatives with whom she was emotionally close.

In the beginning of her dream, being on the mountain ledge symbolized her emotional state. She felt that she was on the edge of deeper depression and needed to make a change. Within six months she had decided to take a two-week trip to the Albuquerque–Santa Fe area to visit her brother and explore her options. A week before departing, she had another vivid dream that helped to confirm her decision to move.

Initiation

Some members of an Indian tribe from the northern Midwest plains are standing before me. I'm taking part in a ceremony and they say, "You are going to New Mexico." They come forward as a group and present themselves to me and tell me to carry something sacred. They say, "You are now qualified to carry the pipe for us." They hand me a medicine bag and tell me that I will have safe pas-

*sage in a canoe. They also say something else
which is confusing: "Buffaloes are not at home in
California."*

Shauna felt convinced that she was making the right
move with her upcoming trip. The Indian men in her dream
reminded her of her interest in Native American spirituality
and New Age practices. She wondered if she would want to
do vocational rehabilitation work with Indians if she moved
to New Mexico. But she wasn't sure that was what the dream
was telling her, since she wanted to change careers if she
moved.

Remembering the part about safe passage in a canoe,
she felt a surge of memories and the presence of the Indians
in the dream began to make sense. When she was young she
used to go on weeklong canoe trips in Canada with her father and brother. During the period after her parents separated, from when she was ten until she was fifteen, she was
sent to a summer camp with Canadian Indian counselors.
The long canoe trips with the Indian guides were her only
positive memories during the miserable years of her parents' divorce and custody battles over her.

As Shauna thought more about this dream, she realized
that the Indians didn't necessarily represent the specific
type of work she would want to do, but rather the positive
experiences of physical and emotional well-being. More
lengthy exploration of this dream persuaded Shauna to
search for some type of work that would give her the sense
of adventure, camaraderie, and creativity that she had felt
during her summer canoe journeys as a child.

Shauna's dreams gave her inspiration to continue a ca-
reer search. Six months later, she was planning the move to
New Mexico and taking courses in art and music therapy.
Shauna felt that combining a desire to help people with an

emphasis on creativity would make her work more emotionally rewarding. She hoped to work with children in hospitals or perhaps on the reservations in New Mexico. She was also intrigued by the possibility of combining her interest in New Age healing and Native American spirituality with future work as a creative arts therapist.

Lindsay had been working in sales for over fifteen years and was deeply discouraged with her work. She had been reading a variety of books on career transitions but hadn't found an inspiration that would help her make a change. After many months of dissatisfaction and searching she had a "big dream" that affected her like a "bolt of lightning" and helped her begin to explore a new direction.

The Dream Team

There are several woman friends meeting with me. I can see their faces and they look familiar but not anyone I really know. It's some sort of sales meeting, although I am not sure what the product is. We are talking in an animated way. They are dividing up the territory in the Bay Area and we eventually spread out to California and the whole country. One woman had a computer system set up and says we will be connected by computer but also by our feelings. It has something to do with the group being all women. There is a feeling of synergy and excitement that is very strong.

Lindsay realized that she had always worked for male bosses and frequently differed with their management style. Now she wanted to take a quantum leap in her career and do something where she was no longer the employee but part of management. She even considered starting her own business.

Inspired by the image of her dream team, Lindsay began to call other women she knew in sales and business with the idea of meeting as a support group to explore alternative forms of employment. Within a month the group had its first meeting. After six months the women were considering forming a company that would be run by women and provide specialized professional services to other businesses owned or operated by women.

While Lindsay was exploring these career options, she changed jobs and was working for the first time with a woman, a noted entrepreneur. Lindsay was still unsure what direction her career transition would ultimately take, but she felt that dreams had given her the inspiration necessary to make the change.

Exploring dreams helps us find and pursue new career directions when we are searching for ways to revitalize our career or change jobs. Occasionally we may discover specific ideas or information that prove useful, such as Donald's dream warning about the travel business or Shauna's image of the California hills turning into the mountains of New Mexico. More often, our dreams spark insights that help us resolve issues that block us from achieving more fulfillment in our present job or help us find the inspiration and motivation to make a change.

CONFRONTING A CAREER IMPASSE

When we take concrete steps to change our job or make a career switch, we encounter both internal and external obstacles. External obstacles might include poor economic conditions, such as a recession or lack of demand for our skills. Internal obstacles include fears of failure, guilt about becoming successful, or a general fear of leaving a secure job and venturing into a new one with no guarantee of success. Exploring dreams can help us understand our reaction to external factors and inner conflicts that may block the success of a career transition.

Rusty had recently made a miraculous turnaround. Although he had a BA in English literature from Stanford, he'd been heavily involved in the drug culture of the late 1960s and early 1970s. His use of marijuana and LSD had initially been connected with radical politics, explorations of Eastern religions, and attempts at establishing a rural communal environment.

While living in a northern California commune in the early 1970s, Rusty got involved with a group that was cultivating marijuana and smuggling various drugs for sale into Los Angeles. Although Rusty was not the ringleader, he delivered drugs to suppliers for about three years. During this time he had access to many drugs and became addicted to heroin.

Rusty was able to extricate himself from the drug ring, but his addiction to heroin continued. He was accepted at a prestigious law school but dropped out after the first month because of his addiction. He tried many jobs, but as his addiction worsened he was never able to hold them. Off and on he drove a cab, did construction work, and worked as a security guard. At times he would deal heroin or other drugs on a small scale to support his habit.

Although he was never arrested, Rusty encountered many dangerous situations because of his drug habit. Finally he was knifed by a drug-crazed customer who was attempting to rob him. Although the knife was aimed at his heart, he ducked and it slashed his arm deeply, requiring many stitches.

The brush with death scared Rusty into changing his life. He entered a rehabilitation program, gave up heroin, and read every book he could find on changing careers. He entered psychotherapy and faithfully attended Narcotics Anonymous. He soon decided to seek certification as a drug counselor so he could help others overcome what had been so devastating for him. He enrolled in a certification program and volunteered with a local clinic. They liked his work so much, they promised him a job when he had obtained his certificate. While in school, he continued to drive a cab at night so that he could attend classes during the day.

In the last month of his one-year program to become a drug counselor, Rusty noticed that he was getting feistier in all of his classes, openly disagreeing with his teachers. He began to have doubts about whether he wanted to go through with his career plans. He noticed that he was driving more recklessly. When he picked up customers in his cab whom he recognized as probable drug dealers, he began to feel temptations to use. He knew something was going wrong, but he wasn't sure what.

A week before graduation, he had a dream that affected him profoundly.

Lead Me Not into Temptation
I pick up four people in my cab and drive them far out of town, down a logging road to a small cabin. I am invited inside and notice a small paper bag. I don't know what it is but I see that it is lots of pills, heroin, and 100 new syringes. The people are grinding up the pills and preparing to shoot the drugs. The mixture is a bright pink color which is very striking to me. They offer me free access to the drugs. I am extremely tempted by the offer. My whole body seems to want the drugs—just the way I used to feel when I needed a fix. I realize no one would ever know that I indulged. I fight the temptation for what seems like a long time. Finally I decide that I am not going to take the drugs or hang around those people. I leave the cabin and get back in my car to drive back to the city.

For Rusty the dream felt like an incredible triumph over the temptation to use drugs, defeat his recovery, and sabotage his career transition. He said, "Thinking about the dream gave me chills. I felt like I climbed over Mount Everest. It showed me that I do have the willpower to delay gratification."

Rusty described a chronic pattern of "opting out" in stressful situations and going on drug binges. He said that he had been able to hold to the dream's image of walking away from temptation; it had helped him settle down and get through his last week of classes.

Although the decisive moment of resisting temptation was the most powerful legacy, Rusty explored other aspects of this monumental dream. In particular, the bright pink color of the drugs fascinated him. Rusty thought of different medicines he had taken. When he was a child his mother used to put pink calamine lotion on his skin and occasionally gave him Pepto-Bismol. Later, in his twenties, he often took Pepto-Bismol for indigestion caused by drug use and poor nutrition. So the pink drug in his dream reminded him of substances he had used to soothe himself over the years.

Rusty felt that he no longer had to soothe himself in that way. His dream was a reminder that he had overcome his addictive tendencies. He completed his certificate program, and three months later passed his probationary period on his new job with excellent reviews. He was thinking of going to graduate school, perhaps to get a doctorate in English literature.

Changing careers involves many stresses that can trip us up. As we prepare to make a change in our job or career, our dreams highlight conflicts from the past and the present that may be holding us back.

RETURNING TO A CAREER OR JOB
AFTER A LEAVE OF ABSENCE

Returning to a former career or job can provoke powerful conscious and unconscious reactions. Although many of the co-workers and job functions may be the same, some aspects of the job may have changed significantly. More important, most people returning from leave have just undergone an important turning point, such as a major illness or period of disability, the birth of a child, a long trip (on a sabbatical, for example), being rehired after a layoff, or returning to a job after attempting a career change (see Edward's dreams in chapter 6).

This scenario is especially relevant for women who return after a maternity leave. Leslie, thirty-four, had been devoted to her career as an associate with an accounting firm in San Francisco. She worked long hours and had received steady promotions. She took pride in her work and had worked until the very day she gave birth to her son, Brandon. She had expected to go back to work half-time when Brandon was six months old and full-time when he was nine months.

A few weeks after the birth she was enthralled by her son but still felt that she'd want to return to work full-time. She was surprised when she saw the grief and tears of other mothers who were forced by their employers or by economic necessity to return after three months. She didn't think she would have that kind of reaction. She planned to be extremely cautious in selecting a day-care arrangement.

About six weeks prior to her return to work, Leslie began to have nightmares about her job. On different nights, she dreamed that her employers revoked her maternity leave, decided not to give her job back, and reprimanded her for poor performance. She began to feel anxious about returning to work. She also began to feel nervous about leaving her son with a stranger. She paid close attention whenever she heard or read anything about child abuse.

On the day of her return to work, Leslie had a nightmare that recurred almost every night in a similar form for a week.

Abandoned by My Firm

*It's my first day back to work. I'm getting off the
subway and have to walk up a long staircase. It's
longer than any I have ever seen, like one of those
steep Aztec pyramids in Mexico. Then I have to go
up an extra-long elevator, much taller than the office I work in, which is on the twelfth floor. When I
get off the elevator, I find out my firm has moved
and no one told me they moved or any details
about where the new office was. I try to call from a
nearby phone but the number has been discon-
nected and there was no forwarding number. I feel
like they had abandoned me and I am very upset.*

Leslie was very edgy that first day back in the office. Although everyone was polite and responsive, she couldn't
stop thinking that she would be fired. And she was feeling
naturally miserable about leaving her six-month-old son
with a stranger.

Leslie was still in an agitated state when she discussed
this dream a week later. She knew that the dream was expressing her anxiety, but she was confused about the deeper
message.

As she explored this dream, many ideas came to her.
The stairs looked just like the ones she had to climb every
day to get to work. Leslie also had a phobia about stairs. Five
years ago she'd fallen down a flight of stairs and broken her
leg. The phobia had gotten so severe, she had sought treatment with a psychologist to help overcome it. Could the
dream be evidence that the phobia was returning? When
she'd been in Mexico recently, she was in fact unable to
climb the steep steps of the pyramid and had watched while
others ascended.

The stairs also reminded Leslie of the "corporate ladder." Leslie had made it partway up the ladder, but now she

wondered if there was going to be anything at the top for her when she resumed climbing. This confirmed thoughts she'd had only recently—maybe the corporate ladder wasn't worth the effort. Her demanding job seemed incompatible with having a child.

The most powerful feeling in the dream was her sense of being abandoned by her firm at the end. They left no word, no forwarding number. The feelings of betrayal she felt were at first directed at the company. They were putting too much pressure on her; they weren't sensitive to working mothers. But as she continued to think about the word "abandonment," a strong association came to her mind: Brandon. She felt she was abandoning her son by going back to work. She began to cry and realized an important message of her dream: It was a reversal. She was being abandoned by her firm, but in reality she felt she was betraying and abandoning Brandon. It was Brandon who couldn't call if he had a problem.

Leslie's dream helped her to acknowledge her grief and guilt about separating from her son. Exploring its meanings helped her to accept how challenging the role changes were, from corporate executive to mother and now working mother. Leslie was also worried about losing her job or missing the inside track on promotions because she no longer worked overtime. At the same time, she wondered if her dream wasn't fulfilling a wish that she would like to abandon her old position and find a part-time job that would allow her to spend more time with her son.

After she had explored the feelings and issues that arose in her dream, Leslie's nightmares stopped and her stair phobia did not return. By acknowledging her hidden guilt and anxiety and focusing on the difficult role change she was going through, she was able to focus on realistic alternatives. She decided to investigate the possibility of permanent part-time status at her firm or at other companies.

Leslie and her husband began to talk about how to balance two careers and a family.

When you return from a leave, the job may be the same but you have changed. Exploring your dreams will help you understand and work through strong emotional reactions to the process of readjusting to your former occupation.

USING DREAMS TO RESOLVE
CAREER ISSUES AND CRISES

Occasionally dreams inspire spontaneous solutions to an impasse at work or present new solutions for creative blocks. More often we must explore our dreams to gain guidance. This can be done through journal work or other creative forms of dream exploration (see chapter 10), discussion with others, or psychotherapy.

Benjamin, a successful New York magazine publisher, emphasized to me the powerful impact of a dream on resolving a career impasse. He made a midlife career change from writing television documentaries to starting his own magazine. His magazine received critical success and was initially profitable. After five years he sold out to a large corporation but was to continue as publisher as part of the deal.

Because of decisions by the parent company and a changing magazine market, the circulation of Benjamin's magazine began to decline. He could see that it was facing a crisis. He was searching for a way to rekindle the spark of his magazine and increase its public appeal. He had read about the problem-solving aspects of dreams and decided to incubate or request a dream that would help him find a new direction. He then had the following dream.

A Message for the President

I am in a theater watching a football game on a large screen. Suddenly I realize that I am the president of a university and I am dressed for that role

*in collegiate-style clothing. Although I know I am
the president, it is strange because at the same
time, I know I am myself. I walk out of the movie
and towards the campus to a convocation on the
quadrangle. There is the traditional raised platform for the faculty, and everyone is dressed in
academic regalia with students sitting on the
grass in rows. I go with someone who is sneaking
around the back of the platform to see how it is
going. Someone who is there tells me emphat-
ically, "You're not doing your job. You should be
there more." These words stay with me and soon
I go to change my clothes.*

Benjamin felt that his dream was an important response to his dream incubation question. He realized that he
had become less involved and more complacent since he
had sold the magazine. He wanted to get more involved
again and decided to attempt to buy back the magazine from
the parent company in order to revive it and take it in a new
direction.

After lengthy negotiations, Benjamin succeeded in buying back his magazine. He implemented many changes, including a new format, and hired many new writers and edi-
tors. At first circulation did not rise and the magazine was
running at a loss. Gradually, however, the magazine achieved
and surpassed its earlier level of success. This time, Benjamin followed the insights he had gained by exploring his
dream and stayed more closely involved in guiding the magazine's management.

DREAMS AS A SOURCE OF CAREER GUIDANCE

Exploring dreams can help us articulate our inner response
to changes and problems at every stage of the career cycle.
Paying attention to the messages of dreams and nightmares

can help us find new directions and solutions to overcome both internal and external obstacles. When we listen for the guidance that dreams offer, we can have a better chance of making our work more meaningful.

The venerable mythologist Joseph Campbell exhorted those of us interested in finding meaningful work "to follow our bliss"—that is, to pursue the activities and career that express our inner needs and bring meaning to our lives. Following work-related dreams can help us follow this advice and resolve our career crises and transitions.

6. Midlife Dreams
The Transition from Old to New Identities

ELENA, A FORTY-YEAR-OLD Mexican-American woman, lived the first half of her life in Mexico. She came to the United States at nineteen to attend college and had risen rapidly in her career until she became executive director of a large social service agency in San Francisco. She and her husband were financially successful, but the materialism and pressured lifestyle felt increasingly empty. She began to despair about the meaning and direction of her life. During a period of soul-searching she had the following dream.

Saving the Children

I am in a large office building like the one where I used to be the director. Just as I am walking in, there is a tremendous earthquake. I know this is the big one. I begin to rush for the exit. As I'm about to run through the doorway, I suddenly realize that the building is just a facade and that inside the modern building is an encampment or little pueblo of adobe houses like the ones my grandparents and cousins live in. I see lots of children in the huts. I know that I have to save them or they will be crushed. I rush into the little village and, using all my strength, I grab as many of the little children as I can carry. Holding all the children, I rush for the door and just make it outside into the sunlight as the brick building collapses behind me.

This dream had a profound impact on Elena. It catalyzed her decision to make a major change in her career and living situation. Within months after this dream, she and her husband had sold their home and moved to a rural area of northern California. Her husband bought a small restaurant, and Elena was student-teaching at a rural public school attended by the children of migrant Mexican farm workers. She was working toward an elementary teaching credential. She was also volunteering at a health clinic that served indigent pregnant women.

At a prenatal discussion group at the clinic where she worked as a translator and advocate for disadvantaged farm workers, Elena recounted her Saving the Children dream as if revealing a precious work of art or a cherished family secret.

Elena explored some of the dream's elements. She had only experienced minor tremors in her life, so the monumental earthquake in her dream didn't seem related to a memory. Rather it felt clearly related to the inner shake-up she was experiencing.

The office building in the dream reminded Elena of the place where she used to work. Reflecting upon the discovery in the dream that the building was only a facade helped her understand why she felt her career success had been felt like a psychological facade. It had not seemed genuine because it did not express the values of her native culture and her childhood.

A house or a building in a dream often represents an image of the self or the body. This rang true for Elena. The little Mexican village inside the modern-looking American building was a perfect metaphor for her identity. The dream helped her understand her need to balance her driven professional side (symbolized by the building) with the earthy, family-oriented part of herself (symbolized by the adobe village and the needy children). Her dream motivated her to escape before being crushed by the facade of her pressured lifestyle.

The theme of saving the children was especially important for Elena. She had been unable to bear children herself, but her career had centered around administering social programs that served children. She had hoped earlier in her career that she could express her interest and concern by developing programs that benefited children, especially minority children. Recently, however, her duties had centered entirely on fund-raising and advocacy. In an era of cutbacks for children's services, she had become quite discouraged. The dream helped her realize that she wanted to work directly with children, and ultimately she decided to get her teaching credential. She and her husband began to consider adopting a Central or South American child.

Saving wounded children is a theme that often occurs in turning point dreams. Although the meaning is unique for each individual, the theme often symbolizes the need to heal or attend to some emotional or physical wound. For Elena, the wound was the loss of some cherished aspects of her cultural and family heritage and the inability to reconcile the two sides of herself: the child who grew up in Mexico and the adult who lived in the United States. The dream showed her she could draw on inner resources that were connected in her mind to the cultural and familial values of her family in Mexico.

Her dream gave her a vision that would guide her in undertaking an earthshaking midlife transition, a vision that helped her find a practical application of her mission of saving children. She would educate and advocate for them directly instead of being an administrator. Even more important, the dream gave Elena a lasting sense of confidence in pursuing a new career and lifestyle.

UNDERSTANDING MIDLIFE CRISES

Carl Jung was the first twentieth-century theorist to focus on midlife as a crucial transition. He emphasized that the midlife crisis was a window of opportunity for self-awareness and personal growth, a time when we are able to become more individuated, to know ourselves better, and to make greater use of our inner resources. He based his formulation on his own wrenching midlife crisis, which led to a profound spiritual renewal and a sense of meaning that inspired much of his later work.

The popularity of Gail Sheehy's book, *Passages: Predictable Crises of Adult Life*, reflected a heightened awareness of an extended turning point that most of us undergo sometime between the ages of thirty-five and fifty. During this midlife phase, many of us go through a period of inner instability. We may question the most fundamental structures and relationships of our lives. Marital conflicts and breakups, career crises, or moves to a new area may occur. For some, the outbreak of midlife angst is clearly connected to another turning point, such as an illness, loss of a job, or a divorce. For others, the origin of the midlife crisis may be invisible at first. It is like a silent alarm from an internal clock that was set years before to go off at midlife.

There is great individual variation as to when midlife transition begins and which issues are most dominant. The state of certain issues in your life influences the midlife transition. These include the current status of your career or relationship, the ages of your children if any, and the incidence of destabilizing events such as losses or major stresses. These and other factors play a part in a complex and unpredictable formula that determines when and how your midlife crisis will begin.

There are also differences between men and women in the timing and psychological focus of the midlife transition. In his influential study of the psychology of men, *The Seasons of a Man's Life*, Daniel Levinson reported that the usual age of the onset of midlife crisis for men was forty to forty-one, with a range between thirty-eight and forty-three. For the men studied by Levinson and his colleagues, the average age for completing the transition was forty-five, with a range from forty-four to forty-seven.

Some women enter midlife following a timetable similar to that described by Levinson for men. For those who have not already experienced a midlife crisis, the onset of menopause may provide a milestone that initiates powerful psychological changes. Conflicts over how to balance career and family often create greater conflict in women than men. But contrary to popular belief, the empty-nest phenomenon of children leaving the home may not be traumatic for all women and may in fact allow them to blossom in other areas, as they're freed from parenting responsibilities.

Some researchers have questioned the universality of midlife crises, implying that such anxiety and painful soul-searching is a luxury of the middle and upper-middle classes and is less noticeable among people whose lives are economically unstable. Other researchers theorize that we go through continuous cycles of stability and instability, so midlife is as likely to contain a crisis as any other life phase. In any case, a life crisis that occurs during the late thirties to early fifties will have its own unique flavor.

My clinical experience has given me strong evidence that people do go through a period of crisis during these years. Often I've observed that a midlife crisis is caused or accompanied by a chain reaction of events: divorce, the death of a parent, children leaving home, career dissatisfaction or conflict, serious illness such as heart attack or cancer. Depression is a frequent complaint of people who consult with me during midlife.

If you have arrived at your forties unscathed, you may cautiously hope you've evaded the anguish of a midlife crisis. Then, suddenly, like an ambush, it strikes. You feel trapped by the structures you have created—career, marriage or relationship, family, and friends. An undercurrent of grief afflicts you as you approach the midpoint of your expected life span. You may feel bitterness about lost opportunities, roads not taken and bright potentials that may never be fulfilled.

Media images of midlife crisis tend to take a pejorative tone that mocks the anguish of the sufferer. Men are pictured as behaving erratically, having affairs with younger women, buying flashy sports cars, and nursing hair transplants. Women are depicted as mourning the empty nest, obsessed with physical signs of aging, and exasperated with men who are emotionally distant. There is a pervasive fear that we will become trapped by foolish choices or indecision, left to spend our days depressed, divorced, or in a dead-end job.

We are vulnerable to many competing emotions and conflicts as well as to the negative effects of our erratic behavior. A passionate affair with a younger person, who seems to love us in all the ways our spouse doesn't, may help rekindle our dormant passion or at least stave off our fears of growing older. On the other hand, an affair may precipitate a divorce that will be followed by years of economic stress, loneliness, and custody battles.

Under optimal circumstances, a metamorphosis has occurred as we emerge from midlife. We have been able to grieve our lost youth, free ourselves of the inner constraints of our parents, master the emotional blocks lingering from childhood, discover new identities, and define ourself in new ways. We have found new friends and new sources of fulfillment and have revitalized our ability to be intimate in love and productive in our work.

In this chapter, we'll look at how we can use dreams to explore and resolve the emotional impasses of midlife and facilitate the discovery of new directions. In particular we'll look at the following ways dreams can be valuable.

- *Acknowledging and coming to terms with powerful emotional reactions that occur at midlife.* These may include grief over the loss of youth, bitterness about lost possibilities and past hurts, feelings of uselessness or hopelessness, an inability to accept the physical aging of our body, or any other reaction or emotion we have long suppressed.
- *Understanding the source of our anxieties,* including a fear of death, a panic about having limited time, and general insecurity about the unknown.
- *Getting an overview of the stages of midlife.* When we feel at sea without a map to guide us, our dreams can help us chart our progress through the stages of falling apart, groping for meaning, and finding solutions to midlife impasses.
- *Reducing our sense of isolation.* Through sharing our dreams we can feel more understood, less alone, and sense the deeper significance of the midlife passage. We can gain a vision of how the second half of life can be a new beginning and not a gradual deterioration.
- *Finding sources of emotional and spiritual renewal,* including inspirations for meaningful and productive new directions in work and revitalized relationships.

ENTERING MIDLIFE: CONFRONTING OUR OWN MORTALITY

Many midlife dreams feature an encounter with death. Vivid dreams of ourselves or those close to us being afflicted with mortal wounds or terminal illnesses symbolize the emergence of feelings of vulnerability and mortality. We face a growing realization that we won't live forever. We see the gray hair, wrinkles, and other signs of aging. We grieve not only the loss of our youthful appearance but the sense that the person we knew as ourself is dying.

In his autobiography, *Memories, Dreams, and Reflections,* C. G. Jung describes in detail the circumstances and dreams that marked the onset of his midlife crisis. At thirty-seven, inspired by his dreams and conscious reflections, Jung broke away from his mentor, Sigmund Freud. He quit his university position, experienced a marital crisis, and entered a period of painful self-examination. During this time Jung felt depressed and profoundly disoriented, questioning his own sanity.

He felt that a series of dreams with death references heralded the beginning of this dark period in his life. In one dream he was exploring a long row of tombs of figures from the distant past—crusaders, knights in armor, and other ancient beings. To his shock, the mummified corpses moved their hands one by one and came back to life. The death imagery was extremely upsetting to him. What was making these ancient souls rise from the dead? Would he soon die, or was he experiencing an emotional death? He searched through all of his childhood memories to comprehend what was happening to him.

He could make no headway in understanding these disturbing dreams until he began to explore them by using painting, writing, and other creative techniques. Slowly he understood the emotional death and painful loss of identity he was experiencing. Further dreams of death, destruction, and barren, frozen scenes confirmed this idea. And yet amidst the tombs there was something that could possibly be revived. This idea gave him hope that there was light at the end of the tunnel—or, in this case, the tomb.

Jung's dream, like others at midlife, contained imagery of tombs and mummies. In this way the unconscious symbolizes that the person at midlife has withdrawn from the outer world and is undergoing a painful inner process, a decaying and destruction of an old way of being.

Phoebe's midlife crisis came on the heels of numerous stressful events that occurred almost simultaneously. At age forty-five, she had finally decided to leave the hospital where she had worked for twenty-two years. She had been suffering from chronic back problems and over the past two years had become dissatisfied with her role as a nursing supervisor. Because she had planned to leave her job and had been training in a new career, she didn't anticipate that leaving the hospital would have a great impact on her. Soon after quitting, however, she became depressed, her back problems increased, and she had a disturbing nightmare.

My Mother Is Dying

Someone comes and says that I have a phone call. When I get to the phone, I can hardly hear the caller. I think that it is my sister. She is telling me that my mom is sick, my mother is dying. I keep trying to find out more but the voice keeps getting fainter and the line is full of static. I try but can't reach her or get a better connection.

Phoebe's real mother was alive and healthy. In the language of her dream, the hospital was the mother that was dying. She had not only worked there but she had been born there, went to nursing school and had her own children there. Leaving was truly the death of an era, an identity, a support network of friends and colleagues, and a second home. Her inability to call represented losing touch with a part of herself that had been so familiar. The (phone) connection with her mother was fading out; Phoebe was experiencing not only the loss of a job but the identity of her career and first half of her life.

Phoebe had kept a dream journal off and on for many years. Over the next few months of turmoil, she searched her dreams for clues to inner guidance, physical and emotional recovery. Her serious back injury gave her time to focus on herself in new ways since in previous years she had been working full-time and raising four daughters. In addition to physical therapy, she began painting her feelings and dreams. Despite her injury, she took a course from a dance therapist. She wanted to understand any psychological basis for her back injury.

During this period, Phoebe began to have many important insights about unresolved conflicts in her previous close relationships. She felt she was finally working out anger toward her ex-husband. At the same time, her current friendships were taking on new dimensions. She wasn't always the chronic giver but was allowing herself to receive; this was an important change.

Three months later, Phoebe was still reeling from the changes but felt she was beginning to turn a corner. On two consecutive nights she had earthquake dreams, a theme that had been rare in her past dreams.

Rebuilding After the Quake

I am in my own home. A large, rumbling, shaking earthquake comes. The house and the entire contents are lifted intact to a green hillside above the lot. Only the cement foundation remains. I bring parts of the house back and try to reconstruct it. The pieces keep falling down. There may have been others helping but it doesn't work.

The Swaying Elevator

I am in a freight elevator with an open iron door. When it moves, I can see out. An earthquake makes the elevator sway severely. The building is still.

*Only the elevator is swaying. There is a guard on
one of the floor landings with his hand reached out
to help me to safety. I just can't reach his finger-
tips. The movements stop and I go down a flight of
stairs and end up on the obstetrical unit of a hospital as if I am in labor.*

As in Elena's case, the dream earthquakes that Phoebe
experienced are evidence of the earthshaking changes she
was undergoing as she entered middle age. In Phoebe's first
earthquake dream, she felt that her house being ripped from
its foundation was an apt metaphor for the loss of identity
she had experienced. Although she was trying to rebuild
with the help of others, she wasn't succeeding as yet in building on the old foundation.

In the Swaying Elevator dream, Phoebe again was unable to benefit from the help that was offered to her in the
moment of crisis. In dreams, the movement of an elevator
between floors of a building is often taken to represent a
transition between two states of consciousness or identity.
That interpretation worked well for Phoebe. She saw the elevator as representing the transition from which she was not
able to exit.

After the painful death and grieving for her old identities, Phoebe was especially intrigued at being transported to
an obstetrics ward. This image gave her hope. Perhaps a rebirth was about to take place. Greater acceptance of her anger and increased ability to be intimate with friends made
her feel that her midlife turmoil was on the verge of resolution. In the weeks that followed these earthquake dreams,
her back began to improve dramatically, she was less depressed, and she resumed taking courses to prepare for a
career change.

For many, the entry into midlife may be punctuated by
conscious and unconscious preoccupations with death, our

own and others'. Heightened awareness of the inevitability of our own death gives the midlife period a special urgency. Dreams of death reflect awareness of our mortality and symbolize the painful loss of old identities as we enter midlife.

CROSSING THE THRESHOLD: IN THE THROES
OF MIDLIFE PASSAGE

The central experience of midlife, according to Murray Stein, is that of liminality. This is an in-between state of suspended identity, during which we become a stranger to ourself, no longer at home in any of the familiar roles or feelings that we used in the past to define ourself. Deriving from the Latin root *limen*, meaning "threshold," the liminal stage is a twilight zone of identity confusion, fluctuating emotions, and erratic behavior. We are grieving the loss of our former self but have not yet discovered a new identity that feels comfortable or familiar.

Judy, a forty-five-year-old divorced single mother, sought psychotherapy soon after her daughter, Corey, went away to college in a nearby city. Judy had been suffering from depression and had started drinking heavily on evenings and weekends. She was concerned about her drinking, which had never before been a problem. She also felt directionless, as if her life no longer had a purpose. After her first psychotherapy session, she had the following dream.

Empty Rooms

I am in the small apartment that I lived in ten years ago just after my divorce when we sold the house. It feels very empty. There is no furniture, the paint is peeling, and the windows are dirty and have cobwebs. It doesn't seem like anyone else is even living in the building. I am searching desperately for my daughter but she isn't there either.

Judy woke up from the dream feeling sad and lonely. As she told it again, the feelings intensified. Through her tears, she confessed that she hadn't expected her daughter's departure to be so upsetting. Judy was struck by the barrenness of the apartment and felt it related to her own emptiness without Corey. Judy began to feel that the image of her daughter in the dream was a displaced image of her own younger self. Everyone had always commented on the striking resemblance between them. The idea that Judy was searching for images of herself from the past resonated deeply.

After her divorce, she had gone back to school and had become a paralegal. She also enjoyed her volunteer work with various political and social organizations, such as a group that provided legal assistance to battered women. Although she was quite attractive, Judy had avoided opportunities to meet men and had not gotten involved in any love relationships.

Through a lengthy exploration, Judy realized that besides being a dedicated mother, she had used her relationship with Corey to protect herself from men and from people in general. Although Corey had long protested her mother's overinvolvement and had even encouraged her to go out and meet men, it wasn't until Corey left that Judy felt the emptiness.

The dream made the desolate feeling even more acute than she consciously admitted. Exploring the dream helped her to acknowledge her grief on a number of different levels. She realized that she had never worked out her feelings of rejection and grief from the divorce. Finally, alone at forty-five, she was grieving the loss of her youth, symbolized in the dream by her daughter.

Judy felt like the apartment in her dream, like an old building that needed fixing and redecorating. Her dream helped her see that she needed to find a new direction for her life now that Corey was gone. As a result of the insights she gained in exploring her Empty Rooms dream, Judy decided that in addition to her psychotherapy she would join a support group oriented toward women at midlife. She realized that hiding the wounds of her divorce had not healed them. It was vital that she decide whether to let people be close to her or to consider remarriage.

Reaching an emotional impasse, such as Judy's inability to resolve fears of rejection, may prevent us from moving across the threshold of midlife and emerging with new solutions. Paying attention to turning point dreams can help us find ways to understand and correct unresolved issues and fears of change that can block our progress.

MEN AT MIDLIFE

In Daniel Levinson's extended study of the seasons of men's lives, 80 percent of the men who participated underwent a turbulent period at midlife. According to Levinson, the psychological distress is caused by wounds from the past that get reactivated as we try to close a chapter of our lives and begin anew. Depression, bitterness, nostalgia for youthful looks and vitality, feelings of uselessness and impotence, and a terror of facing death were all present. Although family and friends often viewed the men as upset or sick, Levinson concluded that this intense self-examination was a normal and necessary part of midlife, ultimately leading to emotional renewal. Levinson describes midlife as involving the following three stages.

Reappraising the Past. In Levinson's midlife schema for men, the first stage is reappraising the past. As a man becomes disillusioned with the structures and relationships in his life, he instinctively looks to the past. He asks himself, What have I accomplished with my life? Am I living up to my potential? Have I allowed myself to open up and be close with my wife, friends, family, and children? Is this the life I want to continue, or do I need to make changes to have a more meaningful future?

Planning and Experimenting. As issues from the past begin to get resolved, there is a stage of planning and experimenting. For some men, this involves dramatic external events such as changing careers, divorcing, remarrying, or moving. For others, the changes may be less visible but just as important, like becoming less preoccupied with work and more involved with family. Or the changes may mean becoming more concerned about making a contribution through creative, spiritual or political pursuits or guiding younger colleagues.

Confronting and Resolving Emotional Polarities. At midlife men often discover that they possess a greater range of emotions. When they are able to acknowledge these powerful feelings, they can enhance their close relationships at home and at work.

Levinson emphasized four emotional polarities that men encounter and struggle with at midlife. The first is *youth versus aging*, which is a confrontation with mortality. Men experience a sense of confusion about still feeling young, yet find themselves increasingly identified as middle-aged. In order to resolve this polarity, a man must confront mortality and make sense of being in-between youth and old age.

The second polarity is *destructive versus creative urges*. This includes coping with anger of lost opportunities, old emotional wounds and poor choices, and becoming more acutely aware of aggressive and malicious tendencies in himself and others. Resolving this polarity requires a greater acceptance of human tendencies toward destructiveness, without sinking into bitterness or cynicism. Instead, he must use the impetus of this conflict to discover new sources of creativity through work, hobbies, recreation, relationships, or endeavors that are socially useful.

The third polarity is acceptance of the *masculine*

versus feminine parts of himself. This includes experiencing vulnerability, dependency, sadness, and warmth, which are feelings traditionally at odds with the stereotypical male image.

The fourth polarity is the tension between *attachment and separateness*. Resolving this issue involves finding a balance between your own needs and those of family, friends, and society. A man needs to pay attention to his inner feelings and needs, and find out what is missing from his emotional life. Paradoxically, turning inward often does not lead to isolation. As he discovers his deeper feelings, he will often find new reserves of energy that lead to new and more passionate involvement with others.

For Edward, exploring and resolving impasses in his relationship with his father was the crucial stumbling block that had to be overcome. Edward, forty-four, a psychologist, had given up his private practice three years earlier to undertake a real estate venture with his brother. After successfully completing one project, he was considering leaving his real estate job and reopening his psychotherapy practice. He began further training to refresh and enhance his skills but was still feeling uncertain about whether to continue in real estate or to return to psychology.

Distressed by his indecisiveness, Edward sought the counsel of friends and family members. In the throes of his confusion and depression, he had the following dream.

Awaiting Court-Martial

I'm in the army and know that I've killed someone. The authorities are on the way to arrest me. I feel incredibly guilty about what I might have done and terrified about being caught and tried.

Edward awoke feeling like he had indeed committed a horrible crime. But what was it? As we explored his dream, the words "court-martial" immediately clicked. Edward had become a conscientious objector during the Vietnam war. This had been a devastating disappointment for his father, a career military officer. Edward had always felt guilty about it and as a result had never broken away from his father's influence.

During his earlier years as a psychologist, Edward had chosen a mentor who was stern and critical—a lot like his father. Recently he had begun training with a new mentor who was much more encouraging and warm in his teaching style and in his technique of doing therapy.

Edward felt that he was beginning to understand his dream "crimes." The murder was the death of his old self. At the same time he felt he had murdered his loyalty to his father. He no longer had to submit himself to stern authorities to atone for his rebellion. And he no longer had to be afraid of being more successful than his father. He had finally begun to free himself from the inhibiting influence of his early paternal relationship.

The insights from this dream inspired Edward to examine his relationship with male authority figures in general. Although the murder theme was repulsive, he realized that he was also confronting and working out his aggressive and destructive tendencies. Daniel Levinson asserts that the resolution of a man's destructive tendencies at midlife helps him find new sources of creativity.

Edward was encouraged by these insights but still feeling confused about whether he was doing the right thing in returning to psychology. Soon he had another dream.

I Can't Find the Therapy Room
I was back at the hospital ward, the first place that I worked as a therapist. I couldn't find a room to meet with patients and I couldn't find my co-therapist to meet with the group or the family I

*was supposed to 'see. It was chaotic, yet I felt a
sense of competence and some sense that it would
work out.*

In this dream, Edward remembered that he'd been very
excited about that first job because it allowed him to be the
coordinator of a treatment team involving nurses, social
workers, and other professionals. For Edward, the dream
was a snapshot of where he was in solving his midlife career
crisis. Emerging from his confusion and disorientation was
a sense of competence. The hospital job had been a rewarding experience that helped him find a positive identity as a
psychotherapist. He was again contemplating a new start in
psychology and seeking a room or a place where he could
feel he belonged.

Although he was still uncertain, this dream confirmed
that returning to work as a psychologist would be a positive
step. The feelings of competence at the end of his dream
gave him the impetus to face the confusing and difficult task
of beginning anew at midlife.

MENOPAUSE: BIOLOGICAL AND
PSYCHOLOGICAL MILESTONE

Psychological studies of menopause have suggested that a
woman's midlife transition is strongly influenced by the biological event of the ending of her reproductive fertility. But
menopause is not necessarily synonymous with midlife crisis for all women. Some women undergo a premenopausal
transition in their late thirties or early forties and have many
reactions parallel to those described above for men. However, for many women, menopause does signal a profound
period of psychological reorganization as well as biological
change.

In her fascinating personal account, *Journey Through*

Menopause: A Personal Rite of Passage, religious studies professor Christine Downing describes a woman's life cycle as three seasons: prior to puberty, the fertile period of menstruation, and the phase from menopause to death. With individual variations, the third season of a woman's life begins between forty-five and fifty, and menopause runs its course over a span of a few years.

The physical changes that women many experience include hot flashes and sweats, headaches, dizziness, insomnia, fatigue, mood swings, and variations in sexual arousal. Some of these symptoms are induced by hormonal changes. Others may be generalized signs of aging or more likely are part of a psychologically induced change provoked by menopause.

According to Downing, many women tend to focus too much on the physical symptoms of menopause and neglect the psychological transformation. She feels that the symptoms that are most important are dreams, nightmares, fantasies, and visions. By attending to their inner reactions, women can understand distressing symptoms and find a deeper meaning in the changes they are undergoing.

Themes of children, babies, fertility, and infertility are often prominent in the dreams of women undergoing midlife crisis. One theme that appears often is that of searching for, rescuing, nurturing, or healing children, often sick or lost babies. For example, Elena's dream of Saving the Children has a theme of the biological clock. Since Elena was infertile, she had to decide whether she would adopt a child or use her work with children as a substitute for childbearing. In Judy's Empty Rooms dream, the search for her daughter was related to the loss of her daughter and the childrearing phase of her life and identity.

At menopause, dreams often focus directly on fertility and childbearing issues. Christine Downing described a series of her own dreams during menopause. A dream just

before her fiftieth birthday, during a period of severe headaches, made her aware of the imminent onset of menopause.

Pregnant with My Fatherless Child
*I am walking with my former husband among
steeply sloping sand dunes like those I remember
from my childhood. From time to time we could
see the ocean, waves breaking high. The wind was
blowing enough to make talking difficult; the dune
grass cut into our calves; the sand shifted under-
foot. We were intent on our walking, giving one another a hand now and then at a particularly tricky
spot, thoroughly enjoying being together. At some
point along the way, when we had slowed our pace
a bit, I said, "You know dear, I think I'm pregnant
again, and this time I don't even know who the father is." Will we keep it? he asked. "We always do,
don't we?" I replied.*

As she thought about the dream, Christine realized that
her period was several weeks overdue. She immediately
connected the dream with a new stage in life, being pregnant
with her menopausal self. Through exploration of this
dream, Downing decided to devote attention to observing
her reactions as the changes unfolded in her body and her
psyche. To honor the importance of her dream, Downing
elaborated fantasies about her dream-child and created rituals to make the transition more special. As the stages of
menopause unfolded, her dreams reflected other themes
that highlighted the loss of biological fertility but pointed to
the emergence of a new source of psychological generativity.

Not all of her dreams reflected positive expectations.
Some revealed emotional turmoil, such as a dream about
watching a decapitated dog actively search for its head. This
grotesque image, she felt, was telling her that although her

mind and body were feeling split, there was still vitality in her body. Or perhaps the dream indicated she was searching for a new mental representation of her body, a new identity for a body that still felt strong and vital but could no longer bear children.

In her book *Change of Life: A Psychological Study of Dreams and the Menopause,* Jungian analyst Ann Mankowitz offers an in-depth exploration of a dream series from a patient whom she calls Rachel. According to Mankowitz, exploring her dreams helped Rachel find guidance and strength through a difficult passage.

On the surface, life seemed normal for the fifty-one-year-old Rachel. She had been married thirty years, had three grown children, and had gone back to school a decade earlier to train as a marriage counselor, which had become a rewarding career. But despite the appearance of stability and fulfillment, Rachel felt an emptiness and a sense that her life lacked direction.

After a year of psychotherapy during which she reported few dreams, Rachel had a profound dream that helped her change her life. We'll look at one of the seven parts of this epic dream.

The Burnt House

I am walking around the house in the country, our family home where we all lived when my children were younger. It's burnt out, destroyed by fire, a blackened empty shell. Part of it looks like dead petrified trees, some of it twisted like flames solidified. I am alone . . . utterly desolate. It's me, my insides, my womb . . . but not just that . . . my past life, my children . . . the whole way of life ended forever . . . but round at the back of the house there is new grass growing and that gives me hope.

Rachel's dream resembles Judy's Empty Rooms dream. In both dreams the image of a dwelling with a barren interior seems linked to the actual event of the children no longer living at home and to the psychological experience of having a womb that will soon be infertile.

In Rachel's dream the damage is more vivid. The interior is burned and petrified. Rachel was shocked by her dream. She associated the fire damage with the hot flashes she'd experienced and to feeling burned-out. Rachel felt that verbalizing her sense of desolation in this segment of the dream helped relieve the self-pity she had been feeling.

Exploring her dream series with her therapist helped Rachel grieve the loss of her youth and her identity as a child-bearing woman. Images such as the green grass growing at the end of the Burnt House dream gave her hope. In the final segment of her epic dream, she is led by male guides to explore the illuminated foundation of a new house that is partially submerged in water. The new foundation suggested a rebuilding that was under way as she moved toward resolving her midlife crisis.

Menopause requires mourning the loss of identity as a woman able to bear children. When a woman's grief can be expressed and resolved, a new birth occurs: the beginning of a new phase of life that offers the excitement and challenge of new roles and identities and new sources of fulfillment.

RETURN FROM LIMBO: NEW IDENTITIES, NEW DIRECTIONS

Carl Jung's midlife crisis lasted nearly seven years. At forty-four, after long solitary hours making paintings based on his visions and dreams, examining his childhood memories, and writing in special journals, he had a dream that signaled the end of his dark night of the soul. In this dream, Jung found himself traveling in the English city of Liverpool, which appeared very sooty and dreary.

The Blooming Magnolia Tree

While walking . . . we found a broad square dimly illuminated by street lights, into which many streets converged. The various quarters of the city were arranged radially around the square. In the center was a round pool, and in the middle of it a small island. While everything was obscured by rain, fog, smoke and dimly lit darkness, the little island blazed with sunlight. On it stood a single tree, a magnolia, in a shower of reddish blossoms. It was as though the tree stood in the sunlight and was at the same time the source of light. . . . I was carried away by the beauty of the flowering tree and the sunlit island.

Jung felt that the dream represented his conscious situation at the time as well as providing a powerful image of future possibilities. He was still feeling gloomy, like the image of the industrial city of Liverpool. He hadn't yet been able to resolve the malaise of his midlife crisis.

The name Liverpool, however, he associated with a pool of life. His exquisite vision of the blooming magnolia on the island in the center of the pool gave Jung a feeling of having achieved the goal of his long exploration. The image of the central tree of life inspired him to develop his theory of the "self" as a part of the mind that when activated gives meaning and purpose to life. Working with the dream centered him emotionally and gave him hope that something beautiful was emerging from his dark journey. In his autobiography, Jung repeatedly emphasizes that the agonies and ecstasies of his dream and visions during his midlife crisis provided him with indelible insights into the mind's functioning that inspired all of his later writings.

After this dream, Jung gave up his intensive artistic exploration and embarked on a much more active schedule of writing, teaching, and traveling. He had returned from the threshold and entered into a new phase of life.

Not every midlife transition ends in such a definitive fashion as Jung's. For some, the end of the transition may coincide with an event such as the resolution of a marital crisis, recovery from an illness, assumption of a new job, or the completion of a creative project. More often the return from the threshold of midlife is gradual and not necessarily marked by one specific event or dream.

For Judy, her Empty Rooms dream came at the beginning of her midlife crisis and also at the beginning of her therapy. After three years of therapy her life had changed dramatically. She had not succumbed to her depression or to drinking. She was still working part-time at her old job as a paralegal but had been accepted to a local law school's evening program. This fulfilled a long-held fantasy. She had been accepted to law school over twenty years earlier but had decided not to go because her husband's job had required them to move frequently. Judy had always done volunteer work in the past, and now she hoped to use her skills as a lawyer to work in a legal-aid clinic or in some kind of public-service position.

Her life was much fuller than in the days of her Empty Rooms dream. Although she was working hard, she had forced herself to develop more social contacts and become involved in a church group, where she had made many friends. Now that Judy had found other interests and friendships, she was putting less emphasis on her daughter, and their relationship had improved.

Near the end of her third year in therapy, Judy had a dream that helped her see how much her life had changed.

Star Student

I'm in one of my law school classes and the professor calls on me to answer a very complicated question, something about discrimination, but

I'm not exactly sure what he wants. I'm very nervous that I'll make a fool of myself. I look down and part of my blouse is transparent, so I'm afraid the class can see my breasts, though no one seems to notice. I start to talk and end up giving a very impressive answer. It's a topic I know a lot about from my work as a paralegal. The professor compliments me on my answer and all the students seem impressed and no one notices my sheer blouse. People come up to me after class and want to meet me as if I could help them with their studies. One man who is about my age seems especially interested to talk, and I feel attracted to him.

Judy was somewhat embarrassed by her dream, especially the part about feeling exposed. She was puzzled by the image of the sheer blouse. When I asked what ideas she had about that, she thought the blouse in the dream looked like one she had recently purchased. It wasn't especially sexy but was very stylish. As her self-esteem had risen and her fears of rejection eased, Judy had begun to pay more attention to her appearance.

In any case, Judy thought there might be a sexual meaning to the dream. The man at the end of the dream was someone in whom she was interested. After talking to him casually a number of times, she'd recently gotten up the nerve to ask him out to coffee. She had begun to date sporadically, but he was someone in whom she might be more seriously interested.

The Star Student dream also helped Judy realize how she had minimized her intellectual abilities and her personal strengths in general. Judy proudly described how she had just received her final grades for the first year of law school and was the third highest in a class of over a hundred. She now felt ready to accept the praise and recognition of her professors and peers.

Judy felt that her Star Student dream was evidence that her self-esteem had significantly improved. She reflected on how anxious she had been while applying to school and during the first term. She had worried about flunking out or being ridiculed by professors. In her dream and in reality, however, she had become a star student. This was shocking to Judy, who had always been nervous about her abilities and never been faced with a challenge as grueling as some of her law school classes.

Judy could see from this dream and from the events in her life that she had made significant changes both externally and internally. Her depression had lifted and her self-image was far more positive. She was excited about her career prospects and began to entertain the possibility of getting involved in a new relationship or even remarriage.

Within three months, Judy had ended therapy feeling that she was well on the road to a new phase of her life. At this time she had not begun menopause, so her midlife transition had resolved itself prior to any biological changes.

For Judy, working with her dreams helped access her feelings and gauge her progress through the stages of her midlife journey. Her daughter's departure helped her understand how she had never resolved the rejection and grief that she'd suffered during her divorce. Through therapy and dream exploration, she was able to find unexpected fulfillments through a career change and the hope of greater ability to be intimate and find a loving relationship.

DISCOVERING A NEW MIDLIFE IDENTITY

During a midlife crisis, a transformation of self occurs. We leave behind the roles, appearances, and infinite possibilities of our youth and enter an in-between period of inner turmoil during which we question many of the givens in our life.

Whether this crisis occurs in our late thirties, forties, or early fifties, its momentous effect shakes up our inner and outer worlds. Whether a midlife crisis is precipitated by a traumatic event, by biological changes, or by pervasive feelings that creep up and surround us, we are in for months and usually years of searching for new directions and structures in our life.

Because the midlife transition has only recently been considered important, there are few rituals and little information and support to guide us. Remembering and observing our dreams can alert us to the onset of a midlife crisis and help us navigate through the early stages of this difficult and confusing transition.

Resolving a midlife crisis requires turning inward, mourning the ending of the era of youth and finding new inspiration to guide the second half of life. Attending to our dreams helps to maintain that inner focus on the thoughts of our heart. Guided by our deeper feelings, we can discover new directions and new sources of fulfillment during this crucial period.

7. Crisis Dreams and Nightmares
Our Inner Response to Trauma

CATHERINE AND RON were on their honeymoon sailing in the Galapagos Islands with a small group of travelers. In the middle of the night they were thrown out of their beds by a tremendous crash. A jagged rock had broken through the hull and into their cabin. Water began pouring in. Naked, they groped for the door and were slammed against the walls of the boat as it repeatedly smashed into the rocks. They barely made it to the upper deck. The boat continued to heave violently. Just as it capsized, Catherine and Ron jumped into the pitch-black waters, professing their love to each other and preparing to die.

Catherine was caught by a rope and drawn under the boat, emerging only after a desperate struggle. Then her body was knocked against the volcanic rocks. Ron and Catherine found each other and struggled up onto the slippery rocks that were lit only by the stars. When they called out to their fellow passengers and crew, miraculously all of them were on the rocks. None of the eighteen on board had been severely injured or killed. Catherine was bruised, had two broken toes, and was covered by spines of the sea urchins that lived on the rocks that had sunk their boat.

When the dawn broke, they could see the pieces of their vessel and debris of their belongings drifting in and out with the tide. Hours later, in shock and scorched by the heat of the equatorial sun, they were rescued.

For weeks, Ron and Catherine couldn't sleep through the night. They would wake up terrified by recurrent nightmares. For the first few nights, Ron jumped out of bed convinced that he was still in the boat and had to escape. He couldn't vanquish the terror he felt. He began to remember the outlines of a dream that he would live with every single night for eight weeks.

The Drowning Waters
I feel water rushing all around me. I'm totally disoriented and can't tell where I am or where I am going. There is no depth or dimension. I feel like I am going crazy or dying. I awake terrified.

With this dream, Ron reexperienced the terror of the shipwreck. He would wake up in a cold sweat with his heart pounding. He couldn't make the memory or the dream go away. In fact, he felt the dream was making the memory worse. At times he wondered whether he was going insane. When his screams awakened Catherine, he would tell her his dreams. But he didn't want to disturb her too much, because she was having her own nightmares.

Catherine's initial nightmares were similar to Ron's. For the first few weeks she dreamed of water rushing over her, overwhelming her. Within a couple weeks, her nightmares became more detailed.

A Tidal Wave Breaches the Sea Walls

I am sitting on a beach and suddenly I see a tidal wave forming in the distance. It is rushing toward me at breakneck speed. I can see a series of walls that were built to hold back the tide. At first it seems like they will be able to hold the water back. But each time the water reaches a wall, I can see it surge relentlessly onward, getting closer and closer until it is just about to crash over me. I wake up panicked.

Although this disturbing dream came almost every night, she felt it gave her some hope that she could overcome the terror she had experienced in the shipwreck. Despite its repetition, the visual image of the walls in her tidal wave dream helped her feel she was beginning to develop some inner protection, some defense mechanism against the terror of drowning. At least there was something that temporarily held back the wave and gave her time to prepare, unlike the real night of the shipwreck.

Two months after the shipwreck, Catherine had a dream that broke the pattern of drowning and tidal waves.

Grandma Becomes a Young Bride

My grandmother tells me she is going to marry Don (my first boyfriend). Although I know she is very old, I'm confused because she looks regenerated as if she is a young woman with rosy cheeks. As she announces her engagement, I feel very happy for her but also confused because I thought she was old and close to death.

She felt sad when she awoke and reflected on her dream. In reality, her eighty-eight-year-old grandmother was near death. Catherine had been extremely close to her. She grew up living in the same house. She had even been named after her.

Catherine knew that the dream was anticipating the loss of her grandmother. Perhaps it represented a wish that her grandmother would find a fountain of youth that would allow her to escape death. But she also sensed it had to do with her own recent marriage. Prior to the shipwreck, her courtship and engagement had made her feel younger and more innocent, as she had felt in her first love affair.

She shared her dream with Ron and explored it with her therapist. She began to think about how the accident had not only ruined her honeymoon but had abruptly ended the joy of her engagement and wedding celebration. She had been harboring a fear that something was lost that could never be regained. The beginning of her marriage had been marked with a terrifying ordeal that she wasn't sure she could erase. Like her grandmother, Catherine had been close to death. The dream of her grandmother's wedding was the first hint that the innocence and happiness of Catherine's engagement could ever be restored.

For Catherine, this dream marked a turning point in her recovery. She associated her exploration of this dream with an alleviation of the depression and lingering terror that had gripped her since the accident and the disrupted honeymoon. When her grandmother died a month later, Catherine used this dream as a positive image that she held with her through mourning.

Catherine continued to have tidal wave nightmares, but they became less frequent and less overwhelming. Many of her dreams, moreover, seemed to refer to the shipwreck in symbolic ways as opposed to the raw terror of her drowning and tidal wave dreams. Slowly, she was recovering from the trauma.

NIGHTMARES: KEYS TO RECOVERY

When we or those close to us experience an event that has lingering psychological side effects, we can expect nightmares within the first few weeks. Often the passage of time, emotional support from others, and our own inner resilience will get us on the road to recovery within a few weeks after a traumatic experience. In some cases, however, it can take months, even years, for the devastating memory and repetitive nightmares to loosen their grip.

It's important to recognize that the nightmares following a traumatic event are not necessarily a sign of pathology but are an unconscious reflection of our attempts to overcome the trauma. These posttraumatic nightmares are a vital source of information that can help us focus our recovery on the issues that have wounded us most deeply.

Posttraumatic Nightmares. When trauma victims reach an impasse in their recovery, they often suffer from persistent, unchanging nightmares that replay the event(s). In his book *The Nightmare: The Psychology and Biology of Terrifying Dreams,* Dr. Ernest Hartmann refers to the phenomenon of unchanging nightmares as *encapsulation.* This is a condition whereby waking consciousness is unable to overcome the overwhelming feelings of vulnerability brought on by the trauma. This failure to cope is reflected in dreams that replay the trauma in an unmodified form, like a terrible television rerun that can't be shut off. Hartmann likens the encapsulation of trauma in repetitive dreams to a physical abscess, a wound that doesn't heal because it is sealed off, with its infection eating away at us.

What Is Posttraumatic Stress Disorder? Recurrent, unchanging nightmares are one of the characteristic symptoms of posttraumatic stress disorder (PTSD), a psychiatric

syndrome that is common to people who have become emotionally devastated after being victimized by events that are
"outside the range of usual human experience." Those who
may suffer from this syndrome include victims of or wit-
nesses to violence; for example, combat veterans, crime victims, battered wives, and children who are physically or sexually abused. It also may afflict the survivors of accidental
or natural disasters such as car and plane crashes, fires, explosions, earthquakes, floods, and hurricanes. Besides insistent nightmares, the syndrome may include depression,
withdrawal, insomnia, and other psychological symptoms.

People with PTSD may also experience severe anxiety, including flashbacks that cause them to remember and
relive the terror. Intrusive memories usually come in the
form of an involuntary mental preoccupation with the most
dreaded and often violent aspects of the trauma. These insistent memories usually alternate with avoidance or denial
of any feelings about the trauma. Avoidance and denial are
defense mechanisms that allow us to shut off memories
that are overwhelming. Unfortunately, these unconscious
mechanisms may protect us too well from our emotionally
devastating memories. If our avoidance and denial are too
strong, we are never able to face and resolve the emotional
wounds resulting from the trauma.

Recovering from PTSD. Why is it nearly impossible for
some of us to overcome the alternating cycle of intrusive
thoughts and denial? The magnitude of the trauma is an important factor. Experiences such as prolonged child abuse,
front-line combat, being the victim of a crime, or experiencing a life-threatening car accident may devastate even the
most stable individual.

Another crucial factor in the way we respond to and recover from traumatic events is whether we have suffered

prior emotional wounds that are parallel. An example of a parallel emotional trauma would be a person who witnessed a murder or other violent crime as an adult and had also seen his father physically abuse his mother as a child. If he has not been able to work out the troubling emotions resulting from the childhood trauma, he will have a more difficult time working out the parallel emotional stumbling blocks caused by the adult trauma.

Another difficult stumbling block is what is known as survivor guilt. This syndrome occurs in people who survive a catastrophe in which other people perish or are seriously injured. The confusion about why we have survived when others close to us have died often leads to an unconscious belief that we deserve to suffer to make up for our good fortune. Survivor guilt can block our ability to recover from a trauma and can lead to depression, self-defeating behavior, or a tendency to be accident-prone.

The inability to rebuild our lives after a trauma can also contribute to the persistence of PTSD. Ron and Catherine were able to return to their home and their careers and begin their marriage with the hope of happiness. On the other hand, a political refugee who was displaced by war in her homeland may never be able to return to her old way of life. She may spend many years facing poverty, discrimination, and culture shock in her new country. She will certainly have a more difficult time recovering and be more vulnerable to nightmares.

Many people who face death are able to make a greater commitment to personal change because of the sense of urgency triggered by their sudden awareness of the finiteness of life. For example, after the shipwreck, Ron decided to pursue a career change to a less pressured field so that he'd be able to spend more time with his children than his father had spent with him.

How Posttraumatic Nightmares Can Be Beneficial. In this chapter we'll explore ways you can break the spell of post-traumatic dreams and nightmares and use them in several constructive ways:

- *As a warning that you're still overwhelmed by the incident.* Dreams after a traumatic experience are normal and may even be a sign of unconscious attempts to master the trauma. But if profoundly disturbing nightmares persist in an unchanged form and are more like a memory than a dream, you may be suffering from PTSD and should seek help soon after the incident. This can help prevent the emotional wounds from becoming encapsulated.

- *As a way to understand what stage of recovery you have reached.* As you recover, your dreams may still be upsetting but they'll often incorporate images and references from the present and from the pre-trauma past. In addition, dreams marking recovery are more illogical, symbolic, and include dreamlike imagery.

- *To help identify unresolved issues from the trauma and from your past.* Long-avoided conflicts from the past will often surface in dreams after a trauma. Dreams spotlight issues such as unresolved grief, survivor guilt, suppressed rage, and terrifying anxieties that must be acknowledged and worked through for healing to occur.

- *To help communicate the emotional magnitude of the traumatic experience and to feel more understood.* Emotional sharing lessens the sense of isolation and prevents the distortions that may set in if the victim withdraws from friends and family.

Exploring your dreams can help heal the wounds of traumatic events. To show you how, this chapter will look at a variety of situations including accidents, crimes, earthquakes, Vietnam combat experience, political terror and torture. These situations may seem extreme if you or someone close to you has not experienced them. But you don't have to be a Vietnam veteran or an accident victim to apply the insights of this chapter. Our responses to other forms of trauma, both major and minor, tend to parallel those discussed here.

DREAMS OF ACCIDENT AND CRIME VICTIMS

When we watch the local news on television, we see an endless series of gory crimes and accidents. When it is someone else's trauma, we can switch off the TV or recycle our newspaper. When the accident or crime victim is ourself or someone close to us, the emotional impact lingers on.

Dreams of accident victims, such as those following Ron and Catherine's shipwreck, give us crucial information and insights about how we are recovering from the trauma. Five months after their shipwreck, Catherine and Ron's nightmares had become infrequent. Then another near-tragedy befell them: their car was rammed head-on by a drunken driver who crossed the median and nearly totaled their car. Both suffered whiplash and bruises but no severe injuries.

The accident plunged both of them into another round of drowning nightmares. Ron would awaken startled, feeling that he was back on the boat and would again have to fight for his life in the dark turbulent sea. For a few weeks the symptoms of PTSD returned. Neither of them could sleep. They suffered from depression and became easily startled. Although the anxiety faded, Ron finds that occasionally he has a similar drowning nightmare, usually at a time of severe stress, sometimes when he's near the ocean and is reminded of the accident by hearing and seeing the waves. Ron has learned to use his occasional nightmares as a warning sign that he's feeling vulnerable.

Sometimes near-misses cause reactions and dreams

similar to those suffered after the original trauma. For example, Tracy and our new baby nearly suffered a head-on collision. A driver veered into their lane and only swerved away at the last second. Although they emerged unscathed, Tracy had nightmares for two to three weeks. On the first two nights after the incident she had a dream that repeated numerous times during the night.

Near-Miss

I am driving with my daughter and a car turns and seems to be heading almost deliberately toward me. The lights are shining into my eyes, blinding me. I can't see well enough to turn and I realize the steering wheel doesn't work the way it is supposed to. I'm helpless and the car is headed straight for us. I try to reach for Zoe to protect her, but it's too dark to see.

The dream recurred in an unchanging form. The first few nights, she woke up several times shaking. The experience in the dream felt real. As we explored the dream, Tracy gradually realized that the part at the end, when she tries to protect Zoe, was the most upsetting. Because of her intense protective maternal feelings, she was harboring a sense of guilt that she had exposed Zoe to mortal danger. By exploring her recurrent dream she was able to ease her feelings of guilt and master the residue of anxiety that the incident left.

Tracy's dreams illustrate a typical reaction to being the victim of an accident or a crime. At first the event is dreamed about in a form that is almost a literal reliving of the incident. Gradually the dreams become less literal and more mixed with symbolism and other events and concerns.

Hartmann stresses that the key to whether an event causes nightmares is the vulnerability of the dreamer. For Tracy, a new mother, her intense protective feelings probably caused her to react more strongly to the near-miss situation.

Psychoanalytic authors Marquis Wallace and Howard Parad describe an extended dream series of a rape victim whom they call Hilda. She was treated with a form of crisis-oriented therapy that utilized dreams as the central focus of discussion. Their approach to crisis therapy seeks to help the client not only to return to her former level of functioning but to use the turning point as an impetus for personal growth.

Hilda, a twenty-five-year-old nursing student, sought therapy two weeks after being raped. She couldn't stop crying and was having severe difficulties concentrating on her studies. She said that her self-esteem was about one on a scale of ten. Her boyfriend broke up with her a week after the rape; she was emotionally estranged from her parents, who lived a hundred miles away. In her first session, she tearfully reported two recurrent dreams.

Seeing My Grave
I am there, but not there. I see my grave. I wonder what it would feel like not to exist. I am afraid of being by myself.

I'm Invisible to Them
I am on a country road. I see a beautiful wheat field. My mother and brother and myself are there. We stop at the top of a hill. It seems that my mother and brother—and father, who suddenly shows up—don't even know that I'm here. I wake up with my mouth open. I am lonely. I have the strange feeling it is easy for them to leave.

Hilda expressed loneliness and anger toward her boyfriend who had rejected her at a moment of need. She also dwelt upon the feeling of being invisible and realized that her parents had not paid much attention to her as a child.

Her sadness alternated with anger at her parents as she explored her long-standing sense of emotional neglect.

Over the course of twenty therapy sessions, Hilda realized that the brutality of the rapist had set off painful memories of insensitive and neglectful treatment by her parents, especially by her stern, alcoholic father. Exploring her dreams not only helped her to express and work out her emotional reaction to the rape, it also accelerated her ability to resolve the sense of being invisible that she carried with her.

The "invisible" dreams, plus others that depicted her father interchanged with her ex-boyfriend, helped Hilda realize that she got involved with men in an attempt to win her father's love. Although she would cling to them, they often treated her poorly. By the end of the therapy she had begun a relationship that had a different quality.

During the course of the therapy, Hilda testified against the rapist at a preliminary hearing. Before, during, and after her testimony, she had nightmares that renewed the terror and invisibility she felt during the rape. After testifying, she dreamed that she reexperienced the rape but was able to run away. Although she was still reliving the trauma, there was now evidence of mastery. Apparently the assertion of testifying, along with the continuing support of the therapist, had altered her dreams. Experiencing the trauma with a new, partially resolved ending is a typical sign that recovery is occurring.

Ultimately, the rapist confessed. After he was sentenced, Hilda felt more secure but continued to have an occasional terrifying dream, such as the following.

Attacked by a Ferocious Bear
A ferocious bear was trying to get me. It attacked. I tried to counterattack but was helpless. I am close to getting eaten and someone is trying to

*help me. The bear claws at me all night, over and
over again. It reminds me of frog and spider
dreams that I used to have.*

The image of the bear provoked incredible feelings of
rage in Hilda. She was angry at her father. Then she became
ferociously angry at the rapist, expressing murderous fantasies toward him. When the therapist suggested that the
bear might represent her own anger as well as an image of
the rapist, Hilda responded positively. She realized that she
had always denied her own anger and made excuses for people who treated her poorly. The dream allowed her a sense of
catharsis and a chance to awaken her assertive side, which
had always been dormant.

At first glance, the image of the ferocious bear would
seem to contradict the idea that Hilda was making progress
in her recovery. But often when we've taken a significant
step toward mastering a trauma, we feel safe to release and
work through more powerful feelings that had previously
been inaccessible. The renewal of nightmares was not a re-
gression but a sign of a greater ability to tolerate and master
the very feelings that had been overwhelming.

POSTEARTHQUAKE DREAMS

Disasters cause us to examine issues in new ways. They
push us to deal with vital issues that we have been neglecting or denying.

Earthquakes and other natural disasters often alter the
lives of those who are injured, suffer property damage, lose
their jobs, or are forced to move. For those who are catas-
trophically affected, severe, recurrent nightmares are common in the weeks and months after the disaster. Even for
those who are less traumatized, the overwhelming force of
nature and the close encounter with death can provoke
strong emotional reactions.

The San Francisco earthquake of 1989 was traumatic for many who lived through it. Even for those who were not injured and only suffered minor property damage, there were lingering images of the fires burning and building and bridges collapsing.

Because of the media exposure, many people dreamed about the collapse of the Bay Bridge and the Cypress freeway structure in Oakland. Others dreamed about the stadium collapsing at the World Series. (In fact, little damage occurred at Candlestick Park.) Other common earthquake dreams were images of huge chasms opening, objects falling, and roofs caving in. Some dreamed of rescuing wounded children and helping them to seek medical treatment.

In the aftermath, a collective case of posttraumatic stress disorder afflicted literally millions of people who were jolted by the quake. Adults and children suffered from diverse symptoms, including nightmares. Many seemed depressed and somewhat dazed at times as they alternated between denying the emotional impact and fearfully reliving it. Even after the San Francisco Bay Bridge was repaired, some people were unable to drive across because of fears that it might collapse if another earthquake struck.

At the moment of the quake, the walls shook in my San Francisco office. Objects and books fell. For what seemed like an endless period (but turned out to be only a few seconds), I felt like the building was about to be torn apart and destroyed. Later I told myself that the earthquake had no major effect on me. I believed that for a few days, until I began to feel aftershocks every time a truck passed by on the street. Like many others, I had gone through an initial period of denial. Soon I could acknowledge the lingering anxiety more freely.

Others had similar periods of initial denial. Raul, a man whose house suffered minor damage, lived near an area where there had been extensive damage and fires. A week after the quake he had the following dream.

Unexpected Quake Damage

I am alone in my bedroom. I look up and see cracks in the ceiling and the walls that I hadn't noticed after the earthquake. I am afraid part of the roof may fall on me.

When he awoke, Raul jumped out of bed and inspected the walls in his bedroom, fully expecting to find the cracks that he saw so vividly in his dream. When he didn't find any, he realized that his earthquake dream was not related to unseen quake damage in his apartment but to emotional damage. He had been denying the impact of the quake.

One week later, more aware of the emotional impact, he noticed that he had become obsessed with looking for damaged buildings in his neighborhood and was quite anxious about subsequent earthquakes causing debris that could injure or kill him. At this point, Raul had passed out of the phase of denial and had moved into a phase of intrusive thoughts and fantasies about the earthquake.

As he discussed his dream, he was struck by how lonely he felt. Raul had recently broken up with a woman he'd been going with for two years. She had often stayed at his apartment, and the dream seemed to be emphasizing the isolation and sadness he'd been feeling. He had tried to deny his grief about the relationship, but the dreams and the earthquake seemed to be forcing him to face his feelings.

The cracks in the bedroom walls were clearly related to working out his fears about the damaging power of the earthquake. But for Raul, they also seemed connected to his problems in the bedroom: he couldn't open up, and he tended to blame his partner instead of considering that he might be afraid of being hurt if he risked intimacy. He hadn't been able to sustain love. Although his recent relationship had been the longest ever, this woman, like the others, ended up leaving because he was not emotionally expressive.

Although his actual earthquake damage had not been

extensive, the unexpected internal damage he discovered was the destructive effect of his fears of intimacy. In addition to helping him become aware of his denial of the impact of the earthquake, discussing his dream helped Raul acknowledge a repetitive pattern in his relationships.

Lynn also dreamed about discovering damage shortly after the earthquake. Her dreams portrayed emotional reactions to the earthquake but also provoked important insights about conflicts in her marriage that were not quake-related.

Impasse on the Higher Road

We are on vacation back East, driving along with my husband, Glen, and his two sons (my step-sons). A car starts to veer toward us and Glen jumps up to a higher road to avoid hitting it. On that road, we immediately come to a pile of debris that seems to be due to an earthquake. There doesn't seem to be a way to get beyond the road-block. I wake up thinking that somehow we need to make a new start.

At around the time of the earthquake, Lynn and Glen had been embroiled over conflicts about Glen's relationship with his ex-wife. Lynn felt that Glen was too easily manipulated by her and was being inconsistent with the children. The strain of these issues was undermining the stability of the marriage. Lynn felt that the damage from the "second earthquake" in her dream was probably a reference to the marital conflicts.

The dream showed the family barely dodging disaster. Lynn felt that Glen's jump to the higher road represented her view of his attempts to rise above the marital conflicts by coming up with magical solutions that didn't really solve them. The earthquake damage was clearly blocking their way, and they had to think of something more practical to get beyond the roadblock in their marriage.

Exploring her dream and the emotional shake-up of the earthquake convinced Lynn that she and Glen needed to confront their marital problems and "find a way to make a new beginning." Lynn wasn't sure how to go about it, but the dream gave her a renewed sense of hope that it would be possible.

For Raul, Lynn, and many others, the earth had shaken but there seemed to be a parallel emotional upheaval. Earthquakes and other traumas shake up our psychological "faults" or vulnerable areas.

After a natural disaster, exploring dreams is an extremely valuable way to resolve lingering anxieties about the disaster itself and to see how the trauma aggravated other stresses and unresolved conflicts. For those who suffer severe damage or injuries, sharing their nightmares as well as conscious feelings is a vital part of recovering and preventing PTSD.

DREAMS AND WAR

A combat-related stress syndrome has been recognized for centuries. In the American Civil War, the term *soldier's heart* was used and the severe symptoms were ascribed to coronary malfunctions. In World War I, the term *shell shock* was indicative of the prevalent belief that brain trauma was the source of the anxiety and nightmares. Finally in World War II, vast numbers of traumatized soldiers made possible a careful study of the symptoms.

It was the acute public reaction to the problems of a large number of Vietnam veterans in the 1970s that led to the inclusion of posttraumatic stress disorder as an official psychiatric diagnosis in 1979. Although organic causes have not been ruled out, the prevailing wisdom is that PTSD is a psychologically induced syndrome that occurs in survivors of severe trauma. For the Vietnam veterans on whom we'll focus, the emotional wounds were compounded by the scorn they received upon their arrival home from a war that our nation lost and would prefer to forget.

In the dreams of combat veterans, we find abundant evidence of how the human psyche copes with overwhelming trauma. Jungian analyst Harry Wilmer has worked extensively with Vietnam combat veterans and conducted a study of 359 dreams from 103 veterans. Recurrent dreams were counted only once; therefore the 359 dreams represent thousands more.

Wilmer found many consistent themes in the veterans' dreams. The most common motifs included killing, being killed, death, dying, being wounded, and committing atrocities. General themes such as being chased, animals, and looming danger took on the characteristics of war scenes. Themes portraying the cycle of service in Vietnam were also common. These included dreams emphasizing approaching combat, direct engagement, returning home, and longing to return to Vietnam.

Out of his research Wilmer observed three stages of impasse and resolution in the dreams that coincide closely with the actual stages of recovery that the veterans had reached.

Stage One Dreams. Wilmer's stage one dreams were characteristic of the men who suffered the most severe symptoms of PTSD. These dreams were more realistic and less dreamlike. They tended to replay horrific events that were witnessed by the dreamer, and the content had little to do with the dreamer's past or present life. Stage one dreams accounted for 53 percent of the total.

A gruesome example was that of a veteran who had been confined to a foxhole for four days with one buddy.

They couldn't even get out to stretch their legs because of the sniper fire. The traumatic nightmare replays an actual memory in an unchanged form.

My Buddy Gets Blown Away

I am talking with my buddy. It is dark. He lights a cigarette and all of a sudden his head blows off. His brains come out all over me. I wake up screaming.

Hartmann believes that soldiers who lose a person with whom they were extremely close are the most vulnerable to the psychologically disabling impact of PTSD. Soldiers who were younger, immature, or had an insecure sense of self are even more at risk because their adult identities had not been fully formed. Often the nightmares would not begin for these men until months or years later, when a subsequent loss, rejection or trauma would trigger the painful memories that had never been dealt with.

Stage Two Dreams. Wilmer found that in the veterans he treated or in those who recovered spontaneously, the imagery in their dreams began to transform as the therapy progressed. In what he describes as the second stage, the nightmares still focus on catastrophic memories, but the content begins to be mixed with events from the present or other eras of the person's life. This indicates that they have begun to resolve their fixation on the terrible events of the past and are dealing more realistically with other pressing issues of their current life.

Dream mastery of trauma usually is characterized by matching emotional challenges with parallel incidents from the past. These stage two dreams reveal the psyche's attempts to transform the trauma into a more symbolic form that can be mastered. They accounted for 21 percent of the total.

Stage Three Dreams. Wilmer's stage three dreams are more like ordinary nightmares, but they tend to have Vietnam as the setting. More metaphorical and dreamlike, they mix in many images of the present and combine them in new ways. There are often attempts by the dreamer to fight back or overcome the dilemmas faced in the dream.

According to Wilmer, the emergence of a stage three dream after prolonged unchanging nightmares is an important part of the healing process. Observing the lessening or ending of their brutal repetitive nightmares helps the veterans to feel understood and to see their inner response to the therapy and healing process. As an example of what he calls "the healing nightmare," Wilmer presents a number of cases of veterans who experienced a transformation in their dream life that correlated with general improvements in their condition.

Jim, thirty-six, had a stage one nightmare for twelve years before beginning therapy. It was always the same: a reliving of an actual ambush in which he led seventeen newly arrived soldiers to their death. Nothing could stop the dream. The incident had forced him to resort to excessive use of alcohol and drugs to blot out the memory. After two months of twice-a-week therapy, his dreams suddenly transformed to stage three—to the shock of Jim and Dr. Wilmer.

Rescuing the Wounded Healer

Everyone is getting killed. Harry (Dr. Wilmer), they got you in the center of the ravine bleeding from gunshot wounds. You are leaning against a tree and crying for help. . . . Now I am standing on top of the ravine and a nurse is with me. She and I slip into the ravine. I hit the Viet Cong over the head with the butt of my rifle and she dresses

*your wounds. I carry you out on my back. Some-
times in the dream, your hands are tied. When I
pull you out, I wake up in tears.*

In the past, Jim had always awakened from his nightmares in a cold sweat, never in tears. It appeared that he had
broken free of his nightly ambush and was beginning to
work through his grief. Although still a nightmare, his Rescuing the Wounded Healer dream reveals a transformation
of his inner life.

The discussion and other therapeutic work with Dr. Wilmer was impacting his dreams. Jim's relationship with his
"healer" was reversed in the dream. Instead of depicting his
sense that the doctor was helping him, Jim became the rescuing hero. He was determined to give his doctor, bleeding
and crying in a ravine, the desperately needed treatment for
his wounds. He would even risk his life to carry him out on
his back. This scene was emotionally parallel to the positive effects Jim was feeling from Wilmer's determination to
heal his emotional wounds.

In addition, saving a man from a combat zone is exactly
what Jim had been unable to do during the ambush. The success of his dream rescue mission suggests that he was finally
overcoming the terrible guilt and achieving a sense of mastery over the incident that had occurred a dozen years earlier.

Jim's example is what Wilmer calls a healing nightmare,
a dream that results in an emotional breakthrough. In the
process of exploring it, Jim gained evidence that he was
deeply engaged in a positive working relationship with his
therapist. He became aware of the emerging grief that he
would have to deal with. It was a grief that until that moment
he had never allowed himself to admit.

He was finally able to allow himself to be taken care of,
to accept nursing and doctoring just as he had provided them
in the dream. The exploration of his Rescuing dream gave

him a feeling that he was regaining control over his waking
life as well as his dream life. This renewed sense of control
and hope for the future were crucial building blocks in his
continued recovery.

NIGHTMARES OF REFUGEES

The nightmares of refugees reveal the emotional scars of political repression, terrorist threats and attacks, and psychological or physical torture. Many refugees are haunted by
persistent nightmares of being threatened or attacked by
murderous troops. Others are plagued by dreams of
wounded children crying out in pain, images of mutilated
bodies, and terrible scenes of destruction.

Psychologist Adrianne Aron has worked extensively
with Salvadoran refugees living in the San Francisco Bay
Area, especially with those who sought political asylum due
to threats against their lives. Almost three-quarters of the
subjects she interviewed spontaneously reported nightmares, and over two-thirds of those were plagued by nightmares of men trying to kill them. In many cases these dreams
were based upon actual experiences of armed threat or
harassment.

One Salvadoran woman, Blanca, had been apolitical.
She was picked up on a Monday and informed that she
would be killed on Friday. She was blindfolded, isolated, and
starved for four days. She heard others being tortured and
shot and fully expected that she too would be murdered. Miraculously her family was able to bribe a guard to secure her
release. Soon she escaped to the United States, carrying
with her the searing memory of her torture. Shortly after her
release from detention, she began having a recurrent nightmare that would plague her for years to come.

Murderers Pursuing Me
*There are armed men coming after me. I am run-
ning, they are getting closer. I don't know what*

*they look like but I can feel them behind me, pre-
paring to kill me. I feel the heat of the blood running down my back and I realize that I have been
shot. Then I wake up.*

The dream depicts Blanca reliving the horrific days
when she fully expected to be murdered. Her unconscious is
frozen in a state of terrified expectation and she is actually
shot in the dream. Blanca awakened screaming from this
dream almost daily for her first two years in the United
States. The content and frequency of her dream are typical
of the dreams of other political refugees. In fact, the nightmares of refugees are so similar that Aron has identified a
two-part pattern that is almost universal.

In the typical first scene of the dream, the victim is usually being chased by armed men, who are often faceless or
unidentified. The dreamer feels their ominous presence
gradually overtaking and preparing to kill him or her. In the
second scene the victims are either shot, beaten, or sub-
jected to other forms of deadly violence. They may respond
by fighting back or trying to disarm the assailant, but they
usually fail; a gun may misfire, or they are paralyzed, or
overwhelmed by superior forces.

Many refugees are unable to gain political asylum or
secure residency status in a new country. They may face de-
portation and the threat of torture or death if they are returned to their homeland. The United States grants asylum
to only about 3 percent of Salvadoran refugees. Until they
obtain residency and/or establish a stable life in their new
country, the nightmares and posttraumatic stress disorder
may continue.

Eventually Blanca married an American citizen, gained
legal status, and began to feel more secure. Six years after
leaving her country, she continues to have this nightmare
when other events in her life are stressful, but the frequency
has been reduced to once a month.

Even when refugees gain residency, they must confront grief and rage over the loss of their family, friends, and career. In addition to the loss of their old way of life, they face overwhelming new problems of acculturation. Many require psychological treatment to shake their nightmares and anxiety.

Julio, a nineteen-year-old Salvadoran, was apolitical. When every male in his family was murdered, he knew that his days were numbered. He fled to the mountains and escaped to the United States. Four times a week for over six years, he was plagued by a repetitive nightmare so upsetting that he rarely slept more than two hours at a time. It was only when he succeeded in winning political asylum in the United States that his nightmares abated and his psychological condition improved.

Arturo served in the Salvadoran air force and continued to work at a military armory in a civilian status after his discharge. He was falsely accused by the national guard of stealing weapons and collaborating with the guerrillas. Although he maintained his innocence he was mercilessly tortured by being burned, shocked, hanged, and beaten.

Arturo's most distressing nightmare, like Blanca's, was an endless replay of being pursued. However, the response to the murderers in the second part of his dream was different. It begins with armed men chasing him with deadly intent. And then . . .

Trying to Fight Back

. . . I stop, because I have a gun. I turn and take aim and shoot at them. But the gun misfires. I wake up.

Although Arturo's dream gun is impotent, at least he wields it in a desperate but futile fight. In reality, Arturo fiercely maintained his innocence and belief that some justice or law would prevail in his favor. In the dreams of many persecuted refugees, they are unable to rearm themselves or fight back. Arturo's fighting suggested some degree of resilience in his spirit.

A number of times Arturo has had apocalyptic nightmares like the following.

The Eve of Destruction

I know the world is going to end because I see the firmament breaking into pieces, floating in an enormous sea. Everywhere, I see people falling into the void. I am standing precariously on a little island.

The dream is reflective of Arturo's perception that his world was being shattered. The island represents a stubborn assertion of innocence in the face of the destruction of his world. Some related dreams portray the Savior's presence at the end of the world. The dreams may reflect Arturo's inner struggle to give a religious meaning to the horrendous torture he was suffering.

Arturo's nightmares gradually became less frequent in the year after he fled his homeland. He dreamed that the Savior appeared and abolished all evil from the world. He was eventually able to achieve political asylum, which gave him some hope that his nightmares would diminish and his life could begin again.

HEALING THE WOUNDS OF TRAUMA

The wounds of trauma are slow to heal. When you become victimized by violence, abuse, accidents, or natural disasters you need empathetic ears to hear your feelings, assist you in rebuilding your life, and help you ease the terror of your nightmares and other anxieties.

It is important not to feel ashamed about seeking help after suffering a trauma. Early intervention that includes individual or group discussion of the traumatic events can head off the development of posttraumatic stress disorder and put you on the road to recovery from your emotional wounds.

Exploring posttraumatic nightmares allows you to gain access to the hidden wounds that paralyze you. As you review the traumatic memories, their grip upon you is loosened. Dreams also provide vital information about what stage of recovery you have reached or whether you are at an impasse in getting over the trauma.

When you listen to the dreams of someone else who has suffered a traumatic experience, remember that you need not feel compelled to offer a sophisticated explanation or analysis. Often the experience that someone is willing to listen and try to understand the victim's troubling feelings help break the spell of posttraumatic nightmares.

8. *Healing Dreams*
Recovering from Injury and Illness

WHEN WE'RE INJURED or ill, our dreams express our deepest fears and help us understand the full range of our emotional reactions. Dreams give us symbolic pictures of the stages of our illness. They can help us participate more actively in selecting the nature of treatment we'll seek and may even help us improve our response. And sharing our dreams allows us to build supportive connections with friends and family at a time when we are most vulnerable.

Breast cancer struck Susan in the prime of life. At thirty-five, she had finally recovered from an emotionally devastating divorce five years earlier. She had also just completed her doctorate in psychology after having made a career change from nursing.

During the first six months of recovering from her mastectomy and going through chemotherapy, Susan began to reach out more to friends for emotional support. She had contemplated joining a support group for women with breast cancer but had been afraid to talk with others for fear of making her own situation seem more real and upsetting to her. While debating whether to enter the support group, Susan had the following dream.

Why Am I Doing This Alone?

I am with a group of women who have been kidnapped and sent to the USSR. A guard is telling us that you have to have special shoes. But I defy him and walk with the other women. The other women go ahead and I fall behind. I suddenly realize that I can catch up and walk with them and ask myself, "Why am I doing this alone?" I call out to another woman and ask to walk with her. Later, we are all in Gorbachev's office and he is talking to Bush and negotiating our release. I am with the other women and we are told that we'll all be let go, and I start hugging the translator and jumping up and down with joy.

Susan's dream helped resolve her immediate dilemma of whether to join the support group. At a deeper level, however, her dream depicted the resolution of old fears about dependence versus independence. Susan was especially moved by the question in her dream, "Why am I doing this alone?" She had always been ready to give to others. As the oldest child, she took care of her younger siblings. As a nurse, she was extremely dedicated to her patients. In her marriage, she always put her ex-husband's needs before her own. In fact, she had been very dependent on him and had grown to resent his dominance. Until her husband left her, she took no steps to develop her more assertive side. Now the cancer and her dreams were pushing her to develop her sense of independence.

She no longer viewed marriage as a threat to her autonomy and began to feel open to the idea of marrying again. Although she was continuing to work in a helping profession, she felt more balanced and less like she needed to be a superwoman in work with clients and relationships with friends. In fact, the illness had made her acutely aware of how precious her family and friends were.

The joy that Susan experienced at the end of the dream was associated with the ending of chemotherapy. After five months of treatment, she has been pronounced cancer-free. Susan had minimized the importance of the end of her treatment, but the dream helped her realize how much of a burden had been lifted when she received a positive prognosis.

Although Susan still experienced bouts of depression and anxieties about the recurrence of the cancer, dreams helped her see that she was actively coping with fears and reaching new dimensions in her personal and professional life.

MAKING THE CONNECTION BETWEEN DREAMS AND ILLNESS

Like other turning points, an encounter with serious illness produces recurring dream images as we respond to the emotional challenges of sickness. Clocks and references to time, for example, are common in the dreams of people who have been diagnosed with a terminal illness. Acute awareness of time in dreams relates to our internal sense of how much time we have left. One person who was given a terminal diagnosis dreamed that he was told it was 11 P.M., indicating that his death was imminent, but when he checked his watch, it was only 9:15. His dream indicated that his internal clock still had time on it, and he ended up living longer than expected.

Other dream images tend to be associated with the physical characteristics of a particular episode of illness. For example, people with cancer often dream of cars going out of control and crashing—symbolizing the deadly, out-of-control growth of cancerous cells. Epileptics may dream of explosions, which may symbolize the sense of fragmentation they feel during a seizure. Women may dream of water spilling out of containers prior to or at the onset of a miscarriage.

In his book *Dreaming with an AIDS Patient*, Jungian analyst Robert Bosnak chronicles a long series of dreams of a man suffering from AIDS. In the period when his patient was approaching death, repetitive dreams of polluted water seemed to symbolize that his inner fluids were contaminated and his condition was deteriorating.

Other dreams of patients with AIDS and cancer contained the theme of a spreading wildfire, symbolizing the consuming destructive power of the disease process. One dream recorded by a colleague was that of William, a Protestant minister suffering from AIDS. William had left the ministry to pursue a secular career in the social services. After contracting AIDS and suffering a near-fatal bout of pneumonia, he had the following dream during a period of remission.

Wildfire in the Church

I am in a church that is on fire. The fire is raging out of control and everyone is fleeing feeling the terrible danger. I look for a place to hide and go up to the pulpit and stand behind the cross thinking I will be safe from the fire there.

This dream inspired William to renew his faith. He decided to halt his other career plans and return to the church. He expressed the hope that his spiritual renewal would help him stave off or recover from AIDS. Unfortunately, the fire had spread too far; within a few weeks William died.

In this chapter, we'll explore how to use our dreams during periods of illness to help us overcome barriers to reaching out to others, to work out the emotional impasses that arise at times of serious illness, to find a sense of meaning during demoralizing phases of an illness, and to transform periods of suffering into opportunities for personal growth.

We'll consider key dreams in various stages of confrontation with life-threatening illness, chronic ailments, injuries, and surgery. In our exploration, we'll look at dreams that

- Occur shortly before the onset of illness and appear to foreshadow the arrival of the illness
- Coincide with the onset or immediate aftermath of an illness, injury, or surgery
- Portray symbolic or direct references to the injured or ill body
- Play a role in triggering episodes of certain disorders: asthma, epilepsy, heart attack, miscarriage
- Depict resolution of emotional blocks related to illness
- Illustrate stages of recovery or deterioration
- Indicate the imminence of death in terminal patients

DREAMS FORESHADOWING ILLNESS

On the verge of serious illness, a compelling nightmare may foreshadow our imminent physical danger. Many people I've worked with have associated a particular dream to the period just before they became aware of their illness. In psychological literature, there are many examples of troubling nightmares in the weeks before the onset of a serious or fatal disease. There is even some scientific evidence that dream content alters dramatically in the weeks prior to the outbreak of a severe illness.

Six weeks prior to her cancer diagnosis, Susan dreamed of a terrible earthquake. Although earthquake dreams are not uncommon—especially for people living in the San Francisco Bay Area, as Susan does—this dream stayed in her mind, troubling her for weeks.

My House Is Crumbling All Around Me

I am in my bed and my house begins to shake. I am not worried at first, but the shaking gets stronger and stronger. I am horrified as I see parts of my house falling down all around me. Despite my terror and the destruction that occurs, I end up being safe.

She tried to reassure herself. What could be wrong? She'd had a mammogram and a full physical just a few months earlier. She had never felt better and was taking care of herself—not overworking, eating a healthy diet, exercising, and feeling fulfilled with her new career.

In the days following her diagnosis and surgery, Susan's earthquake dream kept coming back to her. She knew there was no way of proving it, but it seemed to have predicted a disaster about to strike her.

As she progressed in her recovery from cancer, Susan thought about this dream many times. She thought that the house represented her body. In the dream, as in reality, she couldn't believe the disaster could really be happening. Just as parts of her house broke off, a part of her body had to be removed. The one element of the dream that Susan began to draw solace from was the ending, where she survives despite the destruction. In her more optimistic moments, Susan imagined that she would survive the destructive influence of cancer just as she had survived the earthquake in her dream.

Susan also saw the crumbling house as a metaphor for the upheaval in the stability and structure of her life that was about to occur. In her recovery, she felt she was rebuilding her life on a firmer foundation.

Natalie, like Susan, had no reason to suspect that a cancer was growing inside her. At thirty-two, she had made a successful documentary film and was studying for her doctorate in sociology. She had a steady relationship and was feeling for the first time that she had begun to break free from her mother's stifling influence.

Four months before receiving the shocking diagnosis of malignant cervical cancer, she had a dream that upset her deeply.

The Evil Magician
I'm leading a little girl into an auditorium and somehow she gets lost. As I try to find her, a young man dressed in black leads an older evil-looking magician also dressed in black and has him lie on a couch. Suddenly I can sense which room the little girl is in. I realize to my horror that the magician has annihilated the girl whom I am responsible for. I attack his left arm and touch a green spot on it. I realize that I too am contaminated with the evil power of taking someone's soul, and I'm left with the feeling of being evil.

Dream themes of contamination and poisoning are common in people with cancer and other serious ailments. For Natalie, the dream didn't make sense until after her cervical cancer was diagnosed. Like Susan and others, Natalie later viewed this as a prodromal dream. The term *prodromal* refers to a symptom that appears before the outbreak of a disease that gives some clue to the nature and severity of the illness to come. Prodromal dreams reveal an internal physiological condition often before there is conscious awareness of the illness.

Death and the threat of death may be represented by the intrusion of a stranger and at times by the color black, although this varies in different cultures and individuals. Natalie's evil, murderous magician may have been a personification of the cancer that was growing within her. Later

Natalie came to feel that the magician and the poisonous green spot had other important meanings besides the cancer. They represented her dark side, the part of us that Jung called the shadow, the unacceptable and scorned attributes of our personality. Part of the courageous struggle that Natalie would wage in her fight against cancer would be to overcome the deadly aspect of the poison and to find the green or life-giving aspect of herself.

Dr. Robert Smith of the Department of Psychiatry at Michigan State University has been researching the relationship of dream content to recovery from heart disease and other serious ailments. He has found that men who had dreams featuring death themes and women who dreamed of separation themes recovered more poorly and had a higher death rate.

Other researchers have found a recurrent theme of heat in dreams of people suffering from thyroid disorders. Cancer surgeon Bernie Siegel, in his book *Peace, Love and Healing* described a journalist who had a prodromal dream about being tortured by hot coals placed on his throat, searing his larynx. Simultaneously, his girlfriend dreamed that the two of them were in a bed that was filling up with blood. When they discussed their dreams, he found himself blurting out that he had throat cancer, though no such condition had been diagnosed. Soon he had another dream that featured a group of medicine men circling around him and sticking hypodermics into what they were calling his "neck brain."

A few months later he began having symptoms and went to see a doctor. Upon initial evaluation, all of his tests were normal, and the doctor expressed skepticism about the dream-inspired self-diagnosis. When pressed, the doctor reluctantly scheduled further tests. When they were completed, a diagnosis of thyroid cancer was confirmed.

C. G. Jung and other Jungian analysts have observed that animal themes in dreams may predict illness and also provide an indication of the recovery process. Jung and his colleague Marie-Louise von Franz have written about horse symbolism in dreams as an archetypal or universal symbol of the unconscious or animal life of the body, connected to our instincts and aliveness.

Jung was consulted in the case of Marie, a seventeen-year-old girl who had been diagnosed by one specialist as suffering from a disease of progressive muscle atrophy and by another as suffering from hysteria. When he inquired about her dreams, Marie said she'd been plagued by nightmares. Her recent dreams included one in which her mother was hanged and another about a frightened horse that jumped out a fourth-floor window and ended up mangled in the street below.

In mythology, horses have heralded death, and in reality, horses are subject to stampede behavior. For Jung, the panicked self-destructive horse was a symbol of out-of-control biological forces at work in the girl's body—forces that she was not consciously aware of. Jung felt that the morbid symbolism was forecasting a more serious diagnosis; in fact a fatal prognosis was later confirmed by her doctors.

Von Franz reported another horse dream in a sixty-one-year-old cavalry officer who died unexpectedly of heart failure four weeks after having the following dream, the setting of which was his days in officer training school thirty years earlier.

Discovering the Horse in the Lead Coffin
An old corporal, who in reality had the meaningful name of "Adam," appeared and said to him, "Mr. Lieutenant, I must show you something."

*He led the lieutenant down into the cellar of the
barracks and opened a door—made of lead! The
dreamer recoiled with a shudder. In front of him
the carcass of a horse lay on its back, completely
decomposed and emanating an awful smell.*

For von Franz, the horse in the dream took on further
dimensions because it was intimately connected to the officer's life work as a mounted soldier. In his dream, the horse
may have symbolized the instrument of his work as well as
his life force. The setting of the dream, back at the beginning
of his career, and the death of his horse suggested that his
career cycle was ending.

The value of exploring such dreams is not in making
concrete predictions. Dreaming of a dead horse or an earthquake does not mean we are doomed or will soon be afflicted with a life-threatening illness! But our dreams may
reflect processes in our body of which we are not yet consciously aware. This is especially true if those changes impact our physical survival. Another way of saying this is that
disturbing dreams are an inner warning when we face both
emotional and physical crisis.

Heeding these warnings is not as simple as looking at a
thermometer. Rather than using our dreams to make concrete predictions, we can take the cues we receive to explore
whether there is some aspect of our physical health that we
need to consider. This may help us to discover a health problem sooner through intuitive and emotional reactions to our
dreams.

OUR INNER RESPONSE TO ILLNESS

When we are stricken with an illness or injury, when we receive a diagnosis of a life-threatening ailment, or when we
go through surgery, our dreams express uncensored emotional reactions to the dangerous physical situation we are
enduring. Dreams contain important messages that can

guide the emotional healing that complements any medical treatments we receive.

In some cultures, dreams at the onset of illness are believed to contain crucial information about the healing rituals that are necessary for a cure. For example, according to anthropologist Jackson Lincoln, the Navajo believe that some dreams are the cause of illness either through their content or by their effect on the dreamer. They believe that illness emanates from the spirits of dead men or animals that enter dreams and afflict people.

The Navajo also believe that dreams prescribe specific curing rituals, such as herbal treatments, songs, or ceremonial dances. They used specific dream symbols to select from the repertoire of possible healing techniques. For example, dreams of death (of oneself, neighbors, or others) and dreams of teeth falling out were considered particularly ominous and required a special chant. Other dream symbols called for chants or dances that involved other tribal members and served a function of increasing emotional support for the dreamer.

Western medicine needs to pay more careful attention to dreams in diagnosis and treatment planning as the Navajo do. We would be wise to include a closer look at dreams as part of our approach to treating and healing people during bouts of serious illness.

A dramatic feature of dreams at the onset of illness is that they contain graphic images of biological reactions to the dangers the dreamer is facing. In many instances these images are transparent references to the specific disease. For example, one dreamer with multiple sclerosis, a disease withering the nervous system, dreamed that she stepped on and paralyzed a tarantula.

In my work with cancer patients, I found evidence that specific types of cancer may be represented in dreams by recurrent images related to the site of the cancer and the meaning of the illness to that person. This is consistent with the research of psychologists Meredith Sabini and Valerie Maffly indicating that some forms of cancer may be symbolically linked to unresolved grief and other deep psychological conflicts.

Two of the women I interviewed who suffered from cervical cancer had dreams about their mouth and lips at the onset of their awareness of being ill. Ruth had her dream on the night before going to visit her gynecologist to get the results of a Pap smear that was part of a routine physical. She didn't consciously anticipate that she would be receiving a diagnosis of cervical cancer.

My Dirty Mouth

I am riding in a bus to see my former gynecologist. The bus driver says, "You are disgusting." I realize that my mouth is dirty and there are sores on my skin around my lips and in my mouth. I notice that I am sitting in a section of the bus reserved for handicapped, elderly people.

Ruth was shocked and angry when she received her diagnosis and a recommendation that she undergo a hysterectomy. The images in her dream came to her repeatedly in the days that followed.

At first her Dirty Mouth dream felt like a prediction or even a metaphoric description of her reactions to her illness. She felt that the diseased lips and inside of her mouth were symbolic of the lips of her vagina and interior of her womb. The reference to the elderly section of the bus related to the stigma of feeling ill and old, perhaps even close to death. She also felt humiliated by the bus driver's cruel remarks and frustrated that she was relegated to the disabled section. This reminded her of the difficulties she had experienced with her ex-husband and other men.

Ruth had always been a strong proponent of women's rights. As a journalist, she'd written stories that exposed the way women experienced discrimination in the workplace and in relationships. For Ruth, being yelled at by a cruel male driver and forced to sit separately reminded her of the oppression she felt as a woman and campaigned against in her professional work.

Ruth wondered why the doctor in her dream was her former gynecologist and not her present one. As she thought about this, she remembered that he had left traditional medicine and now practiced a form of alternative medicine that involved the use of imagery and other New Age healing techniques. This part of the dream intrigued Ruth and helped her decide to refuse the hysterectomy and pursue various forms of psychological and alternative treatments.

Natalie was also shocked and overwhelmed when she learned of her malignant cervical cancer. She found herself denying that it was true. After a second opinion, the reality began to set in. "I felt wounded and ashamed, and I felt betrayed that this could have happened to me especially at the high point of my life." Natalie was fiercely determined not to have a hysterectomy despite the opinion of three doctors and her friends and family. Shortly after being diagnosed, she had the following dream.

Oral Birth of My Cat's Kittens
My cat Celeste is having kittens, and I suddenly become her with my own face. My lips become very sensitive and swollen. Out of my mouth comes a gray sac and I see myself giving birth to my cat's kittens.

Natalie felt that her Oral Birth dream was a diagnosis dream that described her condition at the onset of her illness. The swollen lips in her dream seemed to describe her physical state and need for a hysterectomy (the removal of the gray sac). As Natalie explored her dream, it took on meanings that went beyond a mere physical description of the nature and site of her illness. The dream had a malevolent feeling. The oral birth seemed unnatural. Natalie saw herself as unexpressive emotionally, so she was shocked that her mouth would produce something so incredible as the birth of kittens.

Although the dream was frightening, it affected Natalie deeply. She realized that something was changing inside of her. She became convinced that she wanted to marry and have a child. She realized that a good part of her motivation in refusing or delaying the hysterectomy was that she didn't want to foreclose the option of childbirth, even if it meant running the risk of death if the cancer spread.

Like Ruth, Natalie saw this initial dream as revealing crucial psychological blocks that she felt may even have contributed to her illness. She wasn't sure whether emotional conflicts could cause cancer, but she was convinced that awareness of her illness was giving her a powerful impetus to heal emotional wounds that she never before felt the strength to face.

Susan, whose dreams we examined earlier in this chapter, had a series of important dreams just after undergoing a modified radical mastectomy. On the second day after her surgery, Susan had a dream that related to her struggle to adjust to her new body image and to keep up hope in the face of her sudden life-threatening illness. The dreams in this series always featured images of bathing in hot tubs and swimming pools.

The Brutal Stares of the Other Women
I am with my best friend and am changing into a bathing suit so that we can go in a hot tub. I am

changing into a one-piece bathing suit that is low-cut. I feel great and I'm excited to be there. We get in the circular hot tub. There are a few others seated around the edge. Each of them is pushing water in unison with their feet. Two women are staring at me and looking at me funny. I look down at my chest and realize that I only have one breast. I'm frightened and run away. I meet an older woman who reassures me not to pay any attention to their critical stares.

Susan woke up sobbing hysterically. She felt that her dream was exaggerating her loss. She was now different from all of the other women in the hot tub with normal bodies. The terrible loss of her breast seemed hard to bear.

As she explored the different parts of her dream, she began to see it in different ways. The first part of the dream seemed to portray the period just prior to the diagnosis, a time of excitement about her life and possibilities. In the middle of that happy period, the cancer and mastectomy devastated her emotionally.

It was difficult for Susan to break the spell of this nightmare. But as she read it over again and talked about it, she began to think about the end of the dream, when an older woman reassured her and told her not to be swayed by the intolerance of other women or the sense of being different. This figure can be linked to what Jung might have called "The Old Wise Woman," a personification of the feminine aspect of the inner guide or healer within us. Susan was able to receive and be comforted by the inner guidance of the wise old woman in her dream. In reality, Susan was learning to reach out to her friends and rely on them during dark moments of hopelessness.

Susan began to take some comfort in the end of her

Brutal Stares dream. As in her prodromal dream of surviving a cataclysmic earthquake, there is a hopeful note at the end that helped bolster Susan's sense of optimism.

DREAMS AND PSYCHOSOMATIC ILLNESS

There is some evidence that dreams may be implicated in triggering physiological crises in people who are prone to suffer certain ailments, such as asthma, arthritis, miscarriage, and posttraumatic stress disorder (see chapter 7). In most of these cases, it's impossible to distinguish whether the dream triggers the episode of illness or whether the dream portrays the biological distress at the moment it occurs.

Psychiatrist Harold Levitan has conducted extensive research on the dreams of psychosomatic patients and has identified fascinating patterns in the dreams of people who suffer from asthma and arthritis. Levitan believes that for those people who are predisposed to illnesses that may be exacerbated by stress, dreams may trigger an incident of illness.

Levitan focused one of his studies on the dream patterns of people suffering from acute asthma. He identified four highly repetitive themes in the dreams immediately preceding a nocturnal asthma attack. The themes included dreams of being violently attacked by others, dreams of attacking or victimizing someone else, active or passive involvement in incest, and powerful emotions experienced by someone other than the dreamer in the dream.

For asthmatics and others who suffer from psychosomatic illnesses, the dream state may be a time of particular vulnerability, a nocturnal Achilles heel. Levitan believes this to be true because of the emotional impact of how we experience traumatic events in dreams. We are much more likely to witness a brutal attack or even a murder in a dream than we are in waking life. People with psychosomatic disorders tend to be less able to cope with strong emotions such as rage or grief in waking life and are even more overwhelmed by emotion in the sensitive arena of dreams. According to Levitan, an especially violent dream in an asthmatic may actually create a physical reaction that sets in motion an asthma attack.

If you or a friend suffer from asthma, rheumatoid arthritis, hypertension, or other psychosomatic disorders, exploring your nightmares may be difficult, but they can give you important clues as to what underlying emotional issues may trigger an episode of illness. When the nightmares are especially violent and seem to worsen your physical condition, it would be advisable to seek treatment from a mental health professional who can coordinate your treatment with the physician who treats your physical disorder.

OBSTACLES AND BREAKTHROUGHS:
DREAMS AND THE STAGES OF ILLNESS

Monitoring our dreams during bouts of serious illness can provide us with important sources of information. We can see the unfolding stages of our reaction to illness and get a sense of whether we are recovering or have reached an impasse. Occasionally treatment strategies are inspired by or explicitly suggested in dreams.

Toward the end of five months of chemotherapy, Susan was feeling a stronger sense of hope that the treatments would prevent a recurrence. Periodically, however, she had dreams that frightened her and nearly catapulted her into a pit of depression. She dreamed once of a group of women being massacred and another time of women being hanged. She would try to save them but fail. In one dream she was barely able to resuscitate her sister, who had become unconscious while taking a bath. Just before learning the outcome of her chemotherapy, she had the following dream.

The Miracle of the Car Crash

I am buying some plants to give to a friend for his birthday. I get into a long line to pay. The clerk is cleaning up a lot of blood from the counter from a woman who had an abortion. The clerk is sympathetic to the woman. In my left hand, I am horrified to see a bloody towel with the head of a fetus that was aborted. Then the scene switches and I see a guy who I used to go out with. He seems very infatuated with me in an aggressive way. He keeps insisting on a relationship. I feel frustrated and annoyed and ask one of the clerks to call the police. I wait for the police to take me home but I'm still afraid the guy will come back and hurt me. I finally see the police car arrive. Out of the darkness, a bright orange car appears. It is totally out of control and smashes into the garage at high speed. I was shocked by it all. The man from the store goes to check on the driver, who I think must be dead. They come back with a baby who it turns out is unharmed. Everyone is cheering that the baby was healthy.

Susan woke up feeling incredibly relieved. Although some of the imagery was horrifying, she felt that it was a recovery dream, confirming what she knew—that she had survived the fearful "accident" of being hit by cancer.

As Susan explored her dream, she focused on the image of the bloody aborted fetus. It seemed to symbolize the blood and guts of the surgery and her fear it would have been abortive. The man insisting on a relationship reminded her of her ex-husband and other men who had dominated her. Her relationships with men was a crucial psychological issue that the cancer had inspired her to focus on. The

dream suggested to Susan that she had made progress dealing with pushy men. She would no longer tolerate their insensitive advances and would seek help in dealing with this.
In the dream the authority she sought was the police. In waking life, she was finding an inner sense of authoritativeness.

The car crash and its miraculous aftermath were the
most vivid features of the dream. Dream images of cars
going out of control have been associated with the growth of
cancer cells. Susan associated the bright orange car smashing into her garage to the shock of the cancer invading her
body. She viewed the driver who is presumed to be dead as
her own fears of death. The miraculous transformation of
the bloody fetus into an unharmed baby at the end of the
dream is a magical reversal of doom. Despite the gory aspects of the dream, the happy ending gave her hope and reassurance that her own recovery would continue.

John Prendergast's research on dreams of people with
life-threatening illnesses revealed that rebirth imagery is
common in people who have experienced a remission. It is
less common in terminal patients or in those who are entirely well. Dreams of rebirth, miraculous recovery, and ren-
ovation projects in those recovering from life-threatening
illness symbolize the sense of relief, creative renewal, and
triumph over adversity.

After being diagnosed with cervical cancer, Natalie
had a dream that strongly influenced her decision to forgo
surgery and pursue nontraditional treatment approaches.

Finding My Place in the Wave

*I am diving into waves going back from the water
to the beach. I dive into a very large one in slow
motion and sink to the bottom. I find it very peaceful on the bottom. It feels like I will be able to withstand the immersion until I come out of the wave.*

At the beginning of the dream her flexibility of going in and out of the water struck Natalie as out of character. Before her cancer, she had been more rigid personally and the dream portrayed a new image of who she was becoming. Natalie was especially impressed by the image of the wave. She felt that it represented her cancer. It seemed overwhelming, but somehow she was able to slow down the motion, submerge, and trust that she would be able to survive.

Natalie derived from her wave dream a sense that it would be safe to take the risk of delaying the hysterectomy until she was sure that it would be right for her. Because of her refusal to follow the recommendation for surgery, Natalie had great difficulty in finding a doctor who would treat her medically. Doctors feared malpractice suits if her cancer worsened.

Natalie felt that her cervical cancer was "a wound of the feminine," related to the trauma she experienced growing up with her mother. The belief that a cancer can be related to particular psychological conflicts is controversial. However, it is interesting to note that Natalie, Ruth, and other women have linked wounds in their relationship with their mother as causative factors in their cervical cancer.

Jungian analysts have emphasized that there may be a link between the site of a cancer and profound losses. Using evidence from dreams and psychotherapy sessions, they have speculated that the development of cancer may result in part from old emotional wounds such as the death, desertion or emotional unavailability of a parent. Whether these speculations will be proved true remains to be seen. One thing is clear from my own research on cancer patients' dreams: the dreamer often feels a strong subjective sense that the nature of the cancer has a psychological meaning.

In any case, resolving her troubled maternal relationship was a crucial dimension of Natalie's psychological re-covery. She realized that this conflict had held her back from

wanting to have children. She hadn't wanted to risk per-
petrating on anyone else the emotional neglect that she had
suffered. She felt that some of the rigidities in her personality and her inability to express herself were linked to her
mother's insensitivity.

As time passed, Natalie spent many hours grieving the
loss of her grandmother, who had died when she was ten.
This grandmother had been much warmer and more loving
than Natalie's mother. Natalie had internal fantasy dialogues
with her grandmother over whether or not surgery was the
right decision. A crucial turning point occurred for Natalie
after she had the following dream.

Leaving My Mother and Grandmother Behind

*My mother, my grandmother, and I were all taking
my grandmother to a college where she will be
studying. We are looking for her dorm room and I
want to make sure she will be okay. We find the
room and all say goodbye. As it turns out I say
goodbye to both my mother and my grandmother
and leave.*

For Natalie, this dream was pivotal in helping her understand the need to resolve her relationship with her
mother and grandmother. The college setting reminded her
of when she left home for the first time. For Natalie, the
separation from her grandmother felt more like an incor-
poration of her love and support. Leaving her mother, however, symbolized breaking free of the deprivation and rejection she suffered during childhood.

Two years after her initial diagnosis, Natalie married
and gave birth to a daughter. The Oral Birth dream took on a
new level of meaning. She not only learned to express her
feelings; she felt ready to accept the challenge of loving and

caring for her daughter in a way that would be different from the pattern with her own mother.

She ultimately did choose to undergo hysterectomy when her daughter was four months old. Almost eleven years after her initial diagnosis, she hasn't had a recurrence of cancer. Through a confrontation with death, Natalie learned to live by the guidance of her dreams. In so doing, she discovered unexpected new dimensions in her ability to love herself and express love for others.

DREAMS OF PEOPLE APPROACHING DEATH

Recurrent symbols and themes seem to appear in the dreams of people who are approaching death. Some are inspiring images. Others are more disturbing or confusing. Most of the dreams suggest an inner struggle to acknowledge and accept what the dreamer knows is about to happen. Even when the dreamer is consciously denying or fighting the inevitable, the images reveal the psyche's attempt to prepare for a transformative experience.

Carl Jung's last reported dream, just days before his death, featured an image of a mandala (Hindu magic circle) that was similar to the symbolic patterns he observed in his patients during periods of psychological and spiritual growth and change.

The Stone of Wholeness

There was a "great round stone in a high place, a barren square, and on it were engraved the words: And this shall be a sign unto you of Wholeness and Oneness." There were also "many vessels to the right in an open square and a quadrangle of trees whose roots reached around the earth and enveloped him and among the roots, golden threads were glittering."

The image of the gilded tree of life carved on a stone for eternity suggests that Jung had reached an acceptance of his imminent death. The dream reveals a final sense of fulfillment about his lifelong work with the healing power of imagery in dreams, mythology, mysticism, and the arts.

Dying people's dreams contain fewer characters and a greater degree of separation and aloneness. There is often a sense of loss that is not resolved at the end. In some cases, death appears as a stranger approaching or stalking the dreamer. The dreamer frequently is a target of violence or a victim of cataclysmic events such as tidal waves and earthquakes that are symbolic of the overwhelming natural force that is about to overtake him or her.

A dramatic and recurrent theme is that of clocks and the limitations of time. Jungian analyst Marie-Louise von Franz cites the following dream of a man on the verge of death.

The End of Time

He sees the clock on the mantelpiece; the hands
have been moving but now they stop; as they stop,
a window opens behind the mantelpiece clock and
a bright light shines through. The opening widens
into a door and the light becomes a brilliant path.
He walks out on the path of light and disappears.

Von Franz associates the window to an alchemical term, *fenestra aeternitatis*, Latin for "window into eternity." The dream appears to be picturing not only the sense that time has run out, but a view and pathway into an afterlife or other reality.

Despite the alluring light of possible afterlife in the dream above, imagery of rebirth is common in people recovering from serious illness but not in those who are dying.

Life-threatening illnesses can offer us a heightened opportunity for psychological growth and awareness. The sense that death is near may stimulate the desire to resolve important relationships and to express hidden feelings before it's too late. Discussing and exploring our dreams can be very valuable, especially in the days and weeks prior to death. Dream sharing helps the dreamer to process his or her emotional reaction to the imminence of death, to overcome denial and to find the energy to finish old business in the outer and inner worlds.

The following dream series of a man dying of AIDS was related by Dr. Susan Fair. She was therapist to Earl, a thirty-three-year-old black man who had worked for the post office as a supervising clerk for twelve years. At their second meeting, he asked Dr. Fair if she was going to write a book about him. He encouraged her to do so in order for others to benefit from understanding "my awful disease." Earl's story and his dreams are presented here with his permission, as his dying gift to others who suffer from AIDS and to their families and friends.

Earl had been in and out of the hospital for a variety of serious ailments related to AIDS. Early in his therapy with Dr. Fair, Earl's illness worsened and he became bitter and suspicious of everyone who tried to help him. One day he screamed at Dr. Fair and railed at the unfairness of life.

Their work became more intensive when Earl was hospitalized for the final time, two weeks before he died. They met for short periods two or more times a day. Earl began to sense he was failing and said that he had "no more reserves to fight the battle." At times it was difficult for him to speak. He asked Dr. Fair to read to him and suggested *The Wizard of Oz*, which had been a childhood favorite. He wanted her to read only a little bit each time—apparently so that she wouldn't reach the end of the story.

A week before his death, he requested that he be taken off all medication except for pain pills. The next day he made a point of telling her about a vivid dream.

Crawling to Freedom
I am crawling on the dirt floor of a cabin. I have to crawl through it to escape. It reminds me of slaves in the South escaping to freedom through the Underground Railroad.

Earl was frightened by his dream but curious about what it meant. He seemed to perk up as if he had saved up his alertness and strength to tell his dream and explore its meaning. The reference to slaves puzzled him. It reminded him of stories he had read about slaves who made dangerous but successful escapes to freedom with the help of others as they fled the South. For Earl, the metaphor of escape from slavery revealed his sense that he was near death and that the freedom he was seeking might be a release from the slavery of his terribly sick body. He felt that the dirt floor represented the poverty of his childhood and his enslaved ancestors as well as the basic level of existence he was left with.

The crawling escape was scary for Earl. Dr. Fair suggested that it might be an image of dying—going through the feared transition out of the house of his physical being. At the end of their meeting Earl seemed comforted by both the fears he had expressed and the sense of hope that remained after discussing the issue of slavery.

Three days before death, Earl's body was deteriorating fast. He was incontinent and could not get out of bed. But he perked up once again and reported the following dream with a sense of urgency.

A Caged Animal

I am in a zoo instead of a hospital. The same people are around me, the nurses and doctors and patients, but it is a zoo cage instead of a hospital room. It feels very strange that I am in the cage and they are outside. I feel a strong desire to get out and demand that they let me out. They ask me where I would go and I say I don't know. I just want to get out.

Dr. Fair suggested to Earl that his dreams were pictures of his feelings. He said, "I guess I must really feel trapped." Taking the cue from Earl, Dr. Fair further suggested that he might feel that it was hard to watch life going on all around him and see all the people watching who couldn't help. He said this made sense. He talked about his frustration of being weak and no longer able to make his body do what he wanted.

The evening before he died, Earl again became alert when Dr. Fair entered the room. This time he reported what she surmised was a hallucination.

A Feast of Chinese Food

I am wide awake and I look at the hospital table and there is lots of delicious food there—Chinese food like fried rice and pot stickers—my favorite dishes. I can even smell it.

Dr. Fair reassured him that he was probably having a hallucination due to a lack of oxygen. He asked her if the food was really there. She said it wasn't, but that he should enjoy it anyway. He smiled weakly and said that he had always loved Chinese food. She continued her readings of *The Wizard of Oz*. Earl never got to hear the end of the story. He died peacefully the next morning.

WHAT DREAMS CAN TEACH US DURING ILLNESSES

Illness forces us to face the finiteness of our physical existence. Our unconscious becomes sensitized to the physical threat that illness represents. When we sense that we may have less time left, we become concerned with resolving deep conflicts. In this way serious illness can spark a psychological turning point that inspires personal growth.

Dreams can help us turn the suffering of an illness into an opportunity for becoming more fully alive. As we work out solutions to problems from the past and present, we may discover new sources of hope that may influence our ability to recover our physical well-being.

Dreams allow us to monitor vital information (in the form of images and symbols) that can help us understand the emotional factors that influence the onset of and recovery from an illness. They may occasionally foreshadow illness, picturing physical changes in our health that we aren't yet aware of. And they can help us see what stage we have reached in our response to an illness.

It is important to keep in mind that most such dreams are symbolic and should not be taken literally. However, when we use the images, stories, and feelings of our dreams as a jumping-off point for further exploration, we can take advantage of their healing power. Exploring our dreams helps us to tune into the vital resource of our own intuition, allowing us to be more actively engaged in whatever form of medical treatment we seek.

When we or our family members approach death, sharing and listening to dreams can help us overcome denial, resolve lingering issues, and find new sources of meaning even in the final weeks of life.

Listening to the dreams of those who are injured, ill, or dying can enhance the lives of those of us who are well. We can connect more deeply with our friends and relatives at a time of crisis, feel rewarded by our efforts to help, understand our own reactions to illness and death, and witness the drama of emotional healing that may accompany the experience of illness.

Listening to the dreams of the dying doesn't require fancy interpretations. Through our empathic listening, the dying person can feel reassured and understood at a crucial time of fear and confusion.

9. *Grief Dreams*
Resolving the Loss of a Loved One

Doug's father died just six weeks after being diagnosed with pancreatic cancer. In the weeks following his father's death, Doug experienced a terrible case of insomnia. He was waking up and remembering three and four dreams each night. Many of them were nightmares that left him in a cold sweat and terrified to go back to sleep. He said he was "feeling open and raw, as if I had lost a protective coating."

Soon after his father received the terminal diagnosis, Doug had a terrifying dream in which he was trying to erect defenses to shelter his home and his family from imminent nuclear war. At the end of the dream, he heard on the radio that missiles had been launched, and he lay on the floor bracing himself for the explosion. He wasn't sure whether his house would withstand the blast. When he explored this dream, Doug felt that the inevitability of the nuclear attack related to anticipating the pain of losing his father. The house and its defense represented him and his own psychological defenses, which were threatened by the news of his father's grave illness.

After a final unsuccessful operation just prior to his father's death, Doug dreamed that he was attacked by menacing thieves and stabbed with spears. Although the spears went through him, he was somehow able to survive. Doug immediately associated the spears with the surgery. In his dream he was empathizing with the suffering of his father being sliced by the surgeon's knife and barely surviving.

Doug's empathy with his father continued in a powerful dream one month after his father's death. In this dream, Doug's relationship with his young daughter paralleled his own relationship with his father.

Crossing into the Light Without My Daughter

I'm standing in a hallway with my one-year-old daughter in my arms. I'm facing a couple of double swinging hospital doors made of aluminum. I know I have to go through the doors into the room beyond. There are small windows in the swinging doors so I can get a feel for the other room. It is very light in there, like a gymnasium. I am scared to go through the doors because I'm afraid that something will attack me, like some kind of demon that will be very dangerous and that I can't subject my daughter to. She is upset and crying for me and not wanting me to put her down. I know I have to go through the doors and yet can't bring her with me. I am broken up but can't take her. I go through the doors to the brightest place I have ever been to in my life. It opens expansively and is blindingly light. I sense that my deepest fear is there, but don't know how it will materialize. I hear my daughter crying on the other side and I'm terrified. I wake up in a cold sweat.

The dream was excruciating. For Doug, the blinding intensity of the room he had entered and the demonic forces lurking there represented death—the world beyond, where his father had gone. He was troubled by the fact that his dream appeared to portray his own symbolic death. Was it telling him that he too would soon die, leaving his infant daughter fatherless?

As Doug explored his dream, he realized that it had to do with his grief, not any physical danger or illness that he was facing. Through his unconscious empathy with his father, his dreams were allowing him to go in his father's place; to suffer the spears of surgery and the atomic blast of death and ultimately to enter the world of the dead with its mystical blazing light.

As he continued to explore his dream, Doug was most upset about having to leave his daughter behind. Although he had been extremely happy to become a father for the first time at age forty, his dream left him preoccupied with the thought that someday he would have to say goodbye to his daughter, abandon her and travel to the world of death, just as his father had done to him. Doug realized that his daughter's tears and separation anxiety in the dream symbolized his own sadness. He felt that his dreams helped him understand not only his attachment to his father but also the significance of his relationship with his daughter.

Three months after his father's death, Doug continued to have some disturbing dreams about his father, but they were less frequent and their impact did not linger. His insomnia improved and he began to have a series of dreams about remodeling his house—adding rooms, redesigning his study, and fixing up the interior walls. The room with the bright light that represented death in his earlier dreams was beginning to take on a new form, representing growth in his own personality that had been stimulated by his father's death.

RESOLVING GRIEF THROUGH DREAMS

When someone close to us dies, we begin a process of grieving that may last for months or years. Because our culture
tends to deny the profound psychological impact of death
and we lack adequate rituals to guide us through this turning point, we are often at risk during the stages of mourning.
If our grieving does not progress, we may succumb to its
dark, depressive pull and become paralyzed. We may be unable to accept the loss or restore a sense of hope and con-
tinuity in our life. On the other hand, suffering a loss can become a transformative experience that leads to a deeper
experience of meaning and purpose and a positive resolution of our relationship with the person who has died.

The focus of this chapter is on understanding the patterns in dreams during the grieving process. We will look at
how exploring dreams can help us recover from the emotional devastation of loss and transform it into a a new beginning. We'll also examine the symbolic meaning of death
and dead persons in dreams.

During the grieving process, our dreams give us access
to the emotions we endure—sadness, anger, abandonment,
relief. They also help us to see if we are caught in the common impasses of grief—denial, depression, withdrawal,
substance abuse. Our dreams help us to see the slow evolution of our reactions to death and loss, through acceptance,
catharsis, detachment, and finding new involvements and relationships.

Dreams provide crucial guidance in the vulnerable
period of adapting to the death of a loved one. If we pay attention to our dreams we can observe vivid appearances by
the dead person. They may be calling out to us in pain or
sadness or appearing serene in otherworldly surroundings,
suggesting they've made it to a heavenly place of repose.

Early in the grieving process, the appearance of the deceased person in a dream is disturbing. When we awaken,

the contrast between the dream and the fact of the person's death is jarring. The person seems so real in our dreams, more alive than ever. Many cultures accept the notion that through dreams, we have our greatest opportunity to achieve real contact with the spirits of the dead.

In some cultures, events during dreaming are considered to be a crucial part of the process of grieving. Bereaved members of the Negrito tribe of the Philippines do not hold a funeral feast until the dead person appears in several dreams of their close relatives.

In contemporary urban Thailand, after a death, family members discuss their dreams together to hold on to their connection with the deceased. Even the children learn to share their dreams and search for references to the dead person. This informal ritual of dream sharing promotes emotional sharing and facilitates the resolution of grief.

For those people whose religious beliefs include an after-life and possibility of true contact with dead spirits, these dream encounters offer a possibility of working out their unresolved issues with the dead person before their spirit fades. In Thai culture, if one dreams of a relative immediately after his or her death, the dreamer pays the clergy homage to ensure that the relative reaches a safe sanctuary.

If we view the appearance of dead relatives in dreams as a psychological manifestation, dreams can be helpful in many ways during the period of grieving.

We don't have to wait for the deceased person to make an appearance in our dreams to benefit from the wisdom of our dreams. Deeper exploration of almost any of our dreams during the period of acute grief will help us to

- Overcome denial, acknowledge the loss, and mourn more openly
- Express and resolve troubling feelings stemming from the death, such as rage, abandonment, or even relief

- Assess when we are afflicted with depression or suicidal urges
- Relieve guilt and self-reproach connected to the death
- Help us to honor our attachment to the deceased person by reviewing memories and beginning to integrate positive aspects of our relationship with the deceased
- Acknowledge the spiritual dimension of grief
- Confront our own mortality

HOW DREAMS REVEAL THE STAGES OF GRIEVING

Psychological studies of bereavement support the notion that reactions to a death unfold in stages. The most widely accepted explanation of these specific steps comes from the work of Elisabeth Kübler-Ross, M.D. In her book *On Death and Dying*, she proposed five stages of reacting to the inevitability of one's own death, which are also applicable to facing the death of a loved one. The stages are denial, rage, bargaining, depression, and acceptance. It is important to keep in mind that these phases are only guidelines. Not everyone goes through them all, and they may occur in a different order for some people.

Another valuable way to conceptualize the evolution of grieving is as a three-part process that involves (1) overcoming denial and accepting the reality of the loss, (2) letting go of emotional ties to the dead person, and (3) becoming ready to form new relationships and move forward in life.

The stages of grief are clearly seen in the dreams of the bereaved. At first there is an increase in the number of dreams and nightmares that are recalled. Common dream themes in the initial period may include discovering or questioning evidence that the person is actually dead. This theme is related to the struggle to overcome denial and accept the reality of the loss. Dream references to either the

dreamer or the dead person undergoing separation, aloneness, or suffering are also common in the early stage of adjustment. For example, shortly after her mother's death,
Padma, a physician who was raised in India, had repetitive
dreams of seeing her mother dressed in black and appearing
forlorn. She was worried about her mother, who had never
liked to be alone while she was alive. In the dreams she tried
to express her concerns, but her mother was unable to
hear her.

Common dream themes in the middle stages of mourning include struggling to communicate with the dead person
and expressing unresolved feelings of grief, anger, or guilt.
Memories of past losses, such as earlier deaths of important
people, may surface. Evidence of loneliness, depression, and
self-destructiveness may also appear.

Six years after her mother's death, Padma had a dream
that helped her see that she had finally worked out her grief
about the death. It was the first dream in which she experienced a clear resolution.

Ready to Be Reborn

*I can see my mother from a distance. It looks like
the place where we used to spend our summer vacation. She seems younger and more sprightly,
like a time before she became ill. I have a sense that
all her karma had been paid for and she was going
to be reborn into a new life.*

Like my own dream long after my grandfather's death
(see Introduction, "In the Orange Grove with My Grandfather"), Padma's dream gave her evidence that she had
worked out long-standing conflicts about her loss.

When a resolution is reached in the process of letting
go of our attachment to a loved one, dreams can help us to
confirm a sense of resolution. Dreams that herald this
breakthrough may include some of the following themes.

- Peaceful images of the dead person from an earlier era, usually prior to illness or aging
- Appearances of the dead person as an angel, benevolent ghost, or spiritual being from a realm apart from the living
- Words of comfort or reassurance from the dead person or a sense of reassurance from the circumstances that the dead person appears in
- A focus on some positive quality of the dreamer's relationship with the dead person

RESOLVING THE LOSS OF A
PARENT OR GRANDPARENT

The death of a parent or other close relative is usually the first major death-related loss that we experience. Our grieving is influenced by the nature of our relationship with the parent or grandparent, whether the loss was expected, our emotional support network, and the way we have coped with other losses in the past.

Whenever we suffer a loss, our reactions extend beyond the actual loss of visits, phone calls, and letters to and from the person. There are symbolic losses that are crucial to face if we are to transform a period of darkness into one of growth.

With a parent's death, we lose the sense of security that a parent will always be there to protect us and be an emotional or financial safety net. With a parent's death, we confront our own mortality in a more concrete way. Our illusions of immortality are shattered as we are thrust into the role of an elder in our family. There is an awareness that ours will be the next generation to face death.

In the extended period of grieving we must learn to cherish the memory of what our parents gave us. We also must learn to heal wounds from occasions when they failed us by not giving us the quality of empathy, attention, and love that we needed. I have observed that many adults in psychotherapy are caught up in a quest to win the approval and love from their parents that they were denied in childhood as a result of a divorce, severe economic stress, the birth of a sibling, or a parent's substance abuse or other psychological problems. When a parent dies, we must let go of the hidden hope that he or she will someday fill those needs. Facing those unresolved desires may provide a crucial opportunity for psychological growth—to mourn the lost love and find constructive ways to meet our needs in the present.

Terri felt a numbness following her father's death from cancer. She was depressed, empty, and barely able to maintain her responsibilities at work. Her grieving was at an impasse.

When Terri called to make an appointment to be interviewed, she could not remember a single dream in the two months since her father's death. On each of the following three nights, however, she had a series of dreams that she did remember. At the beginning of our first meeting, she said that the act of writing and sharing these dreams with her husband had made her more hopeful that she could overcome her grief and depression.

On the first night, Terri dreamed of her father's car, not his recent car but the one he had when she was ten years old in the period after her parents divorced.

Searching the Trunk of My Father's Car
I am at my father's house, outside, looking in the trunk of his car. The stuff in the car is there for me to take. I'm gathering up things that I could carry out of the trunk: his golf clubs, his satchel, and golf shoes. I am feeling in the dream that I had better take it now because he is going to be gone. But every time I pick anything up it disappears.

The image of her father's old white Cadillac convertible with tall, pointed fins brought back a flood of memories for Terri. It was in that car that she used to spend part of her weekly Sunday visits with her father. He would take her to the golf course, then take her with him in his golf cart despite the rules against it. She even learned to enjoy playing golf with him as she grew older.

The car reminded Terri of the traumatic divorce. After the divorce, the car would always be filled with dirty and clean laundry, golf clubs, and files from his business. It always smelled like cigar smoke. She used to spend a lot of time sobbing in the back seat without her father knowing. She felt caught between her parents' animosity. Her mother constantly expressed hatred toward her father, refusing to speak to him for ten years after the divorce.

Although her father faithfully kept up his visits and did have a great sense of humor, he was never able to express any warmth or love for Terri directly. He always seemed to have a word of criticism about her weight or appearance. In recent years he was incredibly stingy with her. In his will he gave all his money to his second wife. Toward the end, when Terri begged for some special mementos from him, he refused, as if he had some odd mental block about being generous to her. Before he died, Terri had wanted him to give her a special antique set of golf clubs. He gave them instead to a friend. He did give his current golf clubs to Terri's husband. On the day of her father's death, Terri spoke with him and told him she loved him. His response from the delirium of his deathbed was to inquire about her husband's recent golf scores.

For Terri, the disappearing goods in her father's car represented the golf clubs and the many other things her father never gave her. At another level, they represented the direct expression of love and acceptance that he was never able to give.

The next night, Terri again dreamed about her father's old Cadillac. This time it was a more painful image.

Last Chance to Get Anything from My Father's Car

My father's car is moving. The trunk is open but there were fewer things in it: just his golf shoes and clubs and some clothes. I have a sense that this is the last time I'll be able to get anything from the trunk. The car is moving slowly but I have to run faster and faster to try and catch it. I get my hands on some things but end up dropping them and falling behind the car as it moves away. As the dream ends, I have a strong desire to get something, anything, from the car.

Through discussing this dream, Terri could feel the numbness lifting. The deprivation was feeling more acute and the memories more clear. The dream was telling her that her father's old car and its goods were no longer in her grasp. He was gone.

In her third dream, Terri's father appeared to her from the world beyond.

My Father Calling My Name

I hear my father calling me by name . . . Terri, Terri, Terri. I can see his face now. It sounds so familiar, so real. I'm trying to find out where he was calling from. It seems like it is heaven or somewhere high up. I answer: "Dad, how are you?" And he says: "I'm OK. I think that it is harder for Peggy (his current wife) than it is for you." What he seems to mean is that he is in heaven and not suffering pain and grief, but we are. He seems to be living with some peace. I feel like I'm not!

Terri grew angry as she thought more about the end of her dream. Her father was worried about his second wife but not about her. He had been generous with his wife but not with Terri. Ultimately, Terri realized that the reason it had been difficult for her to mourn was that she was angry at him. She had been the one who was always supposed to take care of him and put out the raging fires of her parents' hatred for each other. She had never expressed that anger directly when he was alive, and since his death she had been afraid to stir up old wounds or to break the taboo against being angry at a dead person.

A month after her three-dream series, Terri had a further dream that focused even more clearly on the past. In this dream, she was trying to tell her father what she needed to hear him say before he died. She appeared as a young child pleading with him to say he loved her.

Focusing on her dreams helped her to accelerate her stalled process of grieving. Her dreams precipitated feelings of loss and anger, crystallizing images of what was missing in her relationship with her father. By reexperiencing the lingering pain of her parents' divorce and her father's emotional shortcomings, she began to heal old wounds.

Adam, whose divorce dreams were explored in chapter 4, had two powerful dreams after his father's death. Adam's father and younger uncle were successful dentists who practiced together and were very close. Although it had been hidden and denied for many years, both men were addicted to drugs that were available through their practice. Adam had idealized his father and uncle and was deeply disturbed when he learned of their problem. He couldn't understand their addictive needs or why they would throw away success and happiness.

Adam tried many times to convince his father to straighten out his life. Although he knew intellectually that he wasn't responsible, Adam couldn't shake the feeling that he should rescue his father. As his efforts failed and his father's problems became known publicly, Adam felt as if he was failing the older man. When his father died of an accidental overdose, Adam was devastated. In the weeks following the death, Adam had a recurring dream that upset him greatly.

My Father Is Sucked Down a Manhole
My father is being sucked into a manhole. I am desperately trying to pull him out, but the dark, seething sewage water is sucking him down lower and lower. I strain with all my might but I'm losing my grip and he is sinking. Though I keep struggling for what seems like an eternity, he is finally drawn down into the darkness and swept away.

In the dream, Adam's desperate attempts to rescue his father fail. To Adam, the dark, raging waters of the sewer represent the drugs and depression that captured his father and pulled him down from a life of integrity into one of disgrace.

Adam knew that his feelings for his father were unresolved and that the dream was telling him something about his inability to recover from the death. As the months went by, he began to understand that he needed to get over the guilt that was haunting him about failing to rescue his father. Part of his desperation came from a need to deny his father's fall from grace. He came to accept that his idealization of his father had been crushed, just as his idealization of his ex-wife had been shattered earlier. (See his dream The Fallen Idol in chapter 4.) He had harbored fears that he would meet the same fate as his father: succumbing to alcohol or drugs and seeing his success and connection with his family deteriorate.

As Adam continued to resolve his guilt and ultimately his anger at his father for disappointing him, his dreams began to change. After his uncle's death three years later, Adam's manhole dreams had ceased and the dreams of his father often had a more spiritual quality. One dream in particular was a signal to Adam that he had reached a new level of acceptance and resolution.

Angels Walking

I am seeing my father and his brother walking down the street together arm in arm. They're young again—two beautiful young men. It seems like they are floating along like angels, their feet not touching the ground.

In this dream, his father and uncle are close again and peaceful in a world beyond. Adam felt that he had worked through his guilt and anger so that earlier positive memories of his father were restored. Adam's Angels Walking dream has elements that are often present in the dreams of people who have resolved their grief over a parent or other deceased relative. It usually takes one or more years before this kind of dream appears.

RESOLVING THE LOSS OF A SPOUSE

It's very difficult for widows and widowers to shake loose the cloud of depression and grief that hovers over them. Sarah, who had been married to Harry for forty-nine years, knew that cancer would soon claim his life. During his illness, he prepared her for his departure, teaching her how to manage the family finances and keep up the maintenance of the house. All the practical preparations did not, however, prepare Sarah for the magnitude of the loss she experienced when Harry passed away.

In the months following his death, Sarah had frequent nightmares that Harry had returned to their living room and would move toward her, urgently trying to tell her something. She could never hear or understand what he was saying, because he would vanish before he completed his important message. She would awake from these dreams feeling desolate in the knowledge that he was no longer with her.

Two years after his death, Sarah still thought about Harry many times each day. During this period, a vivid dream helped her see that the acute period of grieving had subsided.

Harry's Comforting Words

I'm dreaming again of Harry. His face, his look are so real that I think he's alive again. I can see him walking toward me with his big blue eyes and his arms outstretched to me. I'm standing up and I say excitedly, "Where did you come from? I thought you were dead!" He hugs me and says, "I just want to make sure that all is well with you, my darling." It felt so good to see him and hear his voice again.

Sarah was shaken by the dream because of how real Harry appeared. She recalled that the previous night, she had stared for a long time at the picture of him in her bedroom. She had even kissed the picture before she went to sleep.

At first, she was saddened by the dream. But as the image of Harry in the dream came to her mind over and over again, she began to feel a sense of comfort. After two years, the voice of her husband had become a concerned voice inside of her. The sense of incompleteness and anguish toward her husband's death was no longer so painful.

Twelve years later, at age eighty-five, Sarah reported that she still drew comfort in thinking about the dream and how real Harry appeared in it. She never again had such a vivid dream of him.

Dina, an emergency room nurse, had been divorced for three years before she met Ricardo, a fellow nurse in her hospital. She had not dated much after her divorce and wanted to be more careful in choosing another partner. However, their relationship progressed quickly and passionately until they became engaged six months after meeting.

Soon after their engagement, Ricardo went on an overnight camping trip with a couple of old friends from college. On the night he was supposed to return, Dina came home from work and found a series of urgent messages on her answering machine from Ricardo's best friend. She knew something was wrong when the friend insisted that he come over to talk with her immediately. She never suspected, however, that her fiancé had died that day. Although he'd been wading in shallow water, he had mysteriously drowned while others were swimming not far away. Dina kept asking Ricardo's friend if he was telling the truth. The words just didn't seem to sink in. That night she had the following dream.

Return of Ricardo

I am at the emergency room. I am lying down feeling very depressed and unresponsive. One of the doctors comes into the room and asks what is going on. He says he got a horrible-sounding message on my machine. Someone takes him into another room to tell him Ricardo died. I see people that look like Ricardo and then I see Ricardo. I am totally in love with him and in awe of him. He checks his mailbox and sees a note that I left for

him there (which I had done the day before he
died). He looks at me but no one else sees him. Sud-
denly he goes out the back door smiling and doing
a dance.

When she awoke from the dream, Dina called Ricardo's
answering machine, which was still on, and told him how
much she loved him. Even though she knew he wasn't there,
she wanted to believe he would get the message.

Dina felt that this first dream had to do with her inability to believe what had happened. She was feeling the
full power of her love for Ricardo as if he were not dead but
only entertaining her with a short visit, then leaving, as he
would sometimes do in the hospital where they worked.

During the weeks following his death, Dina was
wracked with grief. She wanted to deny the obvious. She
imagined seeing him everywhere she went. She spent hours
crying. Dina felt a terrible sense of loss; their love and the
possibilities of their marriage would never develop. She felt
desolate and abandoned, just when she thought she had
found the love of her life.

Despite all her turmoil, Dina reached out to her friends,
calling them in the middle of the night when she was crying,
asking for help in a way she never had before. This was the
first death of anyone close to her. Through her intense grief,
she felt that she came to value her own life and her friends
more. She was beginning to feel acutely alive. She had a new
desire to live and to make the most of her precious time.

As she worked hard to overcome her denial, Dina had
another dream two months after Ricardo's death.

Smelling the Embalming Fluid
I am out at the stables where Ricardo used to take
me horseback riding. Ricardo moves toward me

> *and we start walking together. He is looking at me*
> *but he doesn't say anything so I know he is dead. I*
> *ask him: "What were you doing in the water when*
> *you don't know how to swim?" I remember smell-*
> *ing the smell of the chemicals of embalming fluid*
> *(that I later realized I had smelled at the funeral).*

The anger that Dina felt in this dream had not been accessible to her earlier. Not only was Ricardo unable to swim, but his mother had drowned when he was ten. How could he have been so stupid as to go into the water alone? How could he have left her when their love was still young?

Two months after Ricardo's death, Dina was still grieving, but she felt that she was beginning to recover from the terrible depression that had gripped her. Her embalming fluid dream helped her to see that her denial was beginning to subside. She was now able to express the full range of feelings she had about Ricardo's death.

RESOLVING THE LOSS OF A CHILD

The loss of a child is surely one of the most shattering events within the realm of human experience. In one study of marital stability after the death of a newborn, over 60 percent of the couples who suffered such a loss experienced marital discord that ultimately led to separation or divorce. Furthermore, the incidence of severe psychiatric problems in men and women who suffer such a loss has been measured at over 33 percent.

The research of Jungian analyst Judith Savage has provided us with powerful insights into parents' reaction to miscarriage, perinatal death (during pregnancy and delivery), neonatal death (between birth and four weeks), and infant death, such as in sudden infant death syndrome. Her book *Mourning Unlived Lives: A Psychological Study of Childbearing Loss* explores dreams, fantasies, and mythological parallels that illuminate the process of recovering from the death of a child.

Searching for a lost child is a prominent theme in the dreams of parents who suffer the death of an infant. One such dream reported by Savage was that of Carol, a single mother whose relationship with the child's father ended early in pregnancy. She decided to continue the pregnancy, but her baby died in the twentieth week of pregnancy. This was one of four similar dreams.

Searching for My Baby

The dreams all started in a hospital after the baby was born. A nurse comes to my room to tell me I had a son but she didn't have him. She'd leave the room but never return. Then I'd get out of bed and search the hospital, asking everyone if they'd seen my baby. No one had. Some people helped me, others didn't. I never find him.

According to Savage, searching dreams are common immediately after the infant's death. They often continue for three or four months and only stop when the parents have accepted that the loss is real and that all illusions of having the child return are gone.

Another dream theme observed by Savage is that of reviving or resurrecting a deceased or fragile child. One women had recurring dreams of tiny babies on the verge of death. Using her own breast milk, she was able to save them from the brink of death and nourish them until they reached a normal size.

Renowned pediatricians John Kennell and Marshall Klaus have stressed the importance of parents seeing a dead child as visual proof that the baby has died. In the case of any fetal loss occurring after the infant had begun to move in the womb, they recommend that the baby be shown to the parents to counteract denial and help them speed the mourning process. A private viewing in the hospital or mortuary and a funeral service can make a tremendous difference in the parents' capacity to resolve this traumatic loss.

After the death of a newborn, infant, or older child and after a miscarriage, the parents often experience a tortuous series of dreams that almost always includes themes of guilt and self-reproach. Such a dream was described by Freud in the chapter on "The Psychology of the Dream Processes" in his monumental book *The Interpretation of Dreams*. The dream was that of a father on the night his young son died of a prolonged fever. When the father fell asleep, his son's body was laid out with tall candles surrounding it. An old man was in charge of praying for the boy and watching the candles.

Father, Don't You See I Am Burning?
My child was standing beside my bed and caught me by the arm and whispered reproachfully: "Father, don't you see I am burning?"

When the father awoke, he saw a glare of light coming from his son's room and rushed next door to find that some of the shroud had been burned by one of the ceremonial candles when the old man had fallen asleep. This simple but poignant dream was caused in part by an ability of the brain to sense danger even in the dream state. The words spoken by the dead child, however, may have had many meanings. Freud suggested that they may actually have been spoken by the boy on his dying day as he pleaded for relief from his burning fever. It is likely that the pleading voice of the child also was touched off by a condensation of other memories and feelings. Perhaps this father was experiencing remorse that he hadn't responded many times in the past to his son's emotional needs. Perhaps he was wracked with guilt that he was unable to prevent his son's illness or save him from its ravages. Perhaps the dream was a denial of his son's death in its portrayal of him as still alive and therefore capable of being saved by some heroic effort.

In one of my own cases, Randy and Caroline had been married for one year when Caroline experienced a miscarriage after eight weeks of pregnancy. She'd had an ectopic pregnancy that was misdiagnosed and almost bled to death. It wasn't clear whether she would be able to conceive again. As Caroline recovered slowly over the next month, she mourned the loss of her child as well as the hope for her and Randy to have a child together. Caroline was increasingly upset when Randy seemed to express little emotion about the miscarriage. Randy, too, wondered why he was feeling numb.

Soon after the loss of the baby, Randy had two horrifying nightmares. The first was an image of a woman who was bleeding heavily from a deep gash. The second featured an old, dying woman who needed a hospital bed for which Randy was forced to pay.

Randy was overwhelmed with anguish and unable at first to think about the meaning of these two nightmares. When he did finally explore these dreams, he felt they helped him to understand the core of what was troubling him. He felt that he should have been more upset about the miscarriage. On the surface, Randy was playing the role of the devoted husband. When Caroline accused him of not caring, he felt guilty and began to question whether he really was a callous person. He became preoccupied with self-doubt and wondered whether he could ever be an adequate husband, let alone father.

His dreams showed him that he was, indeed, upset about the loss of the pregnancy. Furthermore, he was even more upset about the fact that his wife had nearly died and was only slowly recovering from the physical trauma. He also felt that his wife's complaints were valid. His dreams helped him to see that he hadn't been able to express his feelings because he was trying to be the strong partner while his wife was physically and emotionally weakened.

As Randy began to face the fears of his initial nightmares, he had the following dream, which illustrates how troubled he still was by his wife's condition. This was the beginning of a series of dreams in which Randy began to resolve the feelings he had been avoiding.

The Great Soccer Player Is Now Tired

An Hispanic woman is being helped to walk by others. She has recently had a baby. Before that, she was a great soccer player. Now she can barely remember what she was doing. She says that she is very tired now.

Randy quickly realized that the great soccer player represented his wife. Not only was she athletic, she was a star player at her job and in performing and caring for him. He had not realized how upset and disoriented he was at seeing her appear weak for the first time.

As he discussed his dreams, Randy began to feel some of the emotions he had unconsciously avoided. He felt fear and sadness about the potential loss of his wife and empathy for her slow recovery. Beyond that, he began to grasp his pattern of avoiding intimacy in relationships because of his fear of becoming too dependent and risking emotional abandonment. With this greater understanding, he felt he could begin to be more responsive to his wife's needs. As Caroline recovered physically, they began to discuss the idea of adopting a child if Caroline couldn't conceive. Six months later, she did conceive and ultimately gave birth to a healthy child.

Like Randy, many of us react with fear and shame at our deep emotional responses to a loss. We feel that we should have it all together; when we don't, we hide our true feelings. Through our dreams we can understand our vulnerability and appreciate our humanness. Dreams show us that our emotional wounds heal slowly.

GRIEVING THE LOSS OF A PET

The death of a cherished pet can be profoundly upsetting and may trigger a grieving process that closely resembles the grief we might feel for a close friend or relative. In fact, many of us form attachments to our pets that fill crucial emotional needs that are not adequately met by human relationships. This is especially true for people who are not in a primary relationship or those who have no children or whose children have left home. Pets are also precious to people who feel inadequate in their social skills or have suffered losses and wounds in earlier relationships. A loyal dog may last through many relationships and always be there for you when you want to play or take a walk. A cuddly cat may meet your needs for affection when your marriage is stressed or when you are feeling neglected in other ways.

A few years ago, when I saw a sign in my veterinarian's office for a grief support group for pet owners, I chuckled and thought to myself: only in California. But when both of our young cats were hit by a car, killing one and nearly crippling the other, I understood how disturbing the death of a pet can be.

This experience helped me understand the dream of a woman who had recently suffered the loss of her fourteen-year-old dog. She had the dream on a Dream Quest wilderness backpacking workshop in the Big Sur region of California. We were camped on a ridge overlooking a mountain called Pico Blanco, which was considered to be a sacred site to the Ohlone Indians. According to legend, it was on that mountaintop that the mythical Coyote was said to have begun their tribe after surviving a great flood.

In the morning, Barbara, forty, recorded this disturbing dream in her journal.

Nursing a Coyote

There is a wild dog nearby, maybe a wolf or coyote. I lie still because I'm not sure if it will attack me. Somehow I fall back to sleep and wake up (still in the dream) and when I awaken the dog is lying asleep on my chest.

When we met as a group to explore her dream, she was initially confused by it, but she soon associated it to her fear of wild animals and to our discussion of the Coyote legend the previous evening. When I asked her to imagine that she was reexperiencing the dream, she began to describe the feeling of the coyote as heavy on her chest. She became tearful as she thought of her dog, Emily, who was a mixed breed but looked a little like a coyote.

Other group members remarked about the paradoxical quality of the dream image: the wild coyote sleeping peacefully on her breast. As Barbara talked further about the sadness she had experienced when Emily died, she realized that the dream also might have something to do with the fact that she'd just turned forty and was childless. The loss of her nurturing relationship with her dog underlined a painful struggle to accept that she did not have a child to nourish and was nearing the age when it would be difficult or impossible to conceive. Her poignant associations led others in the group to grieve over losses of parents, friends, and pets, some of which had occurred years earlier.

Reactions to death are downplayed in our society. Grief reactions to the loss of a pet are generally trivialized. Barbara had hidden her grief about Emily's death and in doing so had begun to experience the depression that often accompanies blocked grief.

For children and others who have an especially strong attachment, focusing on dreams can help in the process of getting over the loss of a special pet. This exploration helped Barbara to see that Emily's death was not a trivial matter and that she needed to mourn the loss of an important companion.

DEATH SYMBOLISM IN DREAMS

We often have dreams that refer to death when there has been no actual death of anyone close to us. Direct and symbolic references to death are a universal theme in dreams. They are psychologically rich with meaning but often misunderstood or interpreted in an overly literal fashion.

We must be extremely cautious in using dreams to make concrete predictions of the future. This is especially true of dreams foretelling death. If most dreams that contain death symbolism were accurate predictions of doom, there would be few of us left on the planet.

Dreams with death symbolism bear important psychological messages. When references to death or death symbolism appear in your dreams, you may want to consider a number of possible avenues for understanding. Keep in mind that we're speaking generally and that your own dreams may relate to issues that are not mentioned here.

When you dream about the death of someone close to you, it may be related to angry or vengeful feelings toward that person. One dreamer who was of a generally aggressive nature dreamed that his father died in an airplane crash. Although the dream may have had other possible meanings to the dreamer, it did seem to relate to rage and even murderous wishes toward his father.

It is important to remind ourselves that dreams exaggerate and distort our feelings and impulses. The appearance of murderous wishes in a dream does not imply that the dreamer is on the verge of committing an act of aggression.

Death dreams may serve as a kind of unconscious self-reproach when we feel that we have failed in our responsibilities to our children or other people for whom we provide care. Ann Faraday, in *The Dream Game,* cites a dream that she had about her young daughter dying of syphilis. Her dream was frightening and puzzling to her until she reviewed her associations. She remembered rolling around on the floor with her daughter the previous night. As she thought about this, she could imagine the critical voice of her mother reprimanding her not to get her daughter so stimulated because she might die of a sexual disease. Although she was able to laugh at the critical voice of her mother, at the same time she knew that she had to be wary of its influence on her relationship with her daughter.

Dreams of death that are not related to an actual death often indicate that a significant change or loss is occurring in a relationship or at work. Viewing death dreams as related to a change in your relationship to yourself and to others will help you understand their meaning. These dreams are also helpful in understanding and working out earlier losses and deaths that may still be troubling.

DREAMS AND RECOVERY FROM LOSS

Dreams help us comprehend all the dimensions of human grieving. Through the window of our dreams, we can better understand our hidden feelings, bring them to the surface, and get the help we need to ease our suffering and get our lives back on track.

Exploring our dreams can also help us to clarify the symbolic losses that always go along with the death of someone close, such as the painful realization of our own mortality or loss of the innocence and open-endedness of youth. It also may include enduring the death of long-held identities and roles, such as being a mother's daughter or a son's father.

In the midst of our sadness and desolation, dreams help us see the spiritual side of our grief, as in Doug's dream of crossing into the light or Adam's image of angels walking. Seeing spiritual elements in our dreams also can help us find meaning and hope in a time of despair.

As at other turning points, dreams during grieving give us confirmation that we are resolving our losses. We can find meaning in the suffering we endure during a period of grief, and our lives can be enriched by the memories we carry with us.

10. *Working with Turning Point Dreams*
Recall, Journals, Symbolism, Groups, and Therapy

Iᶠ ʏᴏᴜ ᴀʀᴇ puzzled about how to understand your own dreams, you're not alone. Most people are baffled by their dreams. They have no inkling of how to decipher the coded messages. Even the gurus of dream interpretation, Freud and Jung, at first could not apply their theories to unravel the mysteries of their own dreams. Consequently, they developed practical techniques for exploring them. Over a period of years, each maintained a journal, observed patterns, and learned by trial and error to connect the feelings and themes in his dreams to important personal issues and turning points. In this chapter, you will follow in the footsteps of the great explorers of the inner world by learning how to focus on your own dreams.

To guide and inspire you to explore your dreams, this chapter presents a series of techniques for

- Increasing your ability to remember your dreams
- Keeping a personal dream journal and dream glossary

- Exploring dreams on your own through creative writing, expressive arts, and other "creative dream work" techniques
- Understanding the symbols, characters, content, and structure of your dreams
- Sharing and exploring dreams with friends and family members
- Participating in a dream-sharing group or workshop
- Working on your dreams with a psychotherapist
- Using dream incubation techniques for problem solving
- Completing the two-week Turning Point Dream Program

At the end of this chapter you'll find the Turning Point Dream Program, a structured two-week procedure for enhancing dream recall and using your dreams to understand and resolve the emotional challenges of past, present, and future turning points. Many of the ideas and exercises presented in this chapter are incorporated in the Turning Point Dream Program.

REMEMBERING YOUR DREAMS

Remembering dreams does not require complicated procedures or high-tech gadgets. Your attitude and receptivity are the most influential factors. If you approach your dreams with an attitude of curiosity and interest, you are likely to succeed no matter what procedures you use.

The right way to remember and document your dreams is whatever way works best for you. Most people prefer to record their dreams in a journal first thing in the morning. Others use a tape recorder or a sketch pad, or simply tell their dreams to a partner or supportive friend.

Probably the single most important thing we can do to enhance our recall of dreams is to *keep pen and paper by the bedside*. A special notebook or journal that is esthetically pleasing can become a treasure chest of your inner life.

Another helpful technique for improving your memory of dreams is to *make a review of the day's events* in the evening before going to sleep. Your review can be written in your journal or shared with your partner. Focus on interactions and events that provoked strong feelings. This can make you more sensitive to the issues you're most likely to dream about and heighten the probability that you'll remember a dream. At the same time as your evening review, you may also want to picture the faces of the people who are most important to you and about whom you are most likely to dream. Visualizing them will sensitize you to the issues and feelings that are dominant in those relationships. This process will help you establish linkages between your dreams and the challenging aspects of your close relationships.

If you are having difficulty remembering your dreams, try to relax in the evening by listening to music, taking a bath, or practicing relaxation or meditation exercises. Avoid alcohol, drugs, and medications, and limit your caffeine intake, as these suppress dreaming. *As you are falling asleep, give yourself a simple suggestion that you will remember your dreams in the morning.* The suggestion strengthens your intention and reminds you to remain alert and ready to receive dreams when you awaken.

Because the last dream period of the night is the longest, you have the greatest chance for recalling a dream in the morning. To maximize your chances for remembering a dream, plan to wake up naturally or set a (nonmusic) alarm about fifteen minutes earlier than your usual wake-up time. If you do awake during the night with a dream, make sure to jot down key phrases or you'll tend to forget it by morning. This is true because immediate memories require ten minutes of wakefulness for our brain to retain them in our long-term memory banks.

When you awaken, reserve a few quiet moments and lie still with your eyes closed or unfocused. You can linger in a half-dream state and your dreams will often stay with you as you make a gentle transition from sleeping to waking. In this half-dream state, you may also see vivid images that are akin to dreams. The imagery can be enjoyable to witness and meaningful in much the same way as your dreams.

Always record a dream, no matter how fragmentary, frightening, or apparently unimportant it may seem. During the night or when you awaken, *begin by jotting down key words and phrases* even if they are not in a logical order. Often, one word or phrase will later trigger the recall of many more details from a dream.

Obstacles to Dream Recall. Many people have difficulty remembering their dreams. They get tripped up by assumptions and attitudes that cause them to dismiss dreams as unworthy of further consideration. Obstacles to dream recall include the beliefs that a dream is

- Fragmentary and therefore useless
- Too trivial or just a repeat of daily events
- Illogical, nonsensical, or confusing
- Bewildering, morally repulsive, or terrifying
- Inadequate in some way; for example, lacking universal symbols or an appealing coherent story line

If you occasionally dismiss your dreams as worthless for any of the reasons above, you increase the likelihood of having difficulty remembering dreams. It's important to value every dream as a potential source of insight and change. If you find yourself tempted to minimize the importance of a particular dream or of your dreams in general, keep in mind that even the tiniest, confusing, mundane dream fragment can have profound meaning.

KEEPING A DREAM JOURNAL

The most valuable book on dreams you'll ever read is the one that you write yourself: your personal dream journal. Writing dreams down reinforces your ability to remember them and activates feelings, associations, memories, and insights that might have been neglected.

The type of journal you select is not a crucial factor. A spiral notebook, three-ring binder, sketch pad, or clipboard will work just as well as a specially purchased journal. A night light or flashlight can be valuable for writing down dreams during the night if you don't want to disturb your spouse or partner.

Don't become so obsessive about writing your dreams and organizing your journal that it becomes a chore. Quality is more important than quantity. One dream explored in depth is more valuable than a month's worth of dreams that remain untouched and invisible in your journal.

A crucial advantage of keeping a journal is that it gives you the opportunity to review a series of dreams. *A dream series presents a more complete view of your inner life than does one dream.* In your journal you can observe recurring characters, emotional themes, and situations that may not have been apparent initially. Often a repetitive theme or character alerts you to a situation or relationship that is unresolved or undergoing transition.

There are many techniques for structuring a dream journal. Most people who maintain an ongoing journal devise their own method of organization. In my workshops I recommend using the following phrase as a mnemonic device for beginning your associations and organizing your journal: REVIEW-KEY-DREAM-FACETS.

1. REVIEW: Go over emotionally charged events of the previous day or two. Picture people's faces and recent interactions with them. Make notes in your dream journal in the evening.
2. KEY: Jot down the key words and phrases that come to mind just as you awake. Use these keys to unlock the rest of your dream. With the keys, you can reconstruct the dream later in the day if your time is limited in the morning.
3. DREAM: Use the keys as a framework for reconstructing your dream. Write as quickly as you can to avoid the temptation to censor or compose your dream. By faithfully writing all elements of the dream, even those that seem disorganized, you can later harvest the richer nuances of meaning.
4. FACETS: This acronym stands for *feelings, associations, characters, ending, title, summary*. This sequence provides a guide for organizing and cataloging your responses to a dream.

F—FEELINGS. Make a note about the positive and negative emotions that arise in the dream, such as sadness, sexual desire, guilt, anger, joy, love. Also note the quality of your mood when you awoke.
A—ASSOCIATIONS. Write down ideas, insights, memories, and hunches that come to mind as you contemplate the dream. It is best to brainstorm and not worry about whether your ideas seem relevant to the dream.
C—CHARACTERS. Identify the characters. Who do they remind you of? How are you relating with them in the dream? Keep in mind that dreams often merge attributes of different people or portray a character as a disguised reference to someone else.
E—ENDING. How does the dream conclude? Is the ending resolved, partially resolved or unresolved? The

degree of resolution correlates with what stage you have reached in resolving the dilemmas that the dream is addressing.

T—TITLE. Create a title for your dream that describes a crucial element and will help you remember it when you're rereading your journal or analyzing a dream series.

S—SUMMARY AND STRATEGIES FOR CHANGE. Summarize the main themes of your dream and try to link them with important issues you're facing in a current turning point or in situations and relationships in your life. Based on your summary of this dream, what ideas or strategies for change can you think of?

CREATIVE DREAM WORK:
TECHNIQUES FOR EXPLORING DREAMS

Once you've remembered or written down a dream, there are many avenues for further exploration. Creating a relaxed, receptive, and dreamy state of mind is an important first step. I call this the Dream Space. The Dream Space is akin to daydreaming. You can enter it by closing your eyes and letting images and characters in your dream come alive. Let your feelings and ideas flow freely without trying to direct or control them.

Freud used a form of the Dream Space when he encouraged his patients to lie on the couch, tell their dreams, and free-associate, allowing their thoughts and feelings to be communicated without censorship. Jung felt that the therapeutic process was enhanced when his patients were able to "dream their dreams onward" or engage in a focused exploration of their dreams.

To help people enter the Dream Space, I invoke the advice of the Story Lady who used to visit my elementary school each week. Before launching into a fanciful story, she would implore all of the children to "stretch your imagina-

tion," to accommodate the poetic license she was about to
take. In a similar fashion we must suspend our desire to analyze and instead enter the storylike world of our dreams.

This approach involves reexperiencing our dreams—
marveling at the visual imagery, being awed by the emotional intensity and humbled by the monsters and gangsters
that pursue us. When we've reexperienced the dream in this
exploratory way, our eventual analysis will be more on target in terms of making connections between our nocturnal
images and waking concerns.

The Dream Space exercise provides a springboard for
deeper exploration of dreams. It can be used on its own or
combined with one or more of the exercises listed below it.

DREAM SPACE

1. Choose a dream that you want to focus on.
2. Find a comfortable, relaxed location where you
   will not be distracted.
3. From your journal, read the dream silently and/
   or review the events and feelings of the dream.
4. Close your eyes and pretend you are reentering
   and reliving your dream.
5. Imagine that you are experiencing the events
   and feelings of the dream as if they were actually happening.
6. Open your eyes and jot spontaneous notes on
   the feelings, associations, and insights that you
   became aware of during the Dream Space exercise.
7. (Optional) Share your feelings and ideas with a
   trusted friend.

From the Dream Space exercise you can branch out in
many directions. The following journal exercises have been
found to be highly effective when used for individual dream

work, dream groups, and workshops. If you are not oriented toward writing, each of them can be adapted for verbal sharing. Choose a dream and try one or more of the following exercises combined with the Dream Space.

AUTOMATIC WRITING

You'll need your dream journal and a timer. Set the timer for five minutes and complete the Dream Space exercise. Write as fast as you can without stopping to think or worry about whether you are making sense.

DREAM DIALOGUE

Choose two characters or two objects in a dream and write a dialogue in the form of a play script. Again, write as fast as you can without censoring or putting your pen down. Take a minimum of five minutes or as long as you need.

DREAMING THE DREAM ONWARD

Reenter your dream using the Dream Space exercise. Continue your dream beyond its ending. You can use a silent fantasy, tell another person as you make it up, or write a new ending in your journal. If the new ending is unresolved, try to imagine a more positive resolution to the dream.

PAST/PRESENT/FUTURE CONNECTIONS

Past: Reenter your dream and allow your imagination to drift back in time. Jot down the first three memories from the past that come to your mind; leave a space after each. Jot down the names of the first three people that come to mind; again leave a space after each.

Present: Experience your dream again and note three events of the last two days that were signifi-

cant to you. Note the names of two or three people
in your present life that come to mind as you think
about your dream. They may or may not appear in
the dream. Leave a small space after each entry.
Future: Once again reenter your dream using the
Dream Space. Write down two or three events
you'll be facing in the near future. Also write down
three people with whom you'll be having important interactions in the near future.
Connections: In the spaces you have left, go back
and jot down notes and phrases describing the
memories and people you have noted. Do any of
your notes generate ideas or insights about how
your dream is connected to your past, present,
and future?

After each of the above exercises, jot down and/or
share further ideas or insights that may have occurred to
you. Discuss them with someone you trust. Do your associations produce links between your dream and any important
relationships, stressful events, or turning points in your life?

UNDERSTANDING DREAM SYMBOLISM

Our dreams and the symbols in them do not have one specific meaning in the way that a riddle has one answer or a
lock has a key. They contain many levels of meaning, some of
which may even be paradoxical. A useful approach is to
view dream work as a journey of discovery on which we encounter many ideas, theories, and hunches that make our
dream more meaningful and our feelings more understand-
able. Keep in mind that enjoying the journey can be as important as arriving at its endpoint.

A valuable principle to keep in mind is what noted
dream author Ann Faraday has playfully called the tingle
test. The tingle test is invoked when you receive an inter-

pretation or reaction about your dream from another person. If you are able to feel a physical reaction, it is likely that the interpretation is one that is deeply relevant to you.

The meaning of every dream symbol is unique to the dreamer and can only be understood within the context of a current life situation and emotional concerns. *The most crucial step toward understanding the symbolism of our dreams is to explore our own associations.* This requires an active involvement on our part that focuses as much on the process of getting to know our feelings and fantasies as it does on decoding a precise bottom-line interpretation. We can be guided by a knowledge of common symbols and themes, but we must be careful to use our own feelings and intuition as the confirmation of any meaning we ascribe to a dream symbol.

In his book *The Dream and the Underworld,* Jungian analyst James Hillman suggests keeping the images and symbols alive rather than reducing them to one bottom-line conclusion. In discussing a dream image of a black dog, Hillman states: "It is better to keep the dream's black dog before your inner sense all day than to 'know' its meaning (sexual impulses, mother complex, devilish aggression, guardian, or what have you). A living dog is better than one stuffed with concepts or substituted by an interpretation."

If we grasp for a "cookbook method" of looking up the meaning in a book on symbolism, we're likely to drift away from the essence of our dream's unique relevance to our life situation. For example, a dream of a knife could be a phallic symbol related to a lack of or excess of masculine potency. But there is a tremendous difference between the likely meaning of a bloody samurai sword versus an antique silver butter knife. The meaning would also be different if the dreamer had recently cut himself or been the victim of a knifing. And what if the dreamer was a knife salesman or a brain surgeon?

I encourage people to interpret dream symbols within the context of how they appear in the dream. Rather than looking at a dream symbol in isolation, *stay with the entire image* and try to get the feel for what it is telling you about your life.

Understanding Dream Characters. Analyzing the meaning of characters and relationships occurring in dreams can be tricky. Are the characters objective representations of that person? Are they telling you something about your current waking relationships? Or are they purely symbolic aspects of your own personality that are projected onto the stage of our dreams? I believe the answer is all of the above.

For example, in my own dream In the Orange Grove with My Grandfather (see Introduction), the encouraging advice from my grandfather was an aspect of our relationship before his death. But beyond symbolizing the resolution of my grief over his death, the dream also represented the grandfather part of me, that aspect of my own personality that experienced inner guidance and was fulfilled in my work of guiding others as a psychotherapist.

A valuable exercise that can be used in your dream sharing is to *pretend that each of the characters and elements in the dream represents a part of your own personality.* Begin with the character or object that was the most vivid or disturbing and ask yourself, How am I like this character? What part of me does this represent? We tend to identify with the perspective of the character that plays us in the dream, sometimes known as the dream ego.

It can be extremely revealing to assume the role of other characters in the dream, particularly those that are the most repulsive or threatening. Jung felt that these unacceptable or alien-feeling parts of our dreams are part of the *shadow,* or the aspect of our personality that remains concealed from the world and from ourselves. If you have a dream with a despicable character or infamous deed, imagine which part of you this dream element may represent. It can be a difficult but rewarding way to get to know hidden, scorned, and upsetting aspects of your personality.

Through a painstaking study of his own and his patients' dreams, Freud described several mechanisms that camouflage the underlying meanings of a dream. These included reversal, displacement, and condensation. Understanding these mechanisms can be especially helpful in revealing the hidden meaning of characters in our dreams.

According to the principle of dream *reversal*, every emotion, symbol, event, object, or character can stand for its opposite. For example, a dream about your husband or wife getting angry at you may be telling you more about your own anger than your spouse's vengeance. For every dream, consider whether the apparent meaning may camouflage a dream reversal. Being aware of reversals can help you hone in on disguised and repressed aspects of important relationships on which your dreams are focusing.

Displacement and condensation often appear together. *Displacement* occurs when one dream character represents another character. Often a character from the past or one who is less important in your present life will serve as a disguised version of qualities that are linked with a person with whom you have had recent meaningful interactions. For example, while writing this section of the book, I had a vivid dream about an old friend whom I have not seen since high school. In the dream I spoke with him and planned to visit him but felt guilty because I had to cancel. When I thought about my old friend, I realized that he reminded me of a colleague with whom I had lunch the previous day. I had been unprepared for the meeting, and although it went well, I felt afterward that I had let him down. In this dream, canceling the visit with my high school friend was a displacement for the feeling that I had disappointed my colleague.

When *condensation* occurs, qualities of one or more people are merged into a dream character, who in turn may be a displacement for people who are important in the present. For example, a dream figure may have qualities of your boss and your father but not be exactly like either one. Or a Sexual Rejection dream that features being jilted by an old girlfriend may be linked with two or three recent experiences of rejection that may not even have been sexual. It's important to keep the mechanism of condensation in mind because often we're tempted to dismiss a possible linkage of a dream character to a waking relationship because the dream character is not exactly like the real person. In fact, most dream characters are a mixture of real perceptions of a person (or people) and aspects of our own personality.

Objective Meanings. Although the bulk of our dream work involves an open-ended exploration of the subjective meanings, occasionally a dream will actually have an important literal or objective meaning. For example, in some cases a dream of a car losing its brakes and going out of control is related to a subjective experience of feeling out of control. As we saw in chapter 8, cars going out of control can even represent the growth of cancerous cells in the body. But if you have a dream of a car going out of control, it may be worth considering whether your automobile's brakes are dangerously worn or whether something else is objectively wrong with your car. It can be important to look at the potential objective meaning of a dream, although most people err on the side of looking too hard for objective meanings and neglecting subjective, symbolic possibilities.

Psychoanalytic Viewpoints. Freud emphasized how our dream images are linked to unresolved conflicts from childhood that continue to haunt us. Freud's psychoanalytic technique utilized the principle of unconscious *wish fulfillment.*

Using this frame of reference, unconscious wishes are taken to be sexual and aggressive needs that were blocked from full expression at key points in early childhood. Therefore, a classical Freudian analysis of the symbols of a dream would emphasize unfulfilled erotic and aggressive desires that are released in the dream and camouflaged in the symbolism.

Some contemporary psychoanalysts see dreams (and the unconscious) as being shaped less by sexual and aggressive instincts and more by images of our relationships with our parents and other caregivers in the first years of life. From this point of view, dreams can reveal vital information about the nature of our present and past relationships with those who are closest to us.

Jungian Viewpoint. Jung shied away from establishing a uniform method of analyzing dreams. He preferred to treat each dream as unique and not necessarily fitting into patterns we might impose. He did, however, establish certain general principles for understanding dreams. A cornerstone of his approach to dream work was the idea that *nearly all dreams are compensatory.* According to Jung, compensation is a psychological mechanism of balance that is inherent in all people and functions actively in our dreams.

A compensatory analysis of a dream may focus on different kinds of issues that have been neglected or exaggerated in our conscious awareness. For example, compensatory dreams may focus on unresolved grief, blocked assertiveness, unexpressed creativity, self-destructive thoughts and behaviors, or other issues.

In order to apply Jung's principle of compensation to understanding our own dream symbols, we must try to make ourselves aware of attitudes and relationships that may be out of balance. For example, if a dream portrays your father having an angry outburst, you might ask yourself if the anger expressed in the dream is compensating for some imbalance of anger or assertiveness in your life. Your father's anger may be exaggerating your own excessive anger or, conversely, might indicate that you are not aggressive enough to stand up for your own rights and needs.

In my experience, restricting yourself to one school of interpretation limits the richness of understanding that you can derive from a dream. When you approach a dream from different angles you are more likely to strike a chord of meaning. Consider the psychoanalytic frame of reference for concealed references to sex and aggression, other unresolved issues from childhood, and images of your experience of self and close relationships with others. Examine the Jungian frame for universal themes such as the great mother, the shadow, the wounded child, and the wise man or woman. Look through the experiential frame to savor the pure emotional experience of the dream. And, of course, use the Turning Point frame to see how you are resolving issues linked to life transitions and traumatic events.

SHARING DREAMS

Sharing our dreams with family or friends can make the dreams come alive. Even when there is no formal analysis, studies have shown that people who are trained to focus on remembering, exploring, and sharing dreams have pronounced therapeutic benefits: improved mood, fewer symptoms of psychopathology, and enhanced problem-solving abilities.

When you relate one of your dreams to a friend, he or she can offer you a fresh perspective and help you see it in a new way. Because the listener doesn't feel the terror of your nightmare, she can help reassure you, relieve your guilt, and see the universal dimension of it. An act as simple as retelling the dream once or twice may unleash hidden feelings and insights. I recommend that you *tell the dream in the present tense as if you were experiencing it for the first time.* Be aware of your feelings and body sensations as you tell it. Be open to any new parts you may remember and to any ideas or insights that may emerge as you retell it. Rather than reading it, tell it from memory and then return to your journal and read it out loud. The parts that you forgot to mention are likely to be significant.

When you listen to someone else's dream, I recommend that you "Welcome the Dream" before offering any kind of analysis or interpretation. Welcoming a Dream means appreciating it as a special gift, a form of intimate sharing that is best received with sensitivity and respect for the person's feelings. Welcoming a dream rather than interpreting or analyzing it will make a friend feel understood, more secure, and encouraged to go on with a deeper exploration of the dream. Be careful not to show off by trying to impose your insights on the other person. Your insights are likely to be colored by your own needs and concerns, and it is best to let others discover the essence of their dreams at a comfortable pace.

When someone shares a dream with you, listen carefully and let yourself empathize with the dreamer as if you were sharing the experience. If you use your imagination and pretend the dream is your own, you can be helpful by communicating your own experience. Because of the universal themes that often appear, you may be deeply affected by another person's dream just as you would by hearing a poem or seeing a movie.

Sharing your dreams regularly with friends or family members can deepen the emotional bonds in the relationships and help to work out conflicts when they arise. If you're married or in a long-term relationship, I recommend sharing dreams on a regular basis. In addition, when parents take an interest in their children's dreams and encourage family dream sharing, the children will grow up placing a high value on dreams and tend to have more frequent recall.

I suggest that couples designate a two-week period in which both partners focus on remembering dreams and sharing them. This can be especially valuable during a turning point in your relationship such as before marriage, moving to a new home, during pregnancy, or a career or midlife crisis. Once you establish a ritual of sharing during a structured period of two or more weeks, you'll be able to rekindle it in the future when an important dream comes or when you hit another turning point.

DREAM GROUPS

Dream-sharing groups have become increasingly popular in the United States and Western Europe. Within hospitals, schools, churches and synagogues, support groups, and workshops, people have used dreams for therapeutic healing, problem solving, personal growth, and spiritual inspiration.

A group of people focusing on a dream energizes both the dreamer and the other participants. Each dream seems to open up a world of unexpected possibilities. The combined life experience of all the members gives the dreamer access to the whole group's repertoire of insights and suggestions. All involved are often amazed by how easily they can be touched by the feelings and conflicts of another dreamer.

My approach to conducting dream groups is closely aligned with the Experiential Dream Group approach of Montague Ullman, M.D., a psychoanalyst and dream researcher and perhaps the most influential proponent of group dream sharing. Ullman stresses two key factors in dream groups: The Safety Factor and The Discovery Factor.

The *Safety Factor* emphasizes the voluntary nature of sharing and gives authority to the dreamer as to when or how to curtail or expand the exploration. Because of the intimate nature of dream sharing, the group members should try to provide an emotionally supportive atmosphere and refrain from subjecting the dreamer to an onslaught of armchair analysis. The members can offer their own emotional responses and should remain open to discovering new truths about themselves. They must be careful not to impose their experience or ideas on the dreamer. Rather, they can offer their responses as possibilities that may or may not strike a chord with the person.

Ullman's *Discovery Factor* emphasizes an atmosphere of playful experimentation with images and feelings that invite the dreamer to respond with new perspectives. Discoveries may occur in the retelling of the dream. They may be sparked by the group's enthusiastic sharing of their emotional response. Or discoveries may occur in an extended discussion and dialogue that ensues. Frequently, discoveries continue after the group meeting or in follow-up discussions.

USING DREAMS FOR PERSONAL PROBLEM SOLVING

Psychologist Henry Reed, Ph.D., developed a contemporary adaptation of an ancient technique for healing and problem solving. He drew heavily upon the incubation ritual that was frequently prescribed by the ancient Greek physician Hippocrates. Seekers would journey to hundreds of different temples dedicated to the god Asklepios, where they would pray for a dream that would heal their body or their soul.

The core of Reed's dream incubation technique is the selection of a crucial life issue that you want to resolve or understand more deeply. The issue might be an impasse in a relationship, a turning point at work, or a serious physical illness. A period of preparation involves focusing on that issue and consciously exploring all possible avenues for resolving it. This exploration process involves working with a guide, therapist, or even a trusted friend. Journal writing is also an effective tool for reviewing and integrating your conscious preparations for dream incubation.

It's best to form a question to ask yourself and to write it in your journal. Open-ended incubation questions are preferable as they allow you to learn something new and unexpected. Examples of questions that might be used: "How do I feel about this career change I am about to embark on?" "Why do I feel stuck in grief about my husband's death?"

Narrowly focused questions that call for a yes or no answer are less valuable. They make you search for fixed answers rather than being open to new perspectives on your question. In fact, the manifest content of an incubated dream doesn't always relate directly to the question you ask. You may discover answers to questions you hadn't thought to ask that are more pressing than the one you consciously selected.

After the review, an incubation ceremony is conducted for one or more nights. The dreamer concentrates on the incubation question and makes a suggestion to himself that he will try to have a dream that will respond to the issues that need resolution. When a dream is received, it is discussed thoroughly and the person is encouraged to translate the exploration into a written summary of the incubation experience.

Just as artists and writers often have inspiring dreams when they are deeply absorbed in a creative project, we increase the likelihood of dreaming about our dilemma in a new and enlightening way when we concentrate on an important issue. Keep in mind that incubation and dream quest do *not* involve controlling our dreams or asking for a yes or no answer to a particular question. When we try to control our dreams, we overlook the essence of what they offer: a glimpse into the unconscious and an encounter with unknown parts of ourselves.

DREAMS AND PSYCHOTHERAPY

Although we have emphasized ways to work with dreams without the guidance of a psychotherapist, many people will seek the services of a mental health professional at some point in their life. As we've seen in the preceding chapters, our dreams can help us realize when we've reached a turning point impasse that calls for professional help. This section seeks to demystify some of the ways psychotherapists work with dreams and offers guidelines to enhance the benefits you can receive from your work with a therapist.

If you are interested in working on your dreams in psychotherapy, be sure to question your therapist as to his or her attitude about dreams. Not all therapists favor the use of dreams. Many who don't are intimidated because they feel they must be experts who always know the correct interpretation. They are unskilled at the kind of experimentation and imagination that dream work requires.

When you begin therapy, be sure to pay special attention to the dreams you have after deciding to enter therapy and after the first few sessions. These initial dreams often contain valuable information about the nature of the impasse you're facing in your life, your attitudes and response to therapy and the therapist, and your hopes for receiving help. In addition, many dreams during the course of psychotherapy are transference dreams; that is, they depict your responses to the therapist and reveal feelings from important past relationships that you may project onto the therapist.

The way your therapist responds to your dreams will influence your inclination to explore them. If the therapist pays little attention, your motivation and your recall will drop drastically. If, on the other hand, the therapist perks up, takes out a note pad and welcomes your dream, you will tend to respond with a wealth of dreams and associations.

It's important to remember that your dreams are a jumping-off point for expanding self-awareness and solving important life problems. Therefore, some dreams may only be discussed briefly but they may spark an extended exploration of a hidden feeling, forgotten memory, or relationship impasse.

On occasion a therapist may feel compelled to offer his or her brilliant interpretation of your dream. This may be more intimidating than helpful. It's better to explore at your own pace and come up with your own insights with the help of your therapist, rather than having them spoon-fed to you in an intellectual form. If your therapist does give you an interpretation that goes way over your head, be sure to question it. Ask for further explanation and make sure it jibes with your own feelings.

Carl Jung was emphatic on this point. He felt that the analyst should refrain from insisting on an interpretation if it did not ring true for the dreamer. According to Jung, dream work was a collaboration between therapist and patient, not a dream solutions expert.

When I offer explanations and interpretations for a dream, it is usually in a tentative form, as a working hypothesis or a series of possibilities. If I say too much or too little or get too excited about my view, I can take the sense of discovery away from the dreamer.

Dreams also can help you decide when to bring your therapy to an end. In general, when you are contemplating leaving therapy, you'll want to consider whether you've made progress or whether you're running away from an issue or feeling that's too painful to face at this point in your life. Looking at your termination dreams can help you and your therapist understand the nature of your decision to leave therapy.

THE TURNING POINT DREAM PROGRAM
As a culmination to our exploration of techniques for remembering, reexperiencing, sharing, and exploring dreams, you may decide to undertake a two-week program for using dreams to resolve the emotional challenges of major life passages, stressful events, decisions, and even minor turn-

ing points that are important at the time they occur. This latter category might include a period of conflict in a relationship, a stressful situation at work, or an illness or accident.

A two-week period is optimal for heightening recall and obtaining a series of dreams that can be viewed as a whole. The appeal of this concentrated period of attention is that it's not intimidating or time consuming, yet the formal two-week structure usually brings fruitful results, even for people who have never before kept a journal or focused on remembering their dreams. When I conducted research on the dreams of expectant fathers, I used a two-week collection period with instructions similar to those given here. Among the forty-eight men who participated, the average number of dreams recalled was more than seven. Few had ever remembered as many dreams prior to that.

The two-week period can of course be extended in further two-week increments or indefinitely if you decide that you enjoy keeping a dream journal. It can be extremely helpful to do the Turning Point Dream Program with a friend or as part of a dream group or class. If you are currently involved in individual or group psychotherapy, sharing the results of this program can be a valuable addition to your work with your therapist.

As a first step, I recommend conducting an emotional review of what stage you have reached in the evolution of the turning point, crisis, decision, or stress you are facing. You can conduct this review on a free-form basis using journal entries, self-reflection, and discussions with friends and/or professionals. To help you with your review, I've developed a three-part Turning Point Life Review Exercise, presented below. The purpose of the exercise is to understand patterns and styles of facing change and to change the way you face change.

The Turning Point Life Review is a valuable prelude to

keeping your two-week dream journal. It can also be used to prepare for incubating a dream response to an important life issue or personal problem.

TURNING POINT LIFE REVIEW EXERCISE

PART I *Review of past turning points*
1. List the major turning points that have occurred in your life as a child and an adult; for example, losses of important relationships, marriage, divorce, moving, leaving home, having children, injuries, illnesses, career decisions and changes, traumatic events, financial or legal problems. In writing the list, leave about a quarter of a page after each turning point.
2. Think about what happened during each turning point listed. What were your immediate reactions? What stages did you go through? What kind of support did you get from family or friends? In the blank space after each turning point, or with your discussion partner, summarize the answers to these questions.
3. Review what you wrote or discussed about each turning point. Summarize any patterns in the impasses, and ways that you found to begin to resolve the emotional challenges. Do you see any patterns in the way you reacted to or resolved past turning points that may apply to the present turning point you are experiencing?

PART II *Turning point emotional inventory*
Use your journal and/or discussions with someone else to complete these questions.

1. *Stresses:* What current stresses are you facing? What are the emotional challenges of this turning point?
2. *Physical symptoms:* Are you having physical symptoms? (for example, headaches, stomach distress, sleep disturbance)?
3. *Psychological symptoms:* Are you experiencing psychological symptoms? (for example, depression, anxiety, phobias)?
4. *Behavior problems:* Are you experiencing behavior problems? (for example, substance abuse, difficulty with anger, antisocial behavior, impasses in relationships)?
5. *Role changes:* How are you handling role and identity changes?
6. *Stage/resolution:* At what stage of the turning point are you? Are you experiencing any degree of resolution of symptoms, impasses, conflicts?

PART III *Life review summary and strategies for change*

Reviewing your responses to parts I and II, summarize the patterns you observe in the ways you have reacted to and resolved past and present turning points. From the patterns you see, is there anything you might do to alter unproductive ways of facing change and to enhance coping strategies that have worked well? Successful strategies might include:

- Reaching out for emotional support or professional help when necessary
- Limiting self-defeating behaviors
- Overcoming denial of powerful emotions such as grief, anger, and guilt

- Learning lessons from past mistakes
- Trying to heal wounds from the past
- Experimenting with new attitudes, activities, and relationships
- Searching for new sources of happiness

Write notes on your summary and strategies for change, and/or set aside time to share your experiences and insights from this exercise with a trusted friend or professional.

TWO-WEEK TURNING POINT DREAM PROGRAM INSTRUCTIONS

Here are instructions for preparing and carrying out the special two-week program for recalling and exploring your dreams.

PART I *Before the two-week period*
1. Complete the Turning Point Life Review (see above).
2. Select a journal or notebook and keep it by the side of your bed each night.
3. Decide on a two-week period to carry out the program. Mark your calendar.
4. Arrange with a partner to share and exchange dreams if desired.

PART II *During the two-week period*
1. Write down every dream you have during the two-week period, no matter how fragmentary or unimportant it may seem at the time.
2. For each dream you recall, use the REVIEW-KEY-DREAM-FACETS procedure described earlier in this chapter.
3. For each dream, complete one of the techniques described in this chapter, such as

Dream Space, Automatic Writing, Dream Dialogue, or Dreaming the Dream Onward.

4. For each dream you remember, use some of the hints for understanding symbolism presented earlier in this chapter in the section "Understanding Dream Symbolism."

PART III *After the two-week period*

1. Read everything you have written, including all the dreams, dream FACETS and other exercises, journal entries, and the insights you have gained from discussions with others during this period.

2. Summarize in your journal and/or discuss with someone the patterns, ideas, and insights that occur to you.

3. Finally, at the end of your review of the two-week period, make one final written or oral summary using the procedures in Part III of the Turning Point Life Review that encourages you to sum up what you have learned and points you in the direction of strategies for change.

Notes

INTRODUCTION

4. I knew from   Patricia Garfield, *Your Child's Dreams* (New York: Ballantine, 1984).   **6.** He called these Archetypal   C. G. Jung, "On the Nature of Dreams," in *Dreams* (Princeton, NJ: Bollingen, 1974).   **6.** With my professor   Raymond de Becker, *The Understanding of Dreams* (New York: Bell, 1968).   **6.** I also drew inspiration   Stephen Larsen, *The Shaman's Doorway: Opening the Mythic Imagination to Contemporary Consciousness* (New York: Harper and Row, 1976).   **6.** Such dreams often defined   Carl O'Nell, *Dreams, Culture, and the Individual* (Novato, CA: Chandler and Sharp, 1976).   **8.** I began to conduct Montague Ullman and Claire Limmer, *The Variety of Dream Experience: Expanding Our Ways of Working with Dreams* (New York: Continuum, 1987). **9.** These workshops combined   Alan Siegel, "Dream Quest: A Wilderness Ritual," *Association for the Study of Dreams Newsletter* 2, no. 3 (September 1985): 1–5.   **9.** According to Freud   Richard Jones, *The New Psychology of Dreaming* (New York: Continuum, 1987).   **10.** Rather, there are   Louis Breger, "The Manifest Dream and Its Latent Meanings," in *The Dream in Clinical Practice*, Joseph Natterson (New York: Jason Aronson, 1980).

1. CAN DREAMS CHANGE YOUR LIFE?

18. During periods of upheaval   Rosalind Cartwright, "Rapid Eye Movement Sleep Characteristics During and After Mood-Disturbing Events," *Archives of General Psychiatry* 40 (February 1983): 197–201.   **25.** Late in pregnancy   Alan Siegel, *Pregnant Dreams: Developmental* and discussing   Alan Siegel, "Pregnant Dreams: The Secret Life of the Expectant Father," in *The New Holistic Health Handbook,* ed. Shepherd Bliss (New York: Viking Penguin, 1985).   **27.** Psychoanalyst and eminent   Ernest Hartmann, *The Nightmare: The Psychology and Biology of Terrifying Dreams* (New York: Basic Books, 1984).   **29.** In a study of pregnant   Carolyn Winget and Frederic Kapp, "The Relationship of the Manifest Content of Dreams to the Duration of Childbirth in Primiparae," *Psychosomatic Medicine* 34, no. 2 (July/August 1972).

2. RELATIONSHIP DREAMS

32. In fact, the innovative research   Dale Westbrook, *Dreams and First Marriage at Midlife Transition* (Ann Arbor, Mich.: University Microfilms International, 1989), 159.   **33.** In fact, over a fifty-year period   Keith Bradsher, "Ditching Your Betrothed May Cost You," *The New York Times,* 20 March 1990.   **41.** "A young attractive woman"   Westbrook, 150. **47.** "My fiancé shows up"   Westbrook, 145.   **48.** In the dream she thought   Patricia Garfield, *Women's Bodies, Women's Dreams* (New York: Ballantine, 1988), 140–141.   **49.** "shock of the unpleasant"   Jung, *Dreams,* 72.   **49.** Or perhaps he had   Edward Whitmont and Sylvia Perera, *Dreams: A Portal to the Source* (London: Routledge, 1989), 25. **50.** The grooms-to-be   Westbrook, 130.   **51.** "I'm naked"   Westbrook, 131.   **51.** "I have been given"   Westbrook, 132.   **52.** "I was scheduled for"   Westbrook, 126.   **56.** "Yolanda and I are" Westbrook, 142.

3. FROM CONCEPTION TO BIRTH

60. "A subterranean channel"   Sigmund Freud, *The Interpretation of Dreams* (New York: Avon, 1965), 437.   **60.** "creature turned out" Freud, 437.   **62.** When fewer distressing   Winget and Kapp.   **64.** Third-trimester examples   Siegel, "Pregnant Dreams: The Secret Life."   **66.** "I dreamed about my breasts"   Myra Leifer, *The Psychological Effects of Motherhood: A Study of First Pregnancy* (New York: Praeger, 1980), 78.   **66.** In Arthur and Libby Colman's   Libby Lee Colman and Arthur D. Colman, *Pregnancy: The Psychological Experience* (New York: Noonday, 1990).   **71.** Studies of pregnant   Patricia Maybruck, "An Exploratory Study of the Dreams of Pregnant Women," Ph.D. diss., Saybrook Institute, San Francisco, 1986.   **71.** In fact, babies are featured   Robert Gillman, "The Dreams of Pregnant Women and Maternal Adaptation," *American Journal of Orthopsychiatry* 38 (1968): 688–692.   **71.** My own research   Siegel, *Pregnant Dreams: Develop-*

mental Processes.   **72.** Early in pregnancy   Eileen Stukane, *The Dream Worlds of Pregnancy* (New York: Quill, 1985), 47–49.   **74.** In retaliation, the dreamer   Colman and Colman.   **80.** Psychoanalyst Robert Gillman's   Gillman.   **81.** Dreams of endangered   Eileen Stukane, *The Dream Worlds of Pregnancy* (New York: Quill, 1985), 74–78. **81.** Dreams that identify   Patricia Garfield, 192.   **81.** In that study Gillman.   **83.** Our dreams reveal   Colman and Colman.   **84.** Dreams are a resource   Siegel, *Pregnant Dreams: Developmental Processes.*   **85.** Until the 1970s   Ray Lacoursiere, "Fatherhood and Mental Illness: A Review and New Material," *Psychiatric Quarterly* 46, no. 1 (1972): 109–124.   **86.** Many men experience   Joy Lewis, "Fathers-to-Be Show Signs of Pregnancy," *The New York Times*, 2 April 1985.   **86.** Studies by Jacqueline Clinton   Jacqueline Clinton, "Expectant Fathers at Risk for Couvade," *Nursing Research* 35, no. 5 (September/October 1986): 290–295.   **86.** Pronounced cases of couvade   W. Trethowan, "The Couvade Syndrome," in *Modern Perspectives in Psycho-obstetrics,* ed. J. Howells (New York: Bruner/Mazel, 1972).   **86.** In addition, couvade rituals   Sam Bittman and Sue Zalk, *Expectant Fathers* (New York: Ballantine, 1980), 10–14.   **90.** Expectant fathers' dreams   James Herzog, "Patterns of Expectant Fatherhood," in *Dialogue: A Journal of Psychoanalytic Perspectives* (Summer 1979).   **92.** It's vital to   Elizabeth Bing and Libby Colman, *Making Love During Pregnancy* (New York: Noonday, 1989). See also Jerrold Shapiro, *When Men are Pregnant: Needs and Concerns of Expectant Fathers* (San Luis Obispo: Impact, 1987).

4. SEPARATION AND DIVORCE DREAMS

99. Many more who are not   "Couples Marrying Older Push Divorce Rate Down," *San Francisco Chronicle,* 31 May 1990. Since the early 1970s, the divorce rate has hovered at 50 percent. After a peak in 1981, divorce rates fell in the 1980s because of the tendency for people to marry at an older age and for couples to live together without getting married. Couples marrying in the 1980s faced a divorce expectancy rate of 51 percent. Two-thirds of all divorces occur within the first decade of a marriage. **99.** Children born in the mid-1980s   Judith Wallerstein and Sandra Blakeslee, *Second Chances: Men, Women and Children a Decade After Divorce* (New York: Ticknor and Fields, 1989), 303.   **99.** This phase of being in shock   Joy Rice and David Rice, *Living Through Divorce: A Developmental Approach to Divorce Therapy* (New York: Guilford, 1986), 21. **100.** Since four out of five   Rice and Rice.   **101.** In this period we have   Wallerstein and Blakeslee.   **104.** The person who leaves

Rice and Rice, 22. **108.** As chair of the Department Lynn Lamberg, "Night Pilot," *Psychology Today* 22, 7/8 (July/August 1988). **109.** According to Cartwright Rosalind Cartwright, "Dreams and Divorce," paper presented at the Association for the Study of Dreams Conference, London, 1989. **110.** In other words, the recovering Cartwright, "Rapid Eye Movement." **110.** "Someone was after me" Rosalind Cartwright, "Affect and Dream Work from an Information Processing Point of View," *Journal of Mind and Behavior* 7, nos. 2 and 3 (Spring and Summer 1986): 411–426. **111.** "I was eating some" Cartwright, "Affect and Dream Work." **115.** In Cartwright's study Irene Trenholme, Rosalind Cartwright, and Glen Greenberg, "Dream Dimension Differences During a Life Change," *Psychiatry Research* 12: 35–45. **115.** Learning to accept Rice and Rice, 66.

5. WORK DREAMS

126. Turning points in the career Samuel Osipow, "Career Issues Through the Life Span," in *Psychology and Work: Productivity, Change and Employment,* ed. M. Pallak and R. Perloff (Washington, D.C.: American Psychological Association, 1986). **126.** For some, experimentation Lisa Grunwald, "Is It Time to Get Out?" *Esquire,* April 1990, 130–141. **134.** "I dreamed that my teeth" Susan Knapp, "Teaching the Use of the Dream in Clinical Practice," in Ullman and Limmer. **150.** More often we must explore Hilda Dahl, *The Lotus and the Pool: How to Create Your Own Career* (Boston: Shambala, 1989). **152.** The venerable mythologist Joseph Campbell, *The Power of Myth* (New York: Doubleday, 1988), 229.

6. MIDLIFE DREAMS

157. For the men studied Daniel Levinson et al., *The Seasons of a Man's Life* (New York: Ballantine, 1978). **157.** Other researchers theorize Janet Giele, "Adulthood as Transcendence of Age and Sex," in *Themes of Work and Love in Adulthood,* ed. Neil Smelser and Erik Erikson (Cambridge, MA: Harvard University Press, 1980). **160.** To his shock C. G. Jung, *Memories, Dreams, and Reflections* (New York: Random House, 1961), 195. **164.** We are grieving Murray Stein, *In Midlife* (Dallas: Spring, 1983), 7–22. **166.** In Daniel Levinson's Levinson, 191–259. **167.** When they are able Samuel Osherson, *Finding Our Fathers: How a Man's Life Is Shaped by His Relationship with His Father* (New York: Ballantine, 1986). **169.** Daniel Levinson asserts Levinson, 197. **171.** With individual variations Christine Downing, *Journey Through Menopause: A Personal Rite of Passage* (New

York: Crossroad, 1989). **171.** Others may be generalized Ann Mankowitz, *Change of Life: A Psychological Study of Dreams and the Menopause* (Toronto: Inner City, 1984); Downing. **172.** "I am walking with" Downing, 21–54. **172.** This grotesque image Downing. **173.** "I am walking around" Mankowitz, 34. **175.** "While walking . . . we found Jung, *Memories*, 223–224.

7. CRISIS DREAMS AND NIGHTMARES

185. In his book *The Nightmare* Hartmann, 214–219. **186.** "outside the range of usual" DSM-III-R *Diagnostic and Statistical Manual of Mental Disorders*, Third Edition-Revised (Washington, D.C.: American Psychiatric Association, 1987), 247–251. **187.** Another difficult stumbling Lewis Engel and Tom Ferguson, *Imaginary Crimes: Why We Punish Ourselves and How to Stop* (Boston: Houghton-Mifflin, 1990). **190.** Hartmann stresses that Hartmann, 192. **191.** She was treated with Marquis Wallace and Howard Parad, "The Dream in Brief Psychotherapy," in Natterson. **191.** "I am there" Wallace and Parad, 418–419. **192.** "A ferocious bear" Wallace and Parad, 422. **197.** Finally in World War II Mardi Horowitz, *Stress Response Syndromes* (New York: Jason Aronson, 1976). **198.** Recurrent dreams were counted Harry Wilmer, "Combat Nightmares: Toward a Theory of Violence," *Spring* (1986). **199.** "I am talking with" Wilmer. **199.** Often the nightmares Hartmann, 192–195. **200.** "Everyone is getting killed" Wilmer, 130–131. **202.** "There are armed men" Adrianne Aron, "The Collective Nightmare of Salvadoran Refugees," paper presented at the Fifth International Conference of the Association for the Study of Dreams, Santa Cruz, CA, June 1988. **204.** "I stop, because" Aron. **205.** "I know the world" Adrianne Aron, personal communication, July 1990.

8. HEALING DREAMS

209. One person who Meredith Sabini, "Dreams as an Aid in Determining Diagnosis, Prognosis, and Attitude towards Treatment," *Psychotherapy and Psychosomatics* 36 (1981): 24–36. **210.** In the period when Robert Bosnak, *Dreaming with an AIDS Patient* (Boston: Shambala, 1989). **210.** Unfortunately, the fire Jane Hawes, Ph.D., personal communication, July 1990. **213.** The term *prodromal* Webster's *New Twentieth Century Dictionary of the English Language Unabridged.* **213.** Prodromal dreams reveal Stukane, 37. **214.** He has found Robert Smith, "Do Dreams Reflect a Biological State?" *Journal of Nervous and Mental Disease* 175, no. 4 (1987). **214.** Other

researchers have Sabini, 26.   **214.** Cancer surgeon Bernie Siegel Bernie Siegel, *Peace, Love and Healing: Bodymind Communication and the Path to Self-Healing: An Exploration* (New York: Harper and
Row, 1990), 64–73.   **215.** Jung felt that the   C. G. Jung, "The Practical
Use of Dream Analysis," in *Dreams*, 106–109.   **215.** "An old
corporal" Marie-Louise von Franz, *On Dreams and Death* (Boston,
Shambala: 1987), 19–20.   **217.** For example, according to anthropologist Jackson Lincoln, *The Dream in Primitive Cultures* (Bal-
timore, MD: Williams and Watkins, 1935).   **217.** They believe that
John Spaulding, "The Dream in Other Cultures: Anthropological Studies
of Dreams and Dreaming," *Dream Works* 1, no. 4 (Summer 1981).   **217.**
Other dream symbols O'Nell.   **217.** For example, one dreamer
J. Kirsch, "The Role of Instinct in Psychosomatic Medicine," *American Journal of Psychotherapy* 3 (1949): 253, as quoted in Sabini.
218. This is consistent with Meredith Sabini and Valerie Maffly, "An
Inner View of Illness," *Journal of Analytic Psychology* 26 (1981): 123.
222. Levitan believes that Harold Levitan, "The Dream in Psychosomatic States," in Natterson.   **223.** According to Levitan Harold Levi-
tan, "The Functions of Dreaming," Audio Digest Psychiatry Tapes
(Glendale, Calif: Audio-Digest Foundation, vol. 11, no. 24, 1982).   **225.**
Dreams of rebirth John Prendergast, *Dreams by People with Life-
Threatening Illness* (Ann Arbor, Mich.: University Microfilms Inter-
national, 1986).   **226.** Using evidence from dreams Selma Hyman,
"Death-In-Life—Life-In-Death: Spontaneous Process in a Cancer Patient," *Spring* (1978): 27–41.   **228.** "great round stone" Marie-
Louise von Franz, *C. G. Jung: His Myth in Our Time* (New York: Put-
nam), 287.   **229.** The dreamer frequently is Prendergast.   **229.**
"He sees the clock" John Sanford, *Dreams: God's Forgotten Language* (New York: Lippincott, 1968), 60.   **229.** Von Franz associates
Von Franz, *On Dreams and Death*, 146.   **229.** Despite the alluring
light Prendergast.

9. GRIEF DREAMS

239. In some cultures O'Nell.   **239.** Even the children Srisakul
Kliks, Ph.D., personal communication, June 1990.   **240.** Not everyone
goes Hans Mauksch, "The Organizational Context of Dying," in *Death:
The Final Stage of Growth*, ed. Elisabeth Kübler-Ross (Englewood Cliffs,
NJ: Prentice Hall, 1975).   **240.** Another valuable way Rice and Rice.
252. In one study of Judith Savage, *Mourning Unlived Lives: A Psychological Study of Childbearing Loss* (Wilmette, IL: Chiron, 1989).
252. Furthermore, the incidence Marshall Klaus and John Kennell,

"Caring for Parents of an Infant Who Dies," in *Maternal Infant Bonding: The Impact of Early Separation or Loss on Family Development* (St. Louis: C. V. Mosby, 1976).   **253.** "The dreams all started" Savage. 254. A private viewing Klaus and Kennell.   **254.** "My child was standing" Sigmund Freud, *The Interpretation of Dreams*.   **259.** If most dreams Ann Faraday, "Death and the Dreamer," in *The Dream Game* (New York: Harper and Row, 1974).   **259.** The appearance of murderous Calvin Hall, *The Meaning of Dreams* (New York: McGraw-Hill, 1966).   **260.** Ann Faraday, in Faraday

10. WORKING WITH TURNING POINT DREAMS

271. Again, write as fast as Alan Siegel, "Dreams: The Mystery That Heals," in *The New Holistic Health Handbook*, 95–101.   **272.** A valuable principle Faraday.   **273.** "It is better" James Hillman, *The Dream and the Underworld* (New York: Harper and Row, 1975), 122–123.   **274.** I encourage people to James Hillman, "An Inquiry into Image," *Spring* (1978): 62–88.   **275.** Through a painstaking Leon Altman, *The Dream in Psychoanalysis* (New York: International University Press, 1975).   **277.** He preferred to treat Jolande Jacobi, ed. *C. G. Jung: Psychological Reflections* (New York: Harper, 1961).   **277.** A cornerstone of Mary Ann Mattoon, *Understanding Dreams* (Dallas: Spring, 1984).   **278.** Even when there is no Harry Fiss, "Current Dream Research: A Psychobiological Perspective," in *Handbook of Dreams: Research Theories and Applications*, ed. Benjamin Wolman (New York: Van Nostrand Rheinhold, 1979)   **278.** Even when there is no Rosalind Cartwright et al., "Focusing on Dreams: A Preparation Program for Psychotherapy," *Archives of General Psychiatry* 37 (March 1980): 275–277.   **279.** Your insights are O'Nell, 64.   **280.** Within hospitals, schools Ullman and Limmer.   **280.** My approach to conducting Montague Ullman, "The Experiential Dream Group," in Ullman and Limmer.   **281.** He drew heavily Henry Reed, "Dream Incubation: A Reconstruction of a Ritual in Contemporary Form," *Journal of Humanistic Psychology* 16, no. 4 (1976): 53–70.   **281.** The core of Reed's Henry Reed, *Getting Help from Your Dreams* (Virginia Beach, VA: Inner Vision, 1985).   **284.** Carl Jung was emphatic Mattoon, 173.

Recommended Reading

CAREER TRANSITIONS

Bolles Richard. *What Color Is Your Parachute?* Berkeley, CA: Ten Speed Press. (This book is updated annually and has an excellent bibliography.)

Dahl, Hilda. *The Lotus and the Pool: How to Create Your Own Career.* Boston, MA: Shambala, 1989.

COPING WITH ILLNESS

Maurer, Janet, and Strasberg, Patricia. *Building a New Dream: A Family Guide to Coping with Chronic Illness and Disability.* New York: Addison-Wesley, 1990.

Siegel, Bernie. *Peace, Love and Healing: Bodymind Communication and the Path to Self-Healing.* New York: Harper and Row, 1989.

Simonton, Carl, et al. *Getting Well Again.* New York: Bantam, 1978.

CROSS-CULTURAL APPROACHES TO DREAMWORK

De Becker, Raymond. *The Understanding of Dreams.* New York: Bell, 1968.

O'Nell, Carl. *Dreams, Culture, and the Individual.* Novato, CA: Chandler and Sharp, 1976.

DREAMS AND PSYCHOTHERAPY

Jones, Richard. *The New Psychology of Dreaming.* New York: Grune and Stratton, 1970.

Jung, C. G. *Dreams.* Princeton, NJ: Bollingen, 1974.

Mahrer, Alvin. *Dreamwork in Psychotherapy and Self-Change*. New York: Norton, 1989.

Mattoon, Mary Ann. *Understanding Dreams*. Dallas: Spring, 1984.

Natterson, Joseph. *The Dream in Clinical Practice*. New York: Jason Aronson, 1980.

DIVORCE AND SEPARATION

Wallerstein, Judith, and Blakslee, Sandra. *Second Chances: Men, Women and Children a Decade After Divorce*. New York: Ticknor and Fields, 1989.

Weiss, Robert. *Marital Separation: Coping with the End of a Marriage and the Transition to Being Single Again*. New York: Basic Books, 1975.

EXPLORING YOUR DREAMS

Association for the Study of Dreams Newsletter. P.O. Box 1600, Vienna, VA 22183.

Delaney, Gayle. *Living Your Dreams*. San Francisco: Harper and Row, 1988.

Dream Network Journal. P.O. Box 1321, Port Townsend, WA 98368. (Lists dream groups being offered throughout the United States.)

Jung C. G. *Man and His Symbols*. New York: Dell, 1964.

Krippner, Stanley, ed. *Dreamtime and Dreamwork*. Los Angeles: Tarcher, 1990.

Reed, Henry. *Getting Help from Your Dreams*. Virginia Beach, VA: Inner Vision, 1985.

Taylor, Jeremy. *Dream Work: Techniques for Discovering the Creative Power in Dreams*. New York: Paulist Press, 1983.

Ullman, Montague, and Zimmerman, Nan. *Working with Dreams*. New York: Delacorte Press, 1979.

GRIEF

Klaus, Marshall, and Kennell, John. *Maternal Infant Bonding: The Impact of Early Separation or Loss on Family Development*. St. Louis, MO: C. V. Mosby, 1976.

Savage, Judith. *Mourning Unlived Lives: A Psychological Study of Childbearing Loss*. Wilmette, IL: Chiron, 1989.

von Franz, Marie-Louise. *On Dreams and Death*. Boston, MA: Shambala, 1987.

Weizman, Savine, and Kamm, Phyllis. *About Mourning: Support and Guidance for the Bereaved*. New York: Human Science Press, 1989.

LIFE PASSAGES AND MIDLIFE

Bridges, William. *Transitions: Making Sense of Life's Changes.* New York: Addison-Wesley, 1980.

Downing, Christine. *Journey Through Menopause: A Personal Rite of Passage.* New York: Crossroad, 1989.

Gould, Roger. *Transformations: Growth and Change in Adult Life.* New York: Simon and Schuster, 1978.

Levinson, Daniel, et al. *The Seasons of a Man's Life.* New York: Ballantine, 1978.

Mankowitz, Ann. *Change of Life: A Psychological Study of Dreams and the Menopause.* Toronto: Inner City Books, 1984.

Sheehy, Gail. *Passages: Predictable Crises of Adult Life.* New York: Bantam, 1976.

Stein, Murray. *In Midlife.* Dallas: Spring, 1983.

Viorst, Judith. *Necessary Losses.* New York: Simon and Schuster, 1986.

MARRIAGE AND RELATIONSHIPS

Guggenbuhl-Craig, Adolf. *Marriage: Dead or Alive.* Dallas: Spring, 1977.

Wile, Daniel. *What to Do After the Honeymoon.* New York: 1988.

NIGHTMARES

Hartmann, Ernest. *The Nightmare: The Psychology and Biology of Terrifying Dreams.* New York: Basic Books, 1984.

Mack, John. *Nightmares and Human Conflict.* Boston: Houghton, 1970.

PREGNANCY

Bittman, Sam, and Zalk, Sue. *Expectant Fathers.* New York: Ballantine, 1980.

Colman, Libby, and Colman, Arthur. *Pregnancy: The Psychological Experience.* New York: Noonday, 1990.

Maybruck, Patricia. *Pregnancy and Dreams.* Los Angeles: Tarcher, 1989.

Siegel, Alan. *Pregnant Dreams: Developmental Processes in the Manifest Dreams of Expectant Fathers.* Ann Arbor, MI: University Microfilms International, 1983.

Stukane, Eileen. *The Dream Worlds of Pregnancy.* New York: William Morrow, 1985.

Reader Feedback

I WOULD APPRECIATE HAVING your responses to this book. In particular I'd like to know:

1. How was the two-week journal program described in chapter 10 valuable to you?
2. In what other ways was the book beneficial?
3. Have you had any dreams that you feel changed your life either in subtle or overt ways?
4. Have you had especially vivid dreams or nightmares when you were going through the acute phase of a turning point like those described in this book?
5. For those who are between ages thirty-five and fifty, have you had any dreams that occurred during a midlife crisis or a period when you were confronting issues associated with a midlife transition?

Please send a complete description of a dream or short dream series, what impact your dream(s) have had, and how you worked with them. Include your age, occupation, gender, and other relevant life circumstances. If you wish, include your name, address, and phone number so that I can contact you if I need further information or to seek your permission to use your dreams in future publications. I would appreciate your responses. Send them to Alan Siegel, Ph.D., P.O. Box 9332, Berkeley, CA 94709-0332.

Index